Fathers of
the Church

To

E.-J., an Early Christian

Fathers of the Church

Tertullian : Cyprian : Arnobius
Lactantius : Ambrose
Jerome : Augustine

A Selection from the Writings of the Latin Fathers

Translated, with an Introduction and Biographical Notices,
By
F. A. WRIGHT
Professor of Classics in the University of London

LONDON
GEORGE ROUTLEDGE AND SONS, LTD.,
BROADWAY HOUSE: 68–74 CARTER LANE, E.C.
1928

PRINTED IN GREAT BRITAIN BY
STEPHEN AUSTIN AND SONS, LTD., HERTFORD

CONTENTS

v

* An asterisk affixed to a title means that the work is given complete.

PREFACE

It was with extreme diffidence that I undertook this volume, and I am fully conscious that it may well seem presumption for a layman thus to trespass. But the work involved has given me, at least, both pleasure and instruction, and I venture to hope that this attempt at appreciation may be of interest to the clergy as well as to the general reader. The writings of the Latin Fathers are so extensive that the very richness of the field is apt to make students satisfied with a cursory inspection of its treasures. Moreover, though there is a full collection of the Latin texts in Migne and in the more recent Vienna edition, English translations are neither very accessible nor very convenient. It seemed to me therefore that a selection in English from the works of some of the great men who made the early Christian church might be both useful in itself and also perhaps lead my readers to make fuller acquaintance with the Fathers here briefly represented. That they were not wholly concerned with problems of abstract theology but deal also with subjects that are still alive to-day will, I trust, be made clear by a glance at the contents of this book.

Fathers of the Church

INTRODUCTION

I

THE period covered by the writers from whom the selections in this volume are made coincides almost exactly with the period of the decline and fall of the Roman Empire. Tertullian was born A.D. 155, in the middle years of the Age of the Antonines, the last period of quiet security that the ancient world was destined to enjoy, and living in Rome during the impressionable season of his early manhood, he saw the prodigious splendour and what must have seemed then the invincible strength of the imperial city. Augustine died barely two centuries after Tertullian ; but in those two centuries the solid structure of Roman dominion had been irretrievably shattered, riven asunder to its very foundations. The military anarchy of the third century, checked for the moment by Diocletian's ruthless tyranny, had broken out afresh after his retirement, and while beyond the frontiers the tide of barbarism rose higher and higher, in all the Mediterranean countries a cloud of despondency and inertia settled darkly upon men's minds. Constantine saved what he could from the wreck ; but before the end of the fourth century the crisis had come. Huns, Goths, and Vandals poured southwards and westwards, devastating the country as they went, and in 410 Alaric captured and sacked Rome. Spain, Britain, and Africa all fell away ; and as Augustine lay upon his death-bed the Vandals were preparing to storm the walls of Hippo.

II

How it was that a civilization which had lasted for so many centuries and had spread over so large a portion of the globe was brought down in such disastrous ruin is a question which has always excited the most lively interest. Economists have argued that the causes were chiefly financial, the constant drain of gold eastwards for the purchase of luxuries, the gradual impoverishment of the land in the countries round the Mediterranean, the economic disadvantages inherent in slave labour, and the heavy taxation rendered necessary by state socialism and a large standing army. Ethnologists for their part declare that the main reason of Rome's decline was not loss of money but loss of racial purity. They point out the fact that as early as 130 B.C. Scipio could remind the voters of the capital that he had brought many of them as slaves to Italy, and they have abundant evidence to show that under the Empire the old ruling families of Latin blood completely died out, and their places were taken by newcomers from all parts of the world. But, granting all this, it is still difficult to prove that the economic difficulties of the Empire were any greater than those of the Republic ; or, again, that the blending of racial stocks which the Empire brought about was in itself necessarily a disadvantage. The real causes seem to have been psychological rather than material, and they may be best studied in the writings of Tacitus and Juvenal and the early Latin Fathers.

For centuries before the birth of Christ the Romans had been working too hard and spending too freely, fighting too much and enjoying too greedily. At first, as Augustine points out, their guiding motives were the virtues of fortitude and duty, piety and self-sacrifice. But later they set their hearts on power and pleasure, and having obtained both found themselves still far removed from happiness. The tedium that comes from satiety and the pessimism that is the child of self-indulgence find full expression in Lucretius, and although the Augustan writers did their best to revive the vigour of the nation, the very fervour of their appeals to the past reveals the insufficiency and demoralization of their own age. Under the Empire the spirit of cheerful hopefulness definitely disappears from Latin literature. Lucan, Seneca, Tacitus, and Juvenal vie with one another in gloom, and their depression only too faithfully reflects the spirit of society around them. It is difficult for us to realize the stagnation of all the higher interests in life that attended the Empire's material prosperity. The Romans had no native religion, except the cult of the Emperor's divinity ; they had none of that political activity which in modern states sometimes takes religion's place ; they had not even the relief that the study of science or philosophy occasionally offers. It is not surprising that the end of Graeco-Roman civilization came when it did : the pagans were too apathetic, the Christians were too absorbed, to take effective measures against the dangers that threatened them, and the real cause of Rome's fall was that her own people did not think it worth while to defend her.

III

Nature abhors a vacuum ; and the gap that was made in the world by the fall of the Roman Empire was slowly but surely filled by the rise of the Catholic Church. It sometimes happens that a farmer will carefully plant a young elm-tree in his field, and that soon afterwards a bird by chance will drop an acorn in the hedgerow close by. The elm is already a strong sapling, and it has every advantage of ground, light, and air ; the acorn is small and insignificant, and it must struggle for existence against a thousand dangers and a thousand rivals. The years pass by ; and the elm becomes a tall tree with spreading foliage,

while the acorn shoot is still hardly to be noticed among the
briars and bushes that cluster round it. But the young
oak is striking its roots deep, and grows sturdier every
summer, and soon, rising above the hedge level, it stretches
its branches out towards its neighbour. By that time the
elm has reached maturity, and begins slowly to decay.
One great bough snaps off, and then another; and at last
on a night of furious storm some tremendous gust brings
the whole tree down uprooted from the ground. Then in
the place where once they stood side by side the oak is
left alone. Not unlike to this was the process of the decay
of Rome and the growth of Christianity.

IV

The date when the Roman Empire showed the first
signs of world decline is also the date when the Christian
Church showed the first signs of world development.
It may well be that the proved failure of materialism turned
men's minds irresistibly to a system based not on strength
but on weakness, not on pride but on humility, not on
force but on love. In any case, the numbers of the
Christians, which were very small during the first century
when all seemed well with Rome, in the first decades of
the third century mounted rapidly to a considerable total.
It is true that even in Trajan's reign (98–117) there were
some provinces in the eastern half of the Empire where
Christianity was well established, and Pliny's well-known
letter to the Emperor gives us definite information as
to the position in Bithynia. " The charge seemed to me,"
he writes, " a thing worthy of consideration, especially
so because of the number of those implicated. Many of
every age, of every rank, and of either sex, are being
brought in to danger and will be brought. The contagion
of this superstition has penetrated not only the cities, but
also the villages and the country districts." In Africa
also even before the end of the second century the

Christians formed a numerous community, and Tertullian's boast, if it be confined to his own country, may not be so extravagant as is sometimes supposed. In the *Apologeticus*, written in 197, he says tauntingly to his pagan adversaries : " We Christians are but of yesterday, and yet we have filled every place that was yours ; cities, islands, forts, assemblies, camps even, wards, councils, the palace, the senate, the forum ; we have left you no place but the temples."

But even if this increase began earlier, it was notably accentuated all over the world in the period between 200 and 250, and Christianity then for the first time became a serious problem for the imperial government. What exactly was the proportion of Christians to the population of the whole empire in 250 is almost impossible to discover. Gibbon's estimate of one-twentieth is probably too low, Stäudlin's estimate of one-half is almost certainly too high ; the probabilities incline to Richter's judgment, who reckons the Christians as one-ninth of the total population at this date. As a matter of fact, the precise ratio is not a thing of very great importance, for the Christians in the middle of the third century exercised an influence in the state out of all proportion to their actual numbers. Gibbon is too coldly impartial to be altogether sympathetic to a religious mind, but his estimate of the secondary causes of the growth of the Church is not without justice : " It will, perhaps, appear that it was most effectually favoured and assisted by the five following causes : (i) The inflexible, and, if we may use the expression, the intolerant zeal of the Christians, derived, it is true, from the Jewish religion, but purified from the narrow and unsocial spirit which, instead of inviting, had deterred the Gentiles from embracing the law of Moses. (ii) The doctrine of a future life, improved by every additional circumstance which could give weight and efficacy to that important doctrine. (iii) The miraculous powers ascribed to the primitive church. (iv) The pure and austere morals of the Christians. (v) The union and discipline of the Christian republic, which gradually formed an independent and increasing state in the heart of the Roman Empire."

V

It was probably the fifth of Gibbon's causes quite as much as their increasing numbers that led the Emperor Decius, in the year 250, to disturb the comparative peace which the Christians had enjoyed since the time of Domitian. The term " comparative " is strictly correct, for Christians were always liable to individual accusation and to sporadic outbreaks of mob violence, and although the persecution of Decius was exceptionally severe, it was by no means the first that a Roman Emperor had initiated. The earliest of which we hear was in the reign of Nero, after the great fire of Rome in 64. Nero himself was suspected of being responsible for the conflagration, and so, as Tacitus tells us : " To rid himself of this odium he inflicted the most exquisite tortures on those men, who, under the vulgar appellation of Christians, were already branded with deserved infamy. They derived their name and origin from Christ, who in the reign of Tiberius had suffered death by the sentence of the procurator Pontius Pilate. For a while this dire superstition was checked ; but it again burst forth and not only spread over Judea, the first seat of this mischievous sect, but was even introduced into Rome, the common asylum that receives and protects whatever is impure, whatever is atrocious. The confessions of those who were seized discovered a great multitude of their accomplices, and they were all convicted, not so much for the crime of setting fire to the city as for their hatred of human kind." The next occasion was under Domitian in 96, when that moody tyrant put to death his own niece Domitilla, Clement then Bishop of Rome, and a large number of other persons

on the vague charge of " atheism and Jewish manners ".
This ranks as the second of the ten persecutions recorded
by church historians, the next four being comparatively
unimportant and that of Decius coming seventh. Decius
considered Christianity to be a real danger to the Empire,
and he determined to organize so searching an investigation
that no loophole should be left for escape. On a fixed day
the inhabitants of every town and village in the Roman
world were required to present themselves before a local
commission appointed for the purpose. As their names
were called each man had to satisfy the judges either that
he had never been a Christian or that he had renounced
the faith. He was then given a certificate, *libellus*, such as
the following : " In the first year of Imperator Cæsar
Caius Messius Quintus Trajanus Decius Pius Felix
Augustus. To the officers in charge of the sacrifices of
the village of Alexander's Isle, from Aurelius Diogenes,
the son of Satabus, of the village of Alexander's Isle, aged
about seventy-two, with a scar on his right eyebrow.
I have always sacrificed to the gods ; and now in your
presence I have sacrificed and made a libation and tasted
of the victims ; and I desire you to subscribe." It had
been arranged by Decius that this procedure should be
followed by a house-to-house visitation, and that everyone
not in possession of a certificate should be brought at once
to trial. Fortunately for the church Decius himself died
before many months had elapsed, and for the moment
the danger passed away. But the Christians were now too
prominent to be left undisturbed. Valerian (253–60)
published two edicts against them, and his policy was
continued by Aurelian (270–5). Finally, Diocletian, in
303, at the instigation of Galerius, began the tenth and
greatest of all the persecutions, which went on throughout
the world for eight years, exhausted every possible measure
of violence, and proved at the end completely ineffectual.

VI

The Great Persecution, if it did nothing else, at least showed that it was impossible to uproot the Christian communities by force. From the blood of her martyrs the Church grew more and more strong, and even Galerius before his death was compelled to recognize defeat and issue an edict of toleration. So we approach the turning point of history; and it may be well here, before Christianity became the religion of the state, to consider some of the reasons which had made the government till then so hostile. The chief, perhaps, was the profound and unbridgeable gulf that separates the pure teaching of Christ from any form of autocratic rule, a gulf that the Romans themselves recognized when the mere acknowledgement of Christianity in a court of law was regarded as a sufficient reason for the death penalty. But there were also some more definite charges on which a Christian might be arraigned; atheism, for example, and pacificism and illegal conspiracy and disloyalty to the Emperor; and on all these four counts it was possible for a lawyer to make out a strong case. There is some exaggeration in Renan's statement: " When a society of men becomes a republic apart in the state, it is a scourge even though it be composed of angels." But it must be confessed that the Christians did tend to make themselves a people within a people. They were not actually disloyal to the Roman government, but they were indifferent to many of the things which the government considered of the first importance and they were strongly disposed to shirk some of the duties which in our time are thought incumbent on all citizens. They willingly paid their full share of the heavy taxation which the imperial system imposed. But they avoided military service; and, although soldiering was then a trade rather than a civic obligation, it was of all trades the one most essential to the safety of the Empire and the one that the government was most anxious to encourage. They were industrious and orderly, and they rendered due obedience to the civil authorities set over them by the state. But they were disinclined themselves to accept any of the numerous public offices which the elaborate organization of Rome rendered necessary, and preferred to devote all their energies to the management of their own independent system.

Towards the end of the third century, in nearly every Roman township there were two separate organizations, the one as elaborate and as well disciplined as the other. The Christian clergy corresponded to the Roman council with its executive, and they exercised the same control over the faithful as the council did over the pagans. Both *clerus* and *decuria* were modelled on the imperial senate, and both alike were called the *ordo* : the Christian congregation bore the same name as the pagan populace, *plebs*. At the head of the Church organization stood the bishop, elected by the Christian community ; a man usually of commanding character, and like all educated Romans familiar with the details of civil administration, military training, and forensic eloquence. Next to him came a stipendiary staff of presbyters, living a sort of collegiate life, and then a set of deacons and subdeacons who administered the more secular affairs of the church. Below them again came an indeterminate number of acolytes, exorcists, readers, and doorkeepers ; very many holy virgins, and widows ; and lastly a great host of needy pensioners who depended upon the church for their livelihood. The organization was the same, whatever the size of the town and its surrounding district, and every Christian community was controlled by a bishop. We know that in Cyprian's time there were at least eighty-seven bishops in Africa alone, and although in each province the bishop of the largest town might take the lead when his brother prelates met in synod, yet each bishop held sole authority over his own church.

VII

Three dates stand out in the history of the ancient world as marking the beginning of a new era : 323 B.C., the death of Alexander, and the beginning of the Hellenistic Age ; 31 B.C., the battle of Actium, and the beginning of the Roman Principate ; A.D. 313, the edict of Milan, and the beginning of state-aided Christianity. The circumstances of the edict's publication by Constantine are romantic and familiar. Just before the battle of the Mulvian Bridge, 312, which made him the master of the West, the Emperor had a vision. He saw in the sky a bright cross, with the words " Hoc vince " upon it, and was bidden by Christ to take the symbol for his standard, and in its strength to conquer. He won the day, published the edict next year, and then, whether from gratitude or from policy, decided to make Christianity the religion of the Empire. The change took place, and at once the Christian faith ceased to be a detestable super-stition and became the official creed. All the stages of the process fall within a comparatively few years, and its later details are so intimately connected with the personality of Ambrose, Bishop of Milan, that they may be more fittingly considered in an account of his life and achievements. But a bare catalogue of the chief measures of administration that ensured the Catholic Church its favoured position may perhaps be useful here. Firstly, by a law of Constantine in 313 the Catholic clergy were freed from all state burdens and obligations, and by a second law in 320 an exception to the laws against celibacy was made in their case, allowing them to inherit property and also permitting wills to be made in favour of the Catholic Church. By these laws the material prosperity of the Church was assured, and by the Council of Arles in 315 and the Council of Nicæa in 325 its spiritual unity was as firmly established as it ever can be by the exercise of temporal power. When Constantine died in 337 the union of church and state was an established fact, and the Holy Catholic Church, the one and indivisible, had definitely come into existence. It is true that neither Constantine nor his immediate successors took any active steps against Paganism, and that there was even a reaction in its favour under the Emperor Julian in 363. But this had no permanent effect, and as soon as the tolerant Valentinian was succeeded by his son Gratian hostilities began. The young ruler was entirely under the influence of Ambrose, and in 382 he was persuaded to renew the struggle against the old religion, which had been suspended during the eighteen years of Valentinian's reign. By an imperial edict the vestal virgins and the various colleges of priests were deprived of their revenues, which passed into the public treasury, and any further allocation of funds for their benefit was prohibited. Furthermore, an order was issued removing from the Senate House the famous statue of Victory, which Julian had replaced upon the altar where it had been set first by Augustus. The pagan Senators regarded the statue as a precious memorial of the glorious Roman past, and led by the orator Symmachus, they addressed an appeal to Gratian. But, although the Emperor himself was inclined to yield, Ambrose was inflexible. " The Emperor who shall be guilty of granting such a concession ", he said, " will find that the bishops will neither endure nor connive at his sin. If he enter a church he will either find no priest or else one who will defy his authority. The Church will indignantly reject the gifts of one who has shared them with heathen temples. The altar disdains the offerings of the man who has made gifts to images." The final result was that the deputation was not even granted an interview, and Ambrose was once more triumphant. The death of Gratian gave Paganism a precarious respite, but under Theodosius its end came. That great Emperor at Ambrose's instigation passed and carried into effect two laws, which, as far as

the state was concerned, put a stop to all religious rivalry.
The first forebade heretics—the Arians coming first in
the long list—to gather together publicly or privately for
worship. The second definitely prohibited the ancient
pagan ritual : " *nullus omnino*—let no man of any sort
sacrifice to senseless images."

VIII

The change from persecution to patronage probably
made no very great difference to the mass of the faithful ;
but to the clergy and especially to the bishops it was an
event of the highest importance. The clergy from the
first had been entrusted with the management of the
church funds—indeed, it was possibly thus that they got
their name, for the word " clerus ", which was the
secondary title for the priestly " ordo ", in Greek commonly
means estate,[1]—but so long as Christianity was a " religio
illicita " those funds must have been small and quickly
expended. But when by Constantine's law the church was
allowed to receive legacies, money quickly poured in, and
a bishop of an important see like Rome or Milan soon found
himself possessed of very large resources. Damasus,
for example, who was Bishop of Rome 366–84, and gained
from his enemies the nickname " auriscalpius
matronarum ", " the matron's ear-tickler," was able with
the help of donations from his wealthy devotees to undertake a whole series of costly architectural schemes. He
drained the Vatican hill, constructing for its flood water
the channel that is still in use. He built the church of
S. Lorenzo in Damazo, and adorned it with all the
splendour of gold and marble. He collected the relics of
the martyrs from every side, and giving each its own
shrine made the Catacombs the spectacle which they are
to-day. Like a medieval pope, he was a generous patron

[1] The three different explanations given by Jerome and Lightfoot
are not very convincing.

of art and letters, himself a writer of very mediocre verse,
and in his time the inheritance of Rome's imperial
traditions, left vacant by the withdrawal of the secular
government, fell completely into the Bishop's hands.
The pagan historian Ammianus Marcellinus, describing
the furious conflicts that attended his election when one
hundred and thirty seven corpses were counted at the end
of the day, adds that the prize was well worth the effort,
seeing that the revenues of the Roman diocese and the
offerings of pious Roman ladies enabled the Bishop to
ride in a carriage and keep as good a table as that of the
Emperor himself.

An equally plain example of the change made in a
bishop's position by Constantine's conversion may be
seen in the lives and letters of Cyprian and Ambrose, men
of somewhat similar character and abilities, the one
Bishop of Carthage in 250, the other Bishop of Milan in
375. Cyprian had no political influence and his correspondence is almost entirely concerned with matters of
church doctrine and discipline, some of them of very
trifling importance. His financial means were limited,
and it was a great achievement when the African community under his leadership raised the sum of £800 to
ransom prisoners taken in a Berber raid. Ambrose, on the
other hand, was one of the great figures in the history of
his day ; he writes to Emperors as an equal, and does not
hesitate to admonish and rebuke. Politically his influence
was very great ; financially the money at his disposal
permitted him to found the library at Milan that bears his
name, to build the great church of S. Ambrogio on the
site of a temple of Bacchus, and to spend large sums in
private and public charity. And Ambrose is only one of
several bishops who suddenly emerge in the fourth
century, equally as prominent in worldly as in clerical
affairs.

The new position of the church imposed upon many of
them an immense burden of secular duties, and, as

Chateaubriand says, a bishop in the fourth century needed to be a diplomat, an orator, a skilled administrator ; he had to rule men, and serve as counsellor to princes. Not only did he baptize, receive confessions, preach, prescribe penances, issue anathemas, and lift excommunications, he visited the sick, ministered to the dying, buried the dead, and gave relief to widows and orphans. He built churches, founded hospitals, ransomed captives, administered the revenues of the church, adjudicated as a justice of the peace in private suits, and arbitrated on the quarrels between different cities. At the same time he wrote treatises on doctrinal theology, combated heresy and paganism, corresponded with churches and bishops, monks and hermits, and sat on innumerable councils and synods. Finally, he was in many cases called in by the Emperor to advise on questions of foreign policy, and sent as ambassador to usurpers and barbarian potentates.

IX

Everything has to be paid for, and the price that the Church paid for its accession of worldly prosperity was a decrease of spiritual fervour and an increase of internal dissension. Constantine had fondly imagined that an officially recognized religion would be a useful instrument of government, and that the Christians, free from all fear of persecution, would devote at least part of their energies to the service of the state. But he was sadly disappointed in his hopes. The Church took with both hands all the favours that he showered upon her ; but even if she had wished she could not render the autocrat the assistance he desired. As for her children, they were too absorbed in theological disputes to have much time to spare for worldly matters. In the interests of the state, as well as in the worldly interests of the Church, unity of belief was essential. But unity of belief was extremely difficult to obtain, and the fourth century was distracted by a succession of controversies and heresies—Homoousian, Homoiousian,

Arianiasm, Donatism, Pelagianism, Manichæism—whose echoes are heard continually in the pages of Ambrose and Jerome and Augustine. While men were so cruelly uncertain of their eternal salvation they could hardly be expected to concern themselves very deeply with the security of the Empire, and few troubled to take any definite steps to avert the menace of the barbarian clouds that were collecting blackly on every frontier. It soon became obvious that Christianity had brought not peace but strife ; and the attempt that the Emperor Julian made to revive paganism was so far justified in that the old worship, in which no one seriously believed, was far more amenable to control than was a faith which seemed to its true votaries the one thing worth living for. Arianism, which proved eventually to be one of the chief obstacles to harmony between the Romans and the Teutons, was an especial cause of difference, and all the authority of Athenasius in the East and Hilary in the West was needed to uphold the validity of the Nicene Creed. There were, of course, some Christians, like Damasus and Ambrose, who took a great part in affairs ; but their energy and abilities were directed to the service of the Church rather than to the service of the Empire. Ambrose is the typical example, and his relations with Theodosius show plainly how things had altered in the course of the two centuries covered by our authors. At the end of the second century the Christians were an obscure and despised sect ; at the end of the third century Diocletian could claim and receive from most of his subjects divine honours ; at the end of the fourth century the ruler of the Empire had to submit humbly to a bishop of the church. The penance of Theodosius is indeed a symbolic act ; it marks the end of the old world and the beginning of the new.

X

Within this period of two hundred years—a space of time more fateful for the European world than any other two centuries in our history—the Latin Fathers who are represented in this volume lived and laboured. Of that period they are now for us the chief witnesses ; for the same blight that crept over Roman life crept over Roman literature, and after the death of Juvenal and Apuleius that great stream seems suddenly to run dry. An exception may be made in the case of the two arts that are, strictly speaking, parasites on life and letters, the art of the lawyer and the art of the grammarian ; for in law and grammar we have the illustrious names of Papinian and Ulpian, Servius and Donatus. But in original literature we find almost nothing. There is one second-rate poet, Claudian, who, in the *Rape of Proserpine*, carries on faintly the tradition of Virgil and Ovid. There is one second-rate historian, Ammianus Marcellinus, who does his best to follow Livy and Tacitus. The rest are chiefly pedantic poetasters or hack-biographers writing with an eye to imperial favour and patronage. And not only are the Christian writers of this age far above their pagan contemporaries ; they can stand comparison with the greatest authors of classical times. There is nothing in Roman oratory finer than Tertullian's *Apologeticus*. There is nothing in Roman philosophy so original as Augustine's *City of God*. And there is no work of Roman scholarship in any way equal to Jerome's translation of the Bible. Nietsche with something more than his usual perversity maintained that Christianity had a weakening influence on men's minds ; but it is plain that nearly all the strongest intellects in this age turned to the Christian faith, and from that faith drew vigour and inspiration.

XI

It would obviously be absurd to maintain that all the Fathers are faultless either as men or as writers. The devil's advocate might plead that Tertullian was a heretic, and Cyprian ran away from danger ; that Arnobius was

a semi-pagan, and Lactantius a simpleton ; that Ambrose
was over-ambitious, that Jerome was irritable and
vindictive, and that Augustine behaved with callous
cruelty to the woman whom he professed to love. In these
statements there is just that grain of truth which gives
venom to a lie ; but all that we really learn from them is
something which we know already : no human being is
perfect. Still, in all these men their weaknesses are so
outweighed by their virtues that only a professional
fault-finder need consider them. It is true that Tertullian
embraced Montanism ; but he also demolished the far
more dangerous heresy of Gnosticism, and the one case
where he too rashly followed his own judgment is of little
importance compared with the services he rendered to the
Church as a founder of doctrine and a defender of
Christianity. It is true also that Cyprian sought a safe
retreat from persecution and had to endure the
reproaches of his adversaries for so doing ; but a few years
later he showed that his retirement was due to caution,
not cowardice, and he crowned a life of usefulness with a
martyr's death. And the same is true of the other five. We
know too little of Arnobius and Lactantius to be able
justly to estimate their personalities ; but Ambrose and
Jerome and Augustine have revealed themselves to us by
act and word, and we can confidently say that all three by
the strength of their faith and by the multitude of their
good deeds richly earned the title of saint which the Church
has bestowed upon them.

XII

In this book, however, we are concerned not so much
with moral character as with literary ability ; and on
this score with us the Latin Fathers have scarcely received
their fair share of appreciation. Classical scholars in this
country have usually been content to leave them severely
alone, and in their case to translate the Latin proverb,

omne ignotum pro magnifico, as " all that I don't know is not worth knowing ". And yet three at least of our seven authors, Tertullian, Jerome, and Augustine, are of the first importance, both for their thought, their matter, and their style ; and they would well repay the close attention that amongst us for so many years has been reserved for their pagan rivals. Augustine, for example, is the great master of assonance, and a study of this one feature of his language would fill a book. He is also the inventor of most of those terms of rapturous piety—*dulcedo*, *interior melodia*, *passio*, *sponsus et sponsa*—which have enriched the devotional literature of the world. Lastly, he is the main link between the Latin of Cicero and the Latin of Erasmus, the chief writer in that language which was for many centuries one of the few unifying forces in Europe.

Jerome is not so elaborate a stylist as Augustine, but he is an excellent writer, fluent, vigorous, and clear. He is most famous as a translator, but he is also a master of intimate narrative, as his letters show, and his descriptions both of persons and places are full of animation. Not only was he a great man and a great saint ; he was one of the greatest of scholars, an example to many a mediaeval monk of the pursuit of learning for its own sake. Erasmus regarded him as a model for young students, and he exhibits so many of the best qualities of Latin prose that a short volume of extracts from his works might well serve as an alternative in our schools to the familiar pages of Cæsar's *Gallic War*.

Tertullian's Latin on the other hand is as hard as Jerome's is easy, and requires some effort on a reader's part. But to anyone who can savour real originality of thought and diction, and can enjoy the spectacle of a most acute intellect forcing language into the moulds he has chosen for it, Tertullian offers an extreme fascination. Like Christianity itself, he appeals not only to the scholar but to the people ; and the language of the people, scarcely heard in Latin literature save in Plautus and Petronius, is the basis of his wonderful fabric of words. But in weaving his web he adds many new strands of his own. His military and legal experiences colour his vocabulary with their technical phrases ; his controversies with the Gnostic heretics enrich his pages with philosophical terms ; his studies in Greek and Biblical literature supply him with endless apt quotations and allusions. And, above all, there is the ardent strength of his spirit, warmed by the hot rays of the African sun, which has made his lovers compare his writing to the black ebony of his native land. In the history of Latin prose there are five names that count : Cato, Cicero, Livy, Tacitus, Tertullian ; and it could be argued that Tertullian is the most original genius of the five. The style declares the man ; and although Tertullian lacks the blunt directness of Cato, the copious eloquence of Cicero, the majestic flow of Livy's narrative, and the fierce rhetoric of Tacitus, there is a fire, a passion, and a reality in his pages which to some readers at least make the writings of his predecessors seem either over-coloured or insipid.

TERTULLIAN

QUINTUS SEPTIMIUS FLORENS TERTUL-
LIANUS (A.D. 155–222) is the first of those great
North Africans to whom in the early centuries of our era
the Latin language, Christian literature, and Catholic
dogma are so deeply indebted. Born at Carthage, where
his father held a military position of some importance, the
youth was destined by his family for a legal career, and
after receiving a sound literary training in Greek and
Latin he pursued his law studies for some years in his
native city and in Italy. It was probably while he was living
riotously at Rome that he became a convert to Christianity,
and returning to Africa took up his new career as a priest
in the young Church. In that career the chief outward
event is his adoption of the Montanist heresy, and this
had such an effect on him in increasing his natural severity
that a brief account of it is necessary.

How it was that a character so vigorous as Tertullian's
should have been led astray from the path of true doctrine
is a difficult question. But it is partly answered by the
nature of Montanism itself ; for Montanism was adjudged
to be a heresy not so much because of any error in its
beliefs as because of the extreme degree to which those
beliefs were carried, and also because of the personal
claims which its adherents were inclined to put forward.
The founder of the sect was a certain Montanus, a native
of Phrygia, and until his conversion a priest of Cybele,
who associated with him in his apostolate two women,
Maximilla and Priscilla. Montanus lived in the latter
half of the second century, and regarded himself as
possessed of the gift of tongues, and the power of prophecy.
He furthermore declared that he was the forerunner of

Christ's second advent to reign upon earth, and that the end of this world was rapidly approaching. In preparation for that great event, he enjoined upon his followers strict rules of fasting, the joyful acceptance of martyrdom, a stern refusal of all carnal pleasures, and a continued protest against what he thought to be the growing laxity of church government. Many forms of sin were held to be deadly and beyond all forgiveness : marriage was allowed but not encouraged ; a second marriage was adultery. These doctrines were given out as coming directly from God, for Montanus maintained that he was, in fact, identical with the Holy Spirit and that his own mortal personality had been annihilated by the constant ecstasy in which he lived.

With all this Tertullian was naturally disposed to agree, and in the treatises of his later life, written after his perversion, we have all the leading ideas of Montanism expounded. The tracts *On Fasting* and *On the Veiling of Virgins* are typical examples of this later manner. But even when the Montanist writings are excluded there still remain a number of treatises of the greatest value, and in making a selection from them the chief difficulty arises from embarassment of choice. The thirty books that are certainly from Tertullian's pen fall into three classes— the apologetic, supporting Christianity against paganism ; the dogmatic, refuting heresies ; and the practical, dealing with questions of morality. To the first class belongs one of his earliest books, the *Apologeticus*, defending Christians against the charges of secret crimes and public offences commonly brought against them, and asserting the superiority of Christianity over all other religions. In the second class comes the longest of his works, the five books *Against Marcion*, filling three hundred closely printed pages in Oehler's edition, in which he both refutes the Gnostic heresy and convincingly shows the intimate con- nection between the Old and the New Testaments. The third class contains the mass of his shorter writings ;

the wonderful satire, *The Cloak versus the Toga*; the practical treatises on *Idolatry* and the *Theatre*; the two intimate essays addressed to his wife; the sermons on *Patience* and *Chastity*; and, what is perhaps as interesting as any, the discourse on *Women's Dress*.

Women's Dress is not artistically flawless, for Tertullian is here somewhat inclined to digression and repetition; but it is a sound piece of moral theology and it has also a strong social and historical interest. Written in the period just before the reigns of Caracalla and Elagabalus, a time when Roman society had sunk to the lowest depths of bestial extravagance, it comes nearly a century later than Juvenal's famous diatribe against women; and it carries on the revolt against feminine pride and luxury that inspired the Roman satirist to his fierce outburst of indignation. But Tertullian's methods are much more peaceful and much more subtle than those which Juvenal uses. Far from descending to wild invective, he treats his " beloved sisters " as reasonable beings, who have indeed erred from the straight path but only require to be shown the true way of Christian life to abandon pomp and luxury of their own accord. In psychological insight also Tertullian is greatly superior and his pages are strewn with shrewd aphorisms. Quotation here is scarcely necessary, but " No woman is ugly to her husband ", " The desire to please in either sex is a natural defect ", and " A woman will desire in thought what she dreads in act ", are three among the many striking sayings which readers will discover.

Apologeticus, " The Christian's Defence," is too long to give in its entirety, but perhaps the selections from it in this volume may reveal something of its wonderful power and passion. As M. de Labriolle says : " It is one of those works which survive the circumstances that gave them birth and enter into the common treasury of civilized nations. Nowhere shall we listen to more fervid demands for justice, tolerance, or the rights of the accused ; to more vivid protestations against the tyranny of unjust laws assumed to be irrevocable ; to a more eloquent defence of Christianity, its moral nobility and the heroism of its martyrs." An English scholar, Mr. R. W. Evans, is equally convinced : " Tertullian not only surpassed his predecessors in information and talent, but was peculiarly fitted by temper to treat such a subject. No one could express in such forcible language the indignant sense of injustice, or represent its detail in a more lively manner. None could press his arguments so closely, and few had so learned an acquaintance with heathenism and could expose its follies with more bitter sarcasm, or whip its wickedness with a heavier lash. The free and elastic vigour of a mind that had still half its strength in reserve pervades the composition ; and if we put the mere mechanism of style out of the question, and consider the copiousness, the variety, the interest of the matter, the skilfulness of selection of topics, and the powerful grasp with which they are handled, together with the greatness of the occasion, it will not be too much to say that it is the noblest oration of all that antiquity has left us."

As for *De Pallio*, " The Cloak," it is certainly the most original piece of Latin that we possess. It is also the most difficult, and the great French scholar, Saumaise, the discoverer of the Palatine Anthology, spent much time and trouble in elucidating the text, and writing a translation in Greek. Its difficulties, however, are not caused by any lack of skill on Tertullian's part, but rather arise from his excess of skill ; for into it he pours all the whimsical and fantastic humour which in his more serious works he has to hold in check. The result is a concentrated blend of satire, history, moralizing and general information ; and in this one short treatise we may see the germ of two of the greatest books in our own literature, Carlyle's *Sartor Resartus* and Burton's *Anatomy of Melancholy*. Its title, indeed, is very inadequate : it should either be called a *Philosophy of Clothes* or else an *Anatomy of Change*. But

short though it is, *The Cloak* is so full of matter that it is
rather difficult to see the wood for the trees, and a brief
analysis of its contents may be useful. The Carthaginian
cloak, according to Tertullian, is older than the Roman
toga, which has taken its place.   This leads to a short
history of Carthage, and then by way of some reflections
on the mutability of fortune, to the first theme, *Change*.
Nature changes, the earth's surface changes, kingdoms
and peoples change. Animals change their shape ; witness
the peacock, the snake, and the chameleon ; men change
their garments. So we come to the second theme, *Clothes*.
Achilles and Hercules changed male for female attire ;
Alexander put on Persian trousers.   Philosophers now
wear purple, slaves dress as knights, respectable women
look like prostitutes, prostitutes like respectable women.
The cloak should suffice for all ; the cloak shall speak for
itself. And with the cloak's eloquent plea for moderation
and simplicity of life the piece ends.

SELECTIONS FROM *THE CHRISTIAN'S DEFENCE*

(I) CHARGES BROUGHT AGAINST THE CHRISTIANS
(Chs. 7, 8, 9)

We are called the worst of criminals from the sacrament of infanticide and our feeding thereon and from the incestuous intercourse that follows the banquets, inasmuch as dogs, our pimps forsooth of darkness, then overturn the lamps and procure for us the shamelessness that suits our impious lusts. And yet we are but called so on each occasion ; you never trouble to unearth the truth of the charges so long made against us. If you believe them to be well grounded, bring them into the light ; if you will not do that, refuse to believe them. We raise a previous objection against you on the ground of concealment of evidence and we maintain that what you dare not disclose does not exist. It is quite a different duty that you lay upon the executioner against the Christians, to force them, not to say what they do, but to deny what they are.

This teaching of ours, as I have already stated, began to be taken into account during the reign of Tiberius. Truth from the first was accompanied by hatred of herself ; from her first appearance she is an enemy. Every stranger is her open foe, the Jews peculiarly so from jealousy, the soldiers from their craving for blackmail, the very members of our household from natural ill-feeling. We are daily besieged, we are daily betrayed, we are raided over and over again in our very meeting places and assemblies. Yet who ever under such circumstances came upon an infant wailing ? Who ever kept back for a judge the bloodstained faces of a Cyclops man or a Siren woman just as he had found them ? Who detected even on our wives any trace of impurity ? Who having discovered such crimes concealed them or sold his complicity when he had the culprits in his grip ?

If we are always in hiding, when was the crime that we commit betrayed ?   Or, rather, by whom could it be betrayed ?   In any case, not by the accused themselves, since even as a matter of form all mysteries are bound to be loyally concealed. The secret rites of Samothrace and Eleusis are hidden in silence ; how much more with regard to ceremonies whose betrayal will call forth human punishment at the moment, while God's vengeance is waiting in the future. Unless therefore they are themselves their own betrayers, it follows that the betrayers must be outsiders.   And, unless the impious are less timid than others, where do outsiders obtain their knowledge, since even religious initiations always exclude the profane and take precautions against the presence of spectators ?

The nature of rumour is known to all. It is one of your own poets who says : " The curse of rumour, swiftest far in flight." Why is rumour a curse ?   Because it is swift ?   Because it gives information ?   Or because it is very often lying ?   Even when it brings some truth with it, it is not free from the flaw of falsehood, for it ever takes away from, adds to, and alters the truth. Moreover, the conditions of its existence are such that it can only last while it is lying, and can only live as long as it does not prove its tale. When it has proved it, it ceases to exist, and as though it had played its part of messenger, hands over the story as fact, and thereafter it is held as fact, and is so called. No one then, for example, remarks : " They say this has happened at Rome," or " Rumour has it that he has obtained a province " ; but : " He has obtained a province," and " This has happened at Rome." Rumour is another name for something uncertain, and has no place where certainty exists. Would any man, save one devoid of sense, believe rumour ? A wise man does not trust what is uncertain.

Anyone can judge that, however great may be the extent to which this story has spread, however great the confidence with which it has been built up, still it must have sprung at one time or another from a single root. Thence it creeps into branching tongues and ears ; and the shield of rumour so effectively hides any flaw in the little seed that no one thinks whether the first mouth may not have sown a lie, a thing that is often brought about by the inspiration of jealousy or the whim of suspicion or the familiar and innate delight that some people take in telling falsehoods. It is a good thing that time reveals all things, as your proverbs and maxims witness, and that nature has so arranged and ordered that nothing is concealed for long, even that which rumour has not spread abroad. There is good reason then for the fact that rumour, and rumour alone for all these years, has had any knowledge of the crimes of the Christians. She is the informer you bring out against us, she who has never been able to prove the tales she has continually shouted and formed into a strong and settled opinion. Let me rather appeal to nature for support against those who assume that her stories deserve belief.

Look, I set before you the reward of these crimes. They promise everlasting life. Believe it for the moment ; for I have a question to ask you. Do you, who believe the promise, think it worth attainment at the price of such a guilty conscience ? Come, plunge the sword into an infant who is no one's enemy, guilty of no crime, the child of all ; or if that is another's duty, stand by while a human creature dies before it has really lived ; wait for the new life to depart ; catch the young blood ; soak your bread in it, and enjoy your meal. In the meantime, from your place at table count the places and mark where your mother and sister are ; make a careful note, so that when darkness falls—thanks to the dogs !—you may not go wrong. You will be guilty of a heinous sin, if you fail to commit incest. Thus initiated and sealed you live for ever. Pray tell me if eternity is worth it. If it is not, it should not be believed to be so. Even if you believed, I deny that you could ever wish it ; even if you wished I deny that you could ever have the power.

Why, then, should others be capable of doing what you cannot ? Why could you not do what others can ? We, I suppose, are of another nature—monstrosities with dogs' heads and feet large enough to serve as sunshades. Our teeth are differently arranged, and our generative organs are different from other men's for the gratification of our incestuous lust. You who believe such things about a fellow man can also do them yourself. You are a human being, and so is the Christian. You who are incapable of the deeds ought not to believe them possible. The Christian is a human being and the same as you.

But perhaps we only trick the ignorant and impose upon them. They were unaware that such charges were made against the Christians, charges which they certainly ought to look into and carefully investigate. Nay, it is the custom, I fancy, when people wish to be initiated, to approach the father of the rites first, and write down a list of the things that need to be got ready. Thereupon he will say : " You will need a little child, still soft, and knowing nothing of death, who will smile under your knife ; also some bread to sop up the blood sauce ; further, candlesticks, lamps, some dogs, and scraps of meat to make them strain and upset the lights ; above all you must bring your mother and sister with you." But suppose that the candidate refuses, or that he has no female relatives. What are solitary Christians to do, pray ? I imagine that every lawful Christian must be either a brother or a son. Suppose even that these preparations are made without the candidates' knowledge. Certainly they must know about them later, and endure them, and pardon them. They are afraid of punishment you will say ; though, if they declared the truth, they would deserve protection, and in any case should rather choose to die than to live with such a consciousness of guilt. And why do they continue to be Christians, if they are afraid? Naturally you would not wish to be for long that which you would never have become if you had known the truth beforehand.

To refute these charges more effectively I will show that these crimes are being perpetrated by you both openly and in secret, which is perhaps the reason why you believe that we are guilty of them, too. In the province of Africa until the time of Tiberius's governorship, young children were publicly sacrificed to Saturn. Tiberius, as my father's soldiers, who performed the task for him, can testify, had the priests themselves crucified at their temple on the same votive trees that had previously given shelter to their crimes. Even now this damnable wickedness continues in secret. It is not the Christians only who despise you ; no crime is rooted out once for all, and a god does not change his ways. As Saturn did not spare his own children, he stuck to his habit of not sparing other people's. Indeed, the parents willingly answered his call, and offered their infants of their own accord, fondling them the while lest they should cry when they were being sacrificed. And yet when a father kills his own child it is a crime far worse than murder.

Among the Gauls adults are sacrificed to Mercury. I leave the stories about the Taurians to the theatres where they belong. Lo, in the deeply religious city of the pious sons of Aeneas there is a Jupiter whom at his own games they drench with human blood. " It is only the blood," you say, " of a criminal condemned to the wild beasts." It is of less value, I suppose, than that of a human being? Is it the viler because it is the blood of a sinner? At any rate, it is the blood of murder that you shed. What a Christian is your Jupiter, the only son of his father, in point of cruelty !

As regards infanticide, however, although child-murder differs from homicide, it makes no difference whether it is

done wilfully or as part of a sacred rite. I will turn to you
now as a nation. How many of the crowd standing round
us, open-mouthed for Christian blood, how many of you
gentlemen, magistrates most just and strict against us,
shall I not prick in your inner consciousness as being the
slayers of your own offspring? There is, indeed, a
difference in the manner of death; but assuredly it is
more cruel to drown an infant or to expose it to cold and
starvation and the dogs; even an adult would prefer to
die by the sword. But for us, to whom homicide has been
once for all forbidden, it is not permitted to break up even
what has been conceived in the womb, while the blood is
still being drawn from the mother's body to make a new
creature. Prevention of birth is premature murder, and
it makes no difference whether it is a life already born that
one snatches away or a life that is coming to birth that one
destroys. The future man is a man already: the whole
fruit is present in the seed.

abortion

With regard to banquets of blood and such like tragic
dishes, you may read whether it is not somewhere recorded
(in Herodotus, I think) that certain tribes used to arrange
the tasting of blood drawn from the arms of men on both
sides as a means of ratifying treaties. Something of the
same kind was tasted also under Catiline. They say, too,
that among certain tribes in Scythia all dead persons are
devoured by their kinsmen. But I am roaming too far
afield.

To-day and here you may know the votaries of Bellona
by the blood from a slit thigh, caught in the palm of the
hand and given them to drink. Again, what of those who
as a cure for epilepsy drain with eager thirst the blood of
criminals slain at the gladiatorial shows, while it is still
running fresh from their throats? What of those who dine
on bits of wild beast from the arena, and seek a slice of
boar or stag? Your boar in the struggle wiped off the
blood which he himself had drawn from a man; your
stag lay wallowing in gladiators' gore. The paunches of

the very bears are eagerly sought while they are still full
of undigested human flesh. Men belch the meat that has
been fed on man.

How far removed are you who eat such things, from
the Christians' feasts. And are those of you less guilty
who with savage lust gloat over human bodies and take
living members within your lips? Are they the less
dedicated to filthiness by human blood, because they only
lick that which may become blood? They make a meal,
not of infants, but of well-grown lads. Your perversities
may well blush before us Christians, who do not reckon
the blood even of animals as an article of food, and abstain
from things strangled and from such as die of themselves,
lest we should be polluted in any way by the blood that is
buried in their flesh. When you are putting Christians
to the test you offer them sausages filled with blood, being
of course, quite sure that the means whereby you would
have them deviate from their faith is to them a thing
impermissible. How absurd it is for you to believe that
they are panting for the blood of man, when to your own
knowledge they abhor the blood of beasts—unless indeed
you have found by experience that human blood is the
more palatable of the two! This thirst for blood should
have been used, like the little altar and the incense box,
as a method of testing Christians. They could then have
been discovered by their craving for human blood in the
same way as by their refusal to sacrifice : if they refused
to taste blood, or if they sacrificed, the charge against them
would be disproved. And in any case you would have no
lack of human blood at the hearing and condemnation of
prisoners.

Again, who are more incestuous than those whom Jupiter
himself has taught. Etesias tells us that the Persians have
intercourse with their own mothers. The Macedonians
also are suspect. On their first hearing the tragedy *Oedipus*
they merely smiled at the guilty man's agony and said to
each other : *Il montait sa mere.* Consider now how easily

possible incest becomes owing to the mistakes for which promiscuous lust gives opportunity. In the first place you expose your children, to be brought up out of pity by some passing stranger ; or you surrender them for adoption by parents better than yourselves. The memory of a family thus cast off must of necessity some time or other be lost, and when once the possibility of mistake has established itself, incest will begin to shoot out its tendrils, and as the family increases the chances of crime increase with it. Furthermore, everywhere at home, abroad, across the seas, lust walks by your side, whose indiscriminate fury can easily beget you children unawares in some place or other from the smallest portion of seed, so that a family thus scattered may in the ordinary intercourse of life meet its own past and yet fail to recognize the mixture of incestuous blood.

We, for our part, are protected from these accidents by a scrupulous and faithful chastity, and we are as safe from the chance of incest as we are from debauchery, and every post-matrimonial excess. Some gain an even greater security, since they repel all the assaults of sin by a virgin continence, old men and yet children. If you realized these faults in yourselves, you would see that among the Christians they have no existence. The same eyes would have reported both facts. The two kinds of blindness easily combine ; those who fail to see what really is, fancy that they see what is not.

(II) The Jews and Christ

(Ch. 21)

The Jews, too, knew, of course, that Christ was to come, seeing that it was to them that the prophets used to speak. Even to-day they are looking for his arrival ; indeed, the

chief ground of disagreement between us and them is the
fact that they do not believe that he has come already.
Two advents of his have been indicated, the first, which has
already been fulfilled, in the humility of his human birth,
the second, which precedes the end of the world, in the
sublimity of his manifested Godhead. The Jews mis-
understand the first of these two, and think the second,
which as having been clearly prophesied they still expect,
to be the only one. It was the deserved result of their sins
that they failed to understand the first advent ; for if they
had understood they would have believed, and if they had
believed they would have attained salvation. They themselves read it in their scripture : *Ye have lost wisdom and
understanding, and the use of your eyes and ears*.[1]

At first the Jews assumed that Christ was merely man
because of his humility, but afterwards they regarded him
as a magician because of his power. By a word he cast out
demons from men, restored light to the blind, cleansed the
lepers, healed the paralytic, and by a word brought back
the dead to life. Even the elements he subdued, quelling
storms and walking upon the waves, showing that he was
the word of God (that is, the Logos), the original, first-
born Word, attended by power and reason and supported
by the spirit, the self same spirit who by a word was
making and had made all things. At his teaching, however,
by which the teachers and chief men of the Jews were
refuted, they were sc angered, especially as large crowds
were turning away to him, that at last they brought him
before Pontius Pilate who was then governing Syria on
behalf of the Romans, and by the fury of their partisanship
forced him to surrender Jesus to them for crucifixion.

He himself had foretold that they would do so ; a small
thing if the prophets had not also foretold it earlier. And,
further, when he was crucified he gave many signs that
tallied exactly with the death they prophesied. Of his own

---

[1] Direct quotations from the Scriptures are in this volume printed
in italic.

accord, anticipating the executioner's duty, he by a word released his spirit. At the same moment the light of day was withdrawn, though the sun was in mid-heaven. Those who did not know that this also had been prophesied with regard to Christ, thought that it was an eclipse : and yet you have this world disaster recorded in your secret books. The Jews then took him down, laid him in a tomb, and surrounded it with a large band of soldiers to keep careful guard. He had foretold that he would rise again from death on the third day, and they feared that his disciples would baffle their suspicions by secretly removing the body. But lo, on the third day there was a sudden earthquake and the heavy stone which had closed the tomb was rolled back ; the guard dispersed in fear, and though no disciples appeared there was nothing found in the tomb except the grave clothes.

None the less, however, the rulers, whose interest it was to spread abroad a wicked tale and seduce the tributary and dependent mob from their faith, put about the report that he had been stolen by his disciples. Nor did he show himself to the crowd, lest the impious should be freed from error, and also that belief, marked out for no small reward, should be won at a hard price. But he lived with certain disciples for forty days in Galilee, a district of Judaea, teaching them what they were to teach. Then, after ordaining them to the duty of preaching throughout the world, he was taken up to heaven in a veil of cloud, much more truly than your Proculus asserted was the case with Romulus. All these facts regarding Christ, Pilate, who was himself now a Christian in his inner heart, reported to Tiberius, then Emperor of Rome.

(III) Demons and their Works

(Ch. 22)

We say, further, that certain spiritual substances exist.
Nor is the name unusual. The philosophers know of
demons, and Socrates himself waited on a demon's
bidding. Why not? A demon is said to have attached
itself to him from childhood, evidently to dissuade him
from good. All the poets know of them, and even the
ignorant rabble make constant use of them for cursing.
They utter even the name of Satan, the prince of this evil
race, as it were from the soul's innate knowledge, as part
of their curse. Plato did not deny the existence of angels
as well ; even magicians are ready to bear witness to both
names. How from angels corrupted of their own free will
a yet more corrupt race of demons arose, condemned by
God together with the founders of their stock and with him
whom we have called their prince, is fully told us in holy
scripture. It will be enough now to explain the way in
which they work.

The business of demons is the destruction of man. Thus
from the beginning of things did spiritual wickedness
aspire to man's ruin. Therefore while they inflict on men's
bodies diseases and cruel accidents, they also inflict on
the soul sudden and strange aberrations of violent madness.
Their subtleness and fineness of texture give them access
to both parts of man. Spiritual agencies have great power,
and being imperceptible both to the eye and to the other
senses they reveal themselves rather in their effect than in
their action ; for example, when fruit or crops are by some
unseen atmospheric blight nipped in the bud, killed in the
seed, and damaged when ripe ; or when the air polluted
in some mysterious manner exhales pestilential vapours.
By the same obscure method of contagion the breathing
of demons and of angels upon us works corruption of the
mind, and brings attacks of raving madness, and disgraceful

paroxysms of folly, and cruel lusts attended by perversities of various kinds. The most signal of these is that error which recommends the pagan gods to the enthralled and deluded minds of men, that it may obtain for itself a diet from the incense and victims offered to their statues and images. What more exquisite pasture could it have than by false trickery to turn men's thoughts away from true divinity!

I will now explain how it works these tricks. Every spirit is winged. So are angels and demons. Consequently, they are everywhere in a moment; to them the whole world is one place; what is happening and where it is being done is as easy for them to know as to report. Their swift flight is thought a divine right, for their real substance is unknown. So they sometimes try to be regarded as the authors of what they report; and they certainly sometimes are the authors of evil, but never of good. Even God's dispositions they picked up in the past from the words of the prophets, and to-day they gather them from the readings of Scripture they hear. Therefore, taking from them certain responses with regard to dates they set themselves up as diviners in thievish rivalry with the divine. Moreover, in their oracles people like Crœsus and Pyrrhus know with what skill they adapt ambiguities to results. But it was in the way we mentioned above that Pythian Apollo reported the boiling of a tortoise with the flesh of sheep : in an instant he had been to Lydia.

(IV) THE SPREAD OF CHRISTIANITY AND ITS RITUAL

(Chs. 37–39)

If we are bidden, as I said above, to love our enemies, whom have we now to hate ? Again, if when we are injured we are forbidden to retaliate lest by such action we should fall to our enemy's level, whom can we injure? Look at the facts yourselves. How often do you vent your rage upon the Christians, in obedience partly to your own feelings, partly to the laws? How often also does the hostile rabble take the law into its own hands and, without regard for you, attack us with stones and fires? They show no mercy to Christians, even when they are dead, but drag them from their rest in the grave and from the shelter of death with all the frenzy of Bacchanals, cutting the corpses up and tearing them to pieces, even though they are already decomposed and no longer entire. Yet what instance did you ever note of our retaliation upon you for injuries inflicted upon us, though we are so united and so stout-hearted even to death that one single night with a few little torches would yield us abundant vengeance, if it were permissible among us to wipe out evil with evil?

Heaven forbid that a sect which follows God should be avenged by torches wielded by men, or that it should shrink from suffering that whereby it is proved. If we wished to play the part of declared enemies and not merely that of secret avengers, should we lack the force that numbers and strength give. Are the Moors, or the Marcomanni, or the Parthians themselves, or any race, whatever its size, that is confined to one place and its own territory, more numerous than we are to whom the whole world belongs? We are but of yesterday, and yet we have filled all that is yours, cities, islands, forts, country towns, assemblies, camps even, tribes, councils, the palace, the senate, the forum; we have left you only the temples. For what war should we not have been fitted and ready, even though we were unequal in forces, we are so willing to be butchered, if it were not according to our teaching more permissible to be killed than to kill? Without taking up arms or rebelling, by the mere fact of disagreement we could have fought against you, using the odium of our separation as our only weapon. If such a mass of men as we are had broken off from you and removed ourselves to some distant corner of the world, the loss of so many citizens, of whatever sort, would assuredly have abashed your rule, nay, rather would have punished it by the mere fact of abandonment. Without doubt you would have quaked at your loneliness, at the silence of business, and the death-like stupefaction of the world. You would have had to look for subjects to rule. More enemies would have remained to you than citizens.

As it is, owing to the multitude of the Christians, you have the fewer enemies, since nearly all the citizens you have in nearly all the cities are Christians. You have preferred to call them enemies of the human race rather than enemies of human error. And yet who but we could have rescued you from those secret enemies that everywhere play havoc with your minds and health, I mean from the attacks of evil spirits, which we drive off without fee and without reward? That alone would have been sufficient as vengeance for us, that an empty tenement was left open to unclean demons. But you, without thinking of the price you owe us for our protection, have chosen to consider as enemies a class of people who are not only harmless but even necessary to you, people who plainly are enemies not of the human race, but rather of human error.

Moreover, ought you not to have shown some leniency and enrolled our sect among those associations that the law allows, seeing that it commits none of the offences that are usually to be feared from illegal clubs? Unless I am mistaken, the reason for forbidding clubs is to be found in forethought for public order, and fear lest the state should be split up into factions. Elections, assemblies, senates, public meetings, even public shows would then quickly have been disturbed by the rival clash of partisans since men had already begun to think their assistance in acts of violence a source of gain to themselves, something that could be bought and sold. All such ardent desires for fame and position leave us cold; we have no need for such combinations ; nothing is more foreign to us than politics. We recognize but one state, the world, and that is common to all.

As for your public shows, we renounce them as completely as we renounce their origin, which we know to be superstitious, and we are indifferent to all the events which serve them as occasions. We have nothing to say or see or hear in connection with the frenzy of the circus, the shamelessness of the theatre, the cruelty of the arena, and the folly of the gymnasium. In what do we offend you, if we prefer different pleasures ? If we do not care to learn the art of enjoyment, that is our loss, perhaps, not yours. We reject what pleases you. Our pleasures give you no delight. But the Epicureans have been allowed to give it as their opinion that the truest pleasure is equanimity ; and for the Christian's pleasure there are the great tasks which he has to do.

I will now at once proceed to explain the actual occupations of the Christian association, and having refuted the idea that they are evil will show that they are good. We are a corporation based on consciousness of religion, unity of discipline, and partnership in hope. We come together in congregation for meeting, so that forming in a band, as it were, we may draw near to God and surround him with prayers and supplications. This violence is pleasing to God. We pray, too, for the emperors, for their ministers and those in authority, for the state of the world, for the peace of the empire, and for the postponement of the end. We come together for the recital of Scripture, if the aspect of affairs requires us either to be forewarned or reminded of anything. We nurture our faith on its holy words, we raise our hope, we fix our confidence, and by inculcation we clinch the teaching of its precepts. Our assembly also is the place of exhortation, correction, and godly criticism. Judgement there carries weight, for it is delivered to those who are sure that God sees them, and if anyone has so sinned as to be banished from the communion of prayer, and assembly and all holy fellowship, the verdict is held to foreshadow the judgement yet to come. We are governed by approved elders, who obtain their office not by purchase, but by the testimony of their fellows : for nothing that is God's is obtainable by money.

Even if we have a kind of treasury, this is not filled up by fees paid as the purchase money of religion. Each of us contributes a small sum once a month or when he pleases, and only if he is both willing and able. No one is forced ; contributions are voluntary, and are regarded as pious investments. The money is not disbursed uselessly on banquets or drinking bouts or eating-houses, but on the feeding and burying of the poor, on boys and girls without means or parents, on old servants and shipwrecked persons, and on any who are in the mines and penal settlements and prisons, provided it be for the sake of God's religion, they thus becoming pensioners of their own confession of faith.

It is the working of this kind of love that brands us most deeply in some people's eyes. " See," they say, " how they love one another ! " for they themselves hate one another. " See how ready they are to die for one another ! " for they will always be more ready to kill one another. They rage at us, too, for calling one another brethren, merely I imagine because with them any name of kinship carries but a semblance of affection. We are, moreover, your brethren also, by right of nature, our common mother, although you are scarce deserving of the name of men, because you are bad brothers. How much more properly are those called and considered brethren who have recognized one Father, namely God, who have imbibed one spirit of holiness, who from one womb of the same ignorance have quaked before one light of truth. We are perhaps regarded as less legitimately brethren, because no tragedy cries out upon our brotherly love, or because we are brothers in our possessions, while with you property usually breaks up all brotherly relationships.

We, who are united in heart and soul, have no hesitation in sharing a thing. Among us all things are common except wives. In this matter alone we dissolve partnership, in which alone all other men practise partnership, not only using their friends' wives but also most submissively lending them their own. Herein, of course, they follow the teaching of ancient sages and philosophers, the Greek Socrates, for example, and the Roman Cato, who, possibly with the ladies' full consent, shared their wives with their friends, the wives whom they had married to bear children to them—and I suppose to other men as well. What care should the dames have for chastity when their husbands gave it away so lightly? A fine example this of Athenian philosophy and Roman respectability! A philosopher and a censor both playing the part of pimp! What wonder is it if the bonds of this sort of love are so often broken?

You cavil also at our little dinners as being extravagant as well as tainted with criminal practices. It was about us, of course, that Diogenes made the remark: " The Megarians buy food as if they were to die to-morrow, but they build as if they were never to die." It is easier to see a mote in your neighbour's eye than a beam in your own. The air is foul with the belching of all your tribes and guilds and wards. The Salian priests need a money-lender when they dine. Public accountants must sum up the money spent on tithes and offerings to Hercules. A levy of cooks is proclaimed for the Apaturia, the Dionysia, and the Athenian mysteries. The firemen come rushing out when they see the smoke of a Sarapis feast. And yet it is only the Christians' dining-room that is objected to. Our dinner shows its character by its name; for the word in Greek means " love ". Whatever it costs, it is a gain to incur expense in the name of religion, since by this refreshment we help the needy, not in the way that parasites with you strive for the glory of enslaving their freedom beneath the sway of a belly filled amid insults, but in the way that with God greater regard is paid to those of modest rank.

Since the purpose of our entertainment is honourable, from that purpose you may judge the rest of the rules we follow. As it is part of our religious duty, it allows nothing base, nothing disorderly. A prayer to God is our hors d'œuvre before the meal begins. Only so much is eaten as to satisfy hunger, only so much is drunk as is expedient for chastity. The guests indulge themselves only so far as is consistent with the remembrance that they must worship God even in the night ; their conversation is such as you would expect from those who know that the Lord hears them. After the lights have been brought in and water for the hands, each one is invited to sing publicly to God, in so far as his knowledge of holy scripture or his own invention enables him : thus we test how he has drunk. In like manner a prayer closes the feast. The meeting then breaks up, not into bands of brawlers nor into gangs for scouring the streets and for outbursts of wantonness, but to continue its care for moderation and chastity, as people may who have fed not so much on baked meats as on instruction.

If anyone complains of our Christian meeting on the same ground as they complain about your clubs, I allow that it would deserve to be made illegal if it were the same as those illegal associations and were worthy of their con-demnation. But, for whose ruin have we ever met ? We are the same when gathered together as we are when dispersed, we are as a body what we are as individuals, injuring no man, paining no man. When worthy and honest folk come together, when the chaste meet in congregation, it should be called not a club, but a council chamber.

(V) Christians and the Emperors

(Ch. 35)

The Christians are regarded as public enemies because they do not offer to the emperors useless, lying, and inconsiderate honours, and because being men of true religion they celebrate the imperial feasts conscientiously rather than wantonly. It is, forsooth, a citizen's bounden duty on such occasions to bring his couches and cooking stoves out into the street, to feast parish by parish, to make the city look like a tavern, to thicken the mud with wine, to rush about in crowds for the perpetration of outrage, insult, and incitement to lust! Is this the way to express public joy by public dishonour? Is conduct, disgraceful on an ordinary day, becoming to the emperor's feast? Are those who observe order out of regard for Cæsar now to abandon it on Cæsar s account? Shall immorality obtain free licence from loyalty, and religion be considered an opportunity for wantonness? Verily we deserve to be condemned! Why do we fulfil the joyful vows we make for the emperor's welfare in a chaste, sober, and honest fashion? Why at his festival do we not cover our doors with laurel-wreaths and shame the daylight with lamps? Respectability forsooth requires that on an occasion of public ceremony you should dress your house up to look like a newly opened brothel!

We Christians do not celebrate the annual festivals of the Cæsars in your company or in your fashion, for neither fitness nor modesty nor chastity allow; and you yourselves are influenced by the opportunities you find for pleasure rather than by any worthier reason. Therefore, we are arraigned on a second charge of sacrilege, in the matter of this second cult of the emperor's majesty. I should like, however to point out the character of your own loyalty and the reality of your professions; and I fear that perhaps those who would not have us be considered as

Romans but rather as enemies of the Roman emperors may in this respect also be found to be inferior to the Christians. I appeal to the citizens of Rome, the native populace of the seven hills, and I charge you to say whether those Roman tongues of yours spare any of your Cæsars. The Tiber is my witness and the wild beasts' training schools. If nature had covered our breasts with some transparent substance through which light could pass, who is there of you whose heart would not reveal the picture engraved upon it of one new Cæsar after another presiding at the distribution of a dole? And that, too, even in the hour when the cry goes up :—

May Jupiter take from my years to add to thine.
The Christian is just as unable to utter such words as these as he is to be hoping continually for a new Cæsar.

" But these people," you say, " are only the mob." Though they are the mob, yet they are Romans, and none more eagerly than the mob demand the Christians for punishment. The other classes of society, no doubt, in proportion to their authority are scrupulously loyal ; there is no breath of disaffection in the senate, the knights, the army, and the palace itself ! Whence then come the Cassii and the Nigri and the Albini ? Whence those who besiege the emperor between the two bay trees ? Whence those who take lessons in gymnastics in order to strangle him ? Whence those who rush sword in hand into the palace, more reckless even than a Sigerius or Parthenius ? They all come from among the Romans, unless I am mistaken, that is, from among the non-Christians. And yet all these traitors up to the very outbreak of disloyalty were sacrificing for the emperor's welfare and swearing by his genius, at home and abroad, and, of course, were giving the name of public enemy to the Christians.

Even those who are now every day being unmasked as the accomplices and abettors of a criminal faction, the gleanings that still remain from the vintage of murder, how they decked out their doors with the freshest and

most luxuriant bay-trees, how they darkened their
vestibules with the tallest and brightest lamps, how they
divided up the market-place among themselves with their
elegant and haughty couches, not that they might assist
at the public rejoicings, but that they might con over their
private prayers at another man's ceremony, and inaugurate
a copy and picture of their own hopes, mentally changing
the name of the emperor! The same loyal services are
paid by those who consult astrologers and soothsayers
and augurs and magicians about the emperor's life, arts
which, as having been introduced by the rebel angels
and forbidden by God, the Christians never use even for
their own concerns. Moreover, who needs to inquire into
the Emperor's health, except the man who meditates or
desires something against it, or who hopes and waits
for something to follow? One does not consult about
friends with the same feeling as about masters. The
solicitude of kinship is of a different order of inquisitiveness
from that of servitude.

(VI) THE CHRISTIANS AND TRADE

(Chs. 42–3)

We are arraigned also on another ground, that of
injuries inflicted; and we are said to be unprofitable in
matters of business. How can this be true of men who live
with you and do not differ from you in food, dress,
furniture, or any of the necessities of life? We are neither
Brahmins nor Indian gymnosophists; we are not exiles
from existence nor wild men of the woods. We remember
the gratitude we owe to God our Lord and Creator:
we reject no fruit of his works: we merely refrain from
excessive or wrong use of them. Therefore, we cannot

dwell with you in this world without frequenting the market and the butcher's stall, the public baths, shops, factories, taverns, fairs, and other places of resort. We sail the sea with you, we serve in the army, we till the ground, we engage in trade as you do, we lend our skill and labour to the public for your profit. How we can seem unprofitable to your business affairs, when we live with you and by you, I do not know.

It may be that I do not frequent your religious ceremonies, but even on that day I am a human being. I do not bathe at dawn on the Saturnalia, for I do not wish to waste both night and day. But I bathe at a proper and healthful hour, and keep myself warm and ruddy; I shall be stiff and sallow enough when I am dead and have had my last bath. I do not recline at table in public at the Liberalia—that is well enough for criminals condemned to the lions when they are having their last meal— I dine wherever it suits me on provisions I buy from you. I do not purchase a garland for my head. What difference does it make to you how I employ flowers which are bought all the same? I think they give greater pleasure when they are left free and unbound and trailing in the air. But even if we combine them in a garland, we know a garland by the nose: those who perfume their hair must please themselves. We do not attend the theatres; nevertheless, if I want anything that is sold at such assemblies I take it freely from its proper place. We absolutely refrain from buying incense; if Arabia complains, the Sabaeans may be informed that their wares are used in greater quantity and at greater cost for the burial of Christians than for the fumigation of gods.

" The temple revenues," you say, " are certainly going bankrupt; it gets worse every day; not one man in a thousand contributes a penny." Well, we have not the means to assist both human beings and your mendicant gods; we think that only those who ask for aid should be given it. Let your Jupiter hold out his hand and take his share ; but in the meantime our charity spends more money street by street than your religion spends temple by temple. The rest of your revenues should thank the Christians, who honestly pay their due share and refrain from defrauding others. If you put down the amount lost to the treasury by your false and lying returns of income, the balance would be easily in our favour, and your complaints on the score of religion would be more than balanced by the advantage you have in other ways.

I will readily acknowledge what sort of people might with truth perhaps complain of Christian barrenness. In the front row will come the pimps, procurers, and bullies ; after them the professional assassins, poisoners, and magicians ; likewise the diviners, soothsayers, and astrologers. To be unprofitable to them is a great profit. And yet whatever loss your business suffers through our sect can be balanced by some protection we afford you.

(VII) THE CROWN OF MARTYRDOM
(Ch. 50 and last)

"Why do you Christians complain," you say, " that we persecute you, if you wish to suffer, since you ought to love those by whom you suffer what you wish ? " Certainly we wish to suffer, but in the way in which a soldier suffers war. Nobody indeed willingly suffers war, since both panic and danger there must inevitably be faced ; but yet the man who just now was complaining about battle fights with all his strength and rejoices when he wins a victory in battle, because he gains both glory and spoil. Our battle is to be summoned before tribunals, where we fight for the truth at the risk of our lives. And our victory is to obtain that for which you strive, a victory which brings

with it both the glory of pleasing God and the spoil of
eternal life. But, you may say, we are convicted ; yes,
when we have won the day ; we conquer when we are
killed, and we escape when we are convicted. You may
call us " faggoted " and " axle-men ", because bound to
a stake half an axle's length we are burned amid heaps of
faggots ; but that is our garb of victory, our chariot of
triumph, our garment decked with palm-leaves. Naturally
therefore we do not please those whom we have conquered,
and so we are regarded as desperate and reckless men.

Among you, however, such desperation and recklessness
raises the standard of virtue in the cause of glory and
renown. Mucius, for example, willingly left his right hand
in the altar fire : " Oh loftiness of spirit ! " Empedocles
freely gave all his body to the flames of Etna for the people
of Catana's sake : " Oh what strength of mind ! " The
queen who founded Carthage flung herself upon the pyre
in accordance with her marriage vow : " What an
encomium for chastity ! " Regulus, rather than be the
one of all the foemen spared, suffered tortures all over
his body : " What a brave man, victorious even in
captivity ! " Anaxarchus, when he was being crushed
to death with a barley pestle, kept saying :—" Pound, pound
away : it is Anaxarchus' coating, not Anaxarchus himself,
that you are pounding " : " What a magnanimous
philosopher who could even joke about such a death
as his ! "

I say nothing of those who bargained for fame with
their own sword or some other gentler form of death. For,
look you, at your hands even rivalries in torture are
crowned. A courtesan in Athens who had already wearied
out the executioner, at last bit off her tongue and spat it
into the face of the cruel tyrant, that with it she might
spit out her voice also, to prevent her giving the names of
the conspirators, even in case she might be overcome and
consent to do so. When Dionysius asked Zeno of Elea
what he had gained from philosophy, he replied :

E

" Contempt of death," and facing the tyrants' scourges with unflinching courage, sealed his opinion with death. Spartan boys, encouraged by the presence of their relatives, endured the cruellest whippings, and the more blood they shed the more glory to their family did their fortitude bring.

In these cases glory was lawful, because it was human, and no imputation of reckless prejudice or desperate conviction was cast upon them when they despised death and every sort of cruelty. They were allowed for country, for empire, and for friendship to suffer what we are not allowed to suffer for God. For all these you cast statues and write inscriptions on their portraits, and engrave them epitaphs to last for ever. Certainly, as far as records can do it, you yourselves confer a kind of resurrection on the dead. But the man who hopes for a real resurrection from God, if he should suffer for God, you deem to be mad. Go on, good governors; the mob will think you all the better if you sacrifice Christians to them; crucify, torture, condemn, destroy us; your injustice is the proof of our innocence. For that reason God allows us to suffer these things. Just recently by condemning a Christian woman to the brothel rather than to the wild beasts, you acknowledged that a stain upon chastity is reckoned among us as more dreadful than any punishment and any death. Your cruelties, though each be more elaborate than the last, do not profit you; they serve rather as an attraction to our sect. The more you mow us down the greater our numbers become; our blood is the seed from which new Christians spring.

Many men among yourselves have written exhortations for the endurance of pain and death; Cicero, for example, in the *Tusculans*, Seneca in the treatise *On Chance*, Diogenes, Pyrrho, and Callinicus. But their words do not find as many disciples as the Christians make by their deeds. The very obstinacy, with which you reproach us, is our best teacher. Who is there that is not roused by the sight of it to ask what there is really within it ? Who does not join us when once he has asked ? Who does not long to suffer, when once he has joined, that he may buy back the whole grace of God and procure all indulgence from Him by the payment of his own blood ? To this action all sins are forgiven. Hence it is that even in court we thank you for your verdict. There is an enmity between what is of God and what is of man ; and when we are condemned by you we are acquitted by God.

WOMEN'S DRESS

PART I

If there lingered on earth a faith equal to the reward of that faith which is looked for in the skies, not one of you, my beloved sisters, I am sure, as soon as she knew the living God and realized her own, that is woman's, condition, would ever have desired to dress in joyful, not to say in boastful, guise. She would, rather, pass her days in squalour and put on the garb of mourning, proclaiming herself an Eve sad and repentant, and by the amendment of her dress seeking to expiate more fully that which she inherits from Eve, the ignominy, I mean, of the first sin and the odium of bringing ruin upon mankind. *In pain and anguish, woman, thou dost bring forth : towards thy husband thou must turn, and he is thy master.* And do you not know that you are Eve ? The judgement of God upon your sex endures even to-day ; and with it inevitably endures your positon of criminal at the bar of justice. You are the gateway of the Devil ; you are the unsealer of the forbidden tree ; you are the first rebel against the divine law ; you are she who persuaded him whom the Devil was not strong enough to attack. So easily did you shatter the image of God in man. Because of your reward, which was death, even the Son of God had to die.

Is not a skin tunic, then, sufficient for you ? Why think of further adornments ? Come now, if at the beginning of the world there had been men of Miletus shearing sheep, Chinese spinning silk from trees, Tyrians dyeing, Phrygians embroidering, Babylonians busy at the loom ; if then there had been pearls shining white, rubies flashing red, and gold starting from the ground, together with the desire to possess it ; if the mirror, too, already had won its boundless licence of deceit, would Eve, methinks, have coveted any of these things, a woman expelled from Paradise and now in the bonds of death? Well, then, if she wishes to live again, she must not desire nor know things which she had not and knew not when she was alive. Therefore, all such gauds are but the baggage of a woman condemned to death, invented, as it were, to grace her funeral procession.

Those, indeed, who first devised these things are held to be damned and sentenced to the penalty of death; for they were the angels who fell from heaven upon the daughters of men, and thereby added fresh shame to womankind. Certain substances well hidden and many arts not well revealed they then first brought out into the light for the benefit of an age much less skilful than ours. They laid bare the working of metals, they divulged the qualities of herbs, they made known the power of incantations, they directed curious research even to the interpretation of the stars. But as a special and, as it were, peculiar gift for women, they offered them the instruments of female pride. They brought the flashing stones that give to necklaces their varied hues, the golden bracelets that are clasped about the arm, the artificial dyes that add colour to white wool, and even the dark powder which enhances the effect of eyelids and eyelashes. The quality of these devices we can tell at once by the quality and condition of their inventors. Sinners could not teach nor offer anything conducive to righteousness, wanton lovers anything conducive to chastity, renegades anything conducive to the fear of God.

If such things are to be regarded as forms of knowledge, a bad teacher must inevitably give bad instruction. If they are held to be the rewards of lust, the reward of foul conduct can never be in itself beautiful. Moreover, why was it of such importance to reveal these things or offer them as gifts? Could not women have found favour among men without brilliant jewellery and ingenious ornaments, seeing that they had stirred the passions of angels while they were unkempt and unadorned, and so to speak still raw and rude ?   Or was it that their lovers would have seemed mean and insulting, if they had enjoyed them without payment and given no presents to the women whom they enticed to their beds ?   But these questions of price are out of place. A woman who had taken an angel for her property could want nothing more ; obviously wedlock had paid her well. It is plain that the angels themselves, who must sometimes at least have remembered the place whence they fell and after the hot fury of their lust sighed again for heaven, made these things the reward for a woman's best gift, regarding her natural grace as the cause of all their trouble. They did not wish women's good fortune to bring them happiness. They meant woman to fall from sincerity and frankness, and so, in company with themselves, incur the anger of God ; for they knew well that vain glory and self-seeking and the desire to give carnal pleasure are all things displeasing to Him.

These are the angels, you must know, whom we are going to judge : these are they whom we renounce at baptism : these are the reasons whereby they have earned judgement from men. What, then, are their things doing in their judges' hands ?   What commerce can there be between those who are to condemn and those who are to be condemned ? No more, methinks, than there can be between Christ and Belial. How, when in the future we mount the tribunal can we consistently give judgement against those whose gifts we now crave ? On that day women will have the same angelic substance, the same sex as men ; and they are promised the same high position as judges. Unless, then, here and now we shall have given a previous verdict by previously condemning those things which hereafter we shall condemn on their persons, it is they who will judge and condemn us rather than we them.

I know that the Book of Enoch, which assigned this

place to the angels, is not recognized by some people,
merely because it has not been received into the Jewish
armoury. I suppose they think that a book written before
the Flood could not have survived a disaster which brought
destruction to the whole world. If that is their argument,
they should remember that Noah, who was the great-
grandson of Enoch, survived the Flood, and that Noah
by family account and hereditary tradition, had heard
of the favour before God which his great-grandfather
enjoyed, and also remembered all his famous utterances,
seeing that Enoch had most straitly enjoined upon his son
Methuselah to hand down the knowledge of them to
posterity. Noah therefore could possibly have succeeded
as trustee to this inheritance ; and, had it not been so,
he certainly would not have kept silence concerning the
dispositions made by God who had preserved him and
the glory of his house.

Even if Noah's position were not so easy, the following
consideration would still support our claim that the book
is genuine. After it had been destroyed by the violence
of the Flood, Noah could quite possibly under inspiration
have given it new shape, just as after the storming and
destruction of Jerusalem by the Babylonians it is generally
agreed that Ezra restored all the monuments of Jewish
literature. In his book Enoch has proclaimed the coming
of Our Lord, and we must not reject anything which has
such a bearing upon us. We read moreover that *every
scripture suitable for edification is divinely inspired*. By the
Jews this book may have been rejected for this very reason,
just as they reject nearly all the other portions of scripture
which sound the coming of Christ. Nor, of course, is it
surprising that they refused to recognize the scriptures
which speak of Him, seeing that they would not recognize
Him when He spoke in person before them. Furthermore,
Enoch has a testimony in the writings of the Apostle Jude.

For the moment, then, let us not brand women's pomp
with any stigma from the condemnation that fell upon its

inventors. Let us not impute anything to the angels save their rejection of heaven and their carnal wedlock. Let us, rather, examine the qualities of these things in themselves, so that we may discover the motives that lead women to desire them. A woman's appearance depends upon two things ; the clothes she wears, and the time she gives to her toilet. Under the first heading comes everything that we call " female finery " ; for the second " female frippery " would be a more appropriate term. The first includes clothes, jewels, gold and silver ornaments ; the second deals with the care of the skin, the hair, and those parts of the body which attract men's eyes. Against the first we bring the charge of ostentation, against the second of harlotry. And so at once now, dear handmaid of God, you may see what of all these things is suitable to the training you must undergo. Our ways are not as theirs, and with us it is your humility and your chastity that will make you precious.

Gold and silver, the chief materials in worldly splendour, must necessarily be the same in nature as that thing from which they come. That is, they must be earth. And earth itself has more to boast of than they, inasmuch as it is only when it has been wept over by penal toil in the laborious hell of some accursed mine, and there left the name of " earth " behind it in the fire, that escaping like a runaway from the mine it passes from torments to ornaments, from punishments to bedizenments, from ignominies to honours. Iron, brass, and other altogether worthless materials are in the same condition with gold and silver as regards earthly origin and metallic treatment, so that in nature's judgement the substance of gold and silver is plainly deemed to have no especial nobility.

But, if it is from the quality of usefulness that gold and silver derive their fame, in that respect both iron and brass are superior ; for their utility is so arranged that not only do they discharge functions of their own more numerous and more necessary to human life, but of themselves they can with juster reason take the place of gold and silver. Rings are made of iron, and the records of antiquity preserve the fame of the brazen vessels that were used for eating and drinking. The insane abundance of gold and silver to-day must be responsible for the fact that with us they serve to make utensils for the privy. Certainly fields are not tilled with golden ploughs nor are ship timbers fastened together by the strength of silver. Hoes plunge not a golden edge into the earth, nails drive no silver points into planks. I pass over the fact that all our needs in life depend on iron and brass, and that without their effective strength the other rich substances, which have to be dug from mines and shaped afresh for every new use, would be helpless. We are now therefore in a position to consider, how it is that such dignity has accrued to gold and silver and why they take precedence over other metals which are closely akin to them in point of origin and are superior to them in point of usefulness.

As for the stones that vie with gold in pride, what am I to interpret them to be but pebbles and counters and particles once more of earth? Yet, though they are only stones, they are never wanted for laying foundations, or building walls, or supporting gables, or strengthening roofs. The only edifice which they know how to rear is the edifice of women's folly. A slow process of polishing is required to make them shine, cunning settings to bring out their brilliance, careful piercing that they may dangle in the light, and from gold they must borrow the meretricious allurement which they in their turn render back. As for the spoils that our love of ostentation fishes from the depths of the British Sea and the Indian Ocean, they are but shell-fish, inferior in flavour, I will not say to the sea-snail and the oyster, but even to the common mussel. Some shell-fish I have known which were true sea fruits ; but if this foreign creature suffers from an internal growth, it ought to be regarded as a defect rather than a glory, and though we call that growth a pearl we should remember that really it is no more than a hard round wart. People say also that as in fishes' brains there is a stony substance, so jewels can be extracted from the foreheads of dragons. This, forsooth, was lacking to the Christian woman, that she should add grace to herself from the serpent ! Is it thus that she will set her heel upon the Devil's head, while from it on her neck or even on her own head she heaps ornaments ?

All these things derive their charm solely from their rarity and strangeness. In their own land they are not held in such esteem. Plenty ever breeds contempt. In some foreign countries, where gold is native and abundant, convicts wear gold chains in prison, and there the wicked are loaded with riches—the more guilty a man is, the more wealth he carries on him. At last a way has been found to make even gold undesirable ! At Rome, too, we have seen the noble family of jewels in our matrons' presence blushing at the contempt which is shown for them by the Parthians and the Medes and the rest of their fellow-countrymen. With them they are regarded generally as unworthy of display ; emeralds are hidden under belts, the sword beneath their cloak alone is conscious of the jewels on its hilt, and the huge pearls upon their shoes desire chiefly to escape the mud. In short, the articles which they jewel most richly are just the things that ought not to be jewelled at all, either because they are not visible or else because being visible they are still treated with obvious contempt.

In the same way the slaves of these barbarians destroy the glory of our coloured robes by wearing the like themselves. Their house walls, too, are not painted but make scornful use of those royal purple and violet tapestries which you laboriously undo and shape afresh for your use. With them purple is held in no more account than red ochre. And rightly so ; for what genuine value is given to cloth by adulteration with false colours ? God likes not that which He himself did not produce. Had He not

the power to order that sheep should be born with purple
or sky-blue fleeces ? He had the power, but He did not
wish ; and what God did not wish certainly ought not to
be produced artificially. Those things are not by nature
best which are not from God, the author of nature. So
we understand they are from the Devil, who is nature's
corrupter. There is no other whose they can be if they are
not God's. What is not God's must necessarily be His
rivals ; and, except the Devil and his angels, rival of God
there is none.

Moreover, even if these substances are of God, it does
not follow immediately that such ways of enjoying them
among men are His. We have to consider not only where
shellfish come from, but also what sphere of decoration
is assigned them, and where they display their beauty.
All the profane delights of worldly shows, as I have shown
in my book on that subject—yes, and even idolatry
itself—derive their existence from things that are of God.
But for all that, a Christian ought not to be attracted by the
frenzies of the circus, or the cruelties of the arena, or the
scandals of the stage, simply because God has given to man
the horse, the panther, and the power of speech. Nor can
a Christian commit idolatry with impunity, on the ground
that the incense and the wine and the fire they feed and
the animals offered as victims are all conditional on God's
will ; since even the material object worshipped is of
God as well. With regard to their active employment
how can the origin of material substances, which descends
from God, excuse the use of them, if that use is foreign to
God and tainted with the guilt of worldly ostentation ?

Certain things have been distributed by God in certain
lands or set in some particular portion of the sea. These
things are mutually strangers one to the other, and they
are reciprocally neglected or desired. They are desired
among foreigners as being rarities : they are neglected,
rightly if anywhere, among their own people where
admiration of their charms has been cooled by familiarity.

The rarity and strangeness of such possessions, arising from their scattered distribution which God ordered according to his good pleasure, always finds favour with foreigners ; and the simple reason that they have not something which God has placed elsewhere arouses in them a burning desire to possess it. This desire leads to another vice, the craving for immoderate possession ; for although having a thing may be in itself permissible, moderation should always be observed. This second vice may be called " ambition ", its name derived from the cupidity " ambient " in men's minds which brings this vice to birth and spurs them on to vainglorious desires, commended neither by nature nor by truth, but suggested by the vicious passion of concupiscence.

There are other faults also inherent in ambition and vainglory. For example, in order to feed their own fire they exaggerate the price of things ; since concupiscence grows by heightening the value of what it covets. A small jewel casket holds a great estate. On a string of pearls ten thousand pounds depend. A woman's soft neck carries forests and islands round about it. The slender lobes of her two ears exhaust a whole bank book, and the five fingers of her left hand make a mock of five full money-bags. So great is the strength of ambition that one frail woman's body suffices to support the enjoyment of all these possessions.

PART II

My sisters and fellow-servants, handmaids of the living God, the right that ranks me with you in fellow-servantship and brotherhood emboldens me, meanest as I am in that fellowship, to address to you a discourse, not one of affection certainly, but in the service of your salvation taking affection's place. That salvation, in the case of men as well as of women, depends chiefly on the observance of chastity. We are all of us the temple of God as soon as the Holy Spirit has entered into us; but the sacristan and priestess of that temple is Chastity, who must allow nothing unclean or profane to enter, lest God who dwells within should be offended and leave the polluted abode. But for the moment we are not speaking of Chastity itself, for the enjoining and exacting of which the urgency of divine precepts is sufficient, but rather of some matters pertaining to it, that is, the fashion in which it behoves you to appear abroad. Very many women—in passing this censure on myself may God allow me to pass it on all—either from simple ignorance or from hypocritical motives have the boldness so to walk in public as though chastity consisted only in the bare integrity of the flesh and in the avoidance of fornication. They seem to think that there is no need of anything further, as regards the manner of their dress, the fashion of their toilet, and the studied graces of form and elegance. In their gait they display the same outward appearance as Gentile women, in whom the sense of true chastity is lacking, inasmuch as in those who know not God, the guardian and teacher of truth, there can be nothing that is true.

If any chastity can be believed to exist among Gentiles it is obviously of a very imperfect and unsteady sort. Up to a certain point it may keep a firm hold upon the mind, but it allows itself to relax into every licence of dress. As is the way with Gentile perversity, in thought it desires that from which in act it would shrink. How few women are there who do not desire eagerly to look attractive to strangers! They carefully have their cheeks painted, and then deny that they have ever excited lust. I grant you that with Gentile modesty it is a familiar thing to shrink from a sin, but still wish to do it; or even not to wish, but still not firmly refuse. Why wonder at that? All things that are not God's are perverse. Let those women beware, who by not holding fast to the whole good lightly mingle with evil that good which they do hold. You, my sisters, in your gait, as in all things, must take a different path from theirs. It is your duty to be perfect, even as your Father is perfect who is in the heavens.

You must know that to perfect, that is Christian, chastity carnal desire of one's body is a thing not only not to be wished but even utterly to be abhorred. The desire to please by outward charms, which we know naturally invite lust, does not spring from a sound conscience. Why should you rouse an evil passion ? Why invite that to which you profess yourself a stranger ? Moreover, we ought not to open a way to temptations which sometimes by their urgency bring about that from which God would save his children, and in any case are a stumbling block to disturb the spirit. We ought to walk in the whole substance of faith with such holiness as to be secure and confident in our own conscience, praying that this may abide in us, but not presuming that it will. He who presumes feels less fear ; he who feels less fear takes less precaution ; he who takes less precaution runs more risk. Fear is the foundation of safety ; presumption is a hindrance to fear. It will be more useful, then, to us if we expect that we may possibly sin than if we presume that for us sin is impossible. Expectation will lead us to fear, fear to caution, and caution to safety. On the other hand, if we presume, there will be neither fear nor precaution to save us. He who acts as though he were secure, and is not at the same time wary, possesses no safe and sure security. But he who is always wary will be able in truth to hold himself secure.

As regards His own servants, may the Lord in His mercy have care that for them it may be lawful even to presume without hurt on His goodness. But why should we be a danger to our neighbour ? Why should we excite in him lustful desires ? In amplifying His law God makes no distinction of penalty between lust and fornication, and it will scarcely be that they escape punishment who have

been to another the cause of perdition. That other, as
soon as he has lusted after your beauty and in his mind
committed the lustful act, perishes ; and you have been
made the sword of his destruction. Though you be
acquitted of actual guilt you will not escape the odium
attaching thereto ; just as when a highway robbery has
been committed on a man's land, the crime itself cannot
be laid to the owner's charge, but still the estate gets a
bad name, and its owner incurs suspicion. Are we to paint
our faces that our neighbours may perish ? Where, then,
is the command : *Thou shalt love thy neighbour as thyself* ?
Nay, you must think not only of yourself, but of your
neighbour as well.

No message from the Holy Spirit ought to be restricted
to the subject immediately before us : it should be applied
and carried out on every occasion when it can be useful.
Since therefore the dangerous pursuit of beauty concerns
others as well as ourselves, you must know now that not
only must you reject any outward show of fictitious and
artificial comeliness, but you must also by negligence
and concealment erase the signs of natural grace, as being
equally dangerous to the eyes of those you meet.
Comeliness, indeed, is not to be censured ; it is the body's
felicity, the last touch to God's handiwork, the goodly
vesture of the soul. But it is to be feared, owing to the
violence and wrongdoing of those who pursue it. So it
was that Abraham, the father of the faith, trembled because
of his wife's beauty ; and Isaac had to purchase Rebecca's
safety by ignominiously pretending that she was his
sister.

Let us grant for the moment that excellence of form
need not be feared, and that it is neither troublesome to
its possessors nor destructive to its desirers, nor perilous
to its associates. Let us suppose that it is not exposed to
temptations and that it is not surrounded by stumbling
blocks. It is enough for us that beauty is not necessary to
God's angels. Where chastity is, there beauty is idle ;

for the proper use and enjoyment of beauty lies in wantonness, unless, indeed, one thinks that there is some other harvest for bodily charms to reap. Should women then augment the beauty that is given them and strive after such beauty as is refused, considering that when they furnish to their neighbour that which is demanded from beauty, they are furnishing it also to themselves?

Someone may say: " Why should we not shut out wantonness and only admit chastity? Would it not be permissible then for us to enjoy the praise due to beauty and to glory in our bodily advantages?" Those whose pleasure it is to glory in the flesh must see to that. We have no desire for such " glory ", inasmuch as glory is the essence of exaltation, and exaltation suits not those who according to God's precepts are professors of humility. Moreover, if all glorying is vain and foolish, how much more so, especially to us, is glorying in the flesh. Even if glorying is allowable, we ought to wish to give pleasure, not in the flesh, but in the good things of the spirit; for it is of spiritual things that we are suitors. Where our work is, there let our joy be. Let us cull glory where we hope to win salvation. Obviously a Christian may glory sometimes, yea, and glory even in the flesh. But that will be when the flesh has endured laceration for Christ's sake, in order that the spirit thereby may win the crown, not in order that it may draw after it the eyes and sighs of youths. A thing that with you in any case is superfluous you may justly disdain if you have it not and neglect if you have. A holy woman may be beautiful by the gift of nature, but she must not give occasion to lust. If beauty be hers, so far from setting it off she ought rather to obscure it.

As if I were speaking to Gentiles, addressing you with a Gentile precept appropriate to all, I would say: " It is your duty to please your husbands, and your husbands alone." The less you trouble to please other men, the more you will please them. Have no fear, blessed sisters; no wife is ugly to her own husband. She pleased him enough when he chose her, whether it was her character or her looks that were the recommendation. Let none of you think that if she refrains from making the best of herself she will incur her husband's dislike and aversion. Every husband exacts chastity from his wife; but beauty a believing Christian does not require; for we are not attracted by the same charms as the Gentiles. An unbeliever on the other hand will regard your beauty with suspicion, owing to the infamous scandals which the Gentiles attribute to us. For whom is it, then, that you nurse your beauty? If it is for a believer, he does not exact it: if for an unbeliever, he does not believe in it unless it be simple. Why are you eager to please either one who is suspicious or else one who does not want such pleasure?

Of course, you must not infer from these suggestions that we should approve of an uncouth roughness in dress. We do not urge that squalour and slovenliness are good things. We merely set forth the limit and bounds and just measure of bodily adornment. You must not overstep the line to which simple and sufficient elegance limits its desires, the line which is pleasing to God. Against Him those women sin who torment their skin with potions, stain their cheeks with rouge, and extend the line of their eyes with black colouring. Doubtless they are dissatisfied with God's plastic skill. In their own persons they convict and censure the Artificer of all things. For when they amend and add to his work they censure Him, taking their additions of course, from the Artificer on the other side—that is, from the Devil. Who could show how to change the body save he who by wickedness transfigured man's spirit? It is he undoubtedly who has devised these ingenious artifices, so that in your own persons it may be seen that you lay hands on God.

Whatever is born is the work of God. Whatever is plastered on it is the work of the Devil. How criminal

F

to superinduce on a divine work Satan's ingenuities!
Our servants do not borrow anything from our private
enemies ; soldiers desire nothing from their general's
foes. It is a transgression for you to ask the use of anything
from the adversary of Him in whose hand you are. Shall
a Christian be helped in anything by the Evil One ? The
name of " Christian ", then, would scarcely continue his :
he would belong to him in whose wisdom he desires to
be instructed.   How alien from your discipline and
professions, how unworthy of the Christian name is it
for you to wear a false face, you on whom frankness in all
things is enjoined !   To lie in your appearance, you to
whom lying with the tongue is unlawful ! To seek after
what is not yours, you who have been bidden to abstain
from what is another's !   To practice adultery in your
looks, you who have set your hearts on chastity ! Believe
me, blessed sisters. How will you keep the precepts of
God, if in your own persons you do not keep his
lineaments ?

I see that some women change the colour of their hair
with saffron dye. They are ashamed even of their own
nation, ashamed that they were not born in Germany or
Gaul ; and so by changing their hair they change their
country !   Evil, most evil is the omen of those flame-
coloured heads, a defilement imagined to be a charm.
Moreover, the force of the cosmetics burns the hair and
ruins it ; the constant application of any sort of moisture,
even though it were undrugged, is harmful to the brain ;
and there is even danger in the warmth of the sun, so
desirable for imparting to the hair vigour and dryness.
What has grace to do with injury ? What has beauty to
do with filth ? Shall a Christian woman put saffron upon
her head, as the Gentiles lay it upon their altars ?   A
substance which is usually burned in honour of the unclean
spirit may be considered part of heathen sacrifice, unless
it is used for honest and necessary and salutary purposes,
to serve the end for which God's creation was provided.

But God says : *Who of you can make a white hair black
or a black white ?* And so women prove the Lord wrong !
" Behold," they say, " instead of white or black, we make
it yellow, a more pleasing and graceful colour." Not but
what those who repent of having lived to old age do attempt
to change from white to black again ! Shame on such
temerity ! The age which we fervently pray to attain
blushes for itself ; a theft is accomplished ; youth, the
period of sin, is sighed after : the opportunity for grave
seriousness is wasted. Far from wisdom's daughters be
such folly ! The more old age strives to conceal itself, the
more it will be detected. This, then, is your idea of true
eternity, hair that is ever young ! This is the incorruptibility which we have to put on for the new house
of the Lord, one guaranteed by cosmetics ! Well do you
hasten to greet the Lord, well do you speed to depart from
this iniquitous age, you to whom the near approach of
your own end seems unsightly !

Of what service to your salvation, moreover, is all the
anxious care you spend in arraying your hair ? You will
not let it have a moment's rest : one day it is tied back,
another day it falls loose ; now it is lifted high, now it is
pressed flat. Some women set their heart on forcing it
into curls ; others let it float waving in the air with a
simplicity that has nothing of virtue in it. Moreover, you
affix huge bundles of false tresses to your heads, making
of them, now a bonnet to enclose and cover over the top,
now a platform jutting out at the back of your neck. All
this striving, be assured, is contrary to Our Lord's precepts.
No one, it has been said, can add one cubit to his stature.
But you strive to add to your weight by fixing on your
necks bunches of hair, which look like round dumplings
or knobs of metal. If you are not ashamed of the
ungainliness of the mass, be ashamed of the defilement
wherewith ye defile yourselves. Fasten not upon a pure
Christian head the spoils of some other woman, who was
perchance foul and unclean, a sinner perchance and marked

out for hell. Cast off from your free persons the trappings
that are the mark of slavery. In vain you strive to catch
men's eyes with your splendours : in vain you employ the
most cunning artists to build up the structure of your curls.
It is God's order that you should be veiled. Methinks
the command was given so that some of your heads should
not be seen !

Oh that on the day of Christian exultation I, most
miserable that I am, may raise my head even from beneath
your heels ! I shall see then whether you will rise with
your powder and rouge and saffron dye and with your
heads lavishly adorned ; and whether it will be women thus
tricked out whom the angels will carry up to the clouds to
meet Christ in the air. If these things are good now and of
God, they will be seen then also in your rising bodies and
will recognize their proper place. But nothing can rise
save pure flesh alone and pure spirit. Whatever then does
not rise in the form of spirit and flesh is damned, because
it is not of God. From things that are damned abstain
even to-day. To-day let God see you in the same guise
as he will see you then.

You will say, I suppose, that I am a man and that from
sex jealousy I am driving women from their own domain.
Are there, then, some things that to men also are not
permissible, if we are godfearing, and have a due regard for
gravity ? There are, indeed ; since in men for the sake
of women, just as in women for the sake of men, there is
implanted by a defect of nature the wish to please. My
own sex recognizes some tricks of beauty which are
peculiarly ours—for example, to cut the beard too sharply ;
to pluck it out in places ; to shave round the lips ; to
arrange the hair and conceal grayness by dyes ; to remove
the first traces of down from every part of the body ; to
fix the hair with womanly pigments ; to smooth the skin
by means of rough powder ; to consult the mirror at
every opportunity and to gaze anxiously into it. But all
these tricks are rejected as being frivolous and hostile

to chastity, as soon as the knowledge of God has destroyed the wish to please by opportunities for wantonness. Where God is, there is chastity ; there, too, is gravity, her helper and ally. How, then, shall we practice chastity without her effective instrument, that is gravity ? Moreover, how shall we make gravity useful in the winning of chastity, unless we made strictness manifest in our face, and in our dress, and in the general aspect of the whole man ?

Therefore, as regards your clothing and all the other baggage wherewith you deck yourselves you, my sisters, also must show the like care in pruning off and retrenching a too redundant splendour. What avails it to exhibit in your face an honest frank simplicity worthy of the divine discipline, and then to invest all the rest of your body with the lascivious absurdities of pomps and delicacies? How close is the connection which these pomps have with the business of wantonness, and how they drown the voice of chastity's teaching, may be easily discerned from the fact that they prostitute the grace of natural beauty by making dress a partner in it ; to such an extent, indeed, that if they be lacking they take from beauty all use and charm, and make of her a shipwrecked sailor, a soldier without a sword. On the other hand, if natural beauty fails, the assistance of outward embellishment supplies a grace, as it were, of itself. Those periods of life, in fact, which are at last quiet and sheltered in the haven of moderation, the splendour and dignity of dress lure away from their repose, disturbing the strictness of age by the calls of appetite and making the seductive charms of apparel a compensation for the chill of advancing years.

Therefore, blessed sisters, take not to yourselves such robes and garments as play the part of pimp and pandar ; and if there be any of you whom reasons of birth or riches or past dignities compel to appear in public so gorgeously arrayed as not to appear to have attained wisdom, take heed to temper this mischief, lest under the pretext of necessity you should seem to give full rein to licence. How

will you be able to fulfil the precepts of humility which
our people profess, if you do not moderate the enjoyment
of your wealth and elegances, which tend so much to vain
glory ?   Glory is wont to exalt, not to humble.

"Shall we not use what is our own ?" you say.   Who
forbids your using it ?   But it must be in accordance with
the apostle's word that bids us : *to use this world as if
we abuse it not ; for the fashion of this world is passing away*.
And, again, *those who buy must so act as if they possessed not*.
Why so ?   Because he had laid down the premiss, saying,
The time is drawing short.   If, then, he shows that even
wives are so to be had as though they be not had, owing to
the straits of the times, what would he think of these
vain appliances that wives now use ?   Are there not
many men who consent and seal themselves to the eunuch
state for the sake of God's kingdom, relinquishing of
their own accord a pleasure which is both so strong and,
as we know, permissible ?   Are there not some who deny
themselves things which God created, abstaining from wine
and animal food, the enjoyment of which involves no danger
or trouble, offering a humble soul as sacrifice to God by
this chastisement of appetite ?   You women have already
had sufficient enjoyment of your wealth and your delicacies,
you have squandered the fruit of your dowries enough in
the days before you knew the discipline of salvation.
We are they upon whom the ends of the world have come.
Before the universe existed we were predestined by God
for the extreme limit of time.   God has trained us that we
may chastise and, so to speak, castrate this age.   We are
the circumcision, spiritual and carnal, of all things ; for
both in the spirit and in the flesh we circumcise the world.

Was it God, forsooth, who showed men how to dye
wool with the juices of herbs and the saliva of shellfish ?
He forgot, perchance, when he was bidding the universe
to come to birth, to order purple and scarlet sheep !   It
was God, too, I suppose, who invented the manufacture
of garments, which, light in themselves, are still heavy in

price ; God who devised the gold settings that encircle and enhance the brightness of jewels ; God who introduced the tiny wounds that ear-rings require, regarding it of such importance that His own work should be spoiled and innocent children tortured and made to suffer at once, that from the scars on their body—born, forsooth, for the steel—should hang some or other of those grains which the Parthians, as we see, use for studs upon their very shoes ! Why, even the gold itself, whose glory so enthrals you, serves a certain tribe, as Gentile literature tells us, for chains !

So certain is it that not reality but rarity makes these things seem precious. The labour involved in the arts invented by the sinful angels when they revealed these substances joined with their rarity raised the price of them, and also raised in women's hearts a desire to possess things that cost so much. But if the same angels who disclosed these substances and their attractions—I speak of gold and bright shining jewels—and also taught men how to work them, and soon among other things instructed them in the use of belladonna and the dyeing of fleeces ; if these angels, I say, have been condemned by God, as Enoch tells us, how shall we please God while we delight in the things of those angels who because of them provoked the anger and the vengeance of God ?

But, granted that God foresaw all this and that God allowed it ; granted that Esaias rebukes no purple garment, reprobates no headdress, represses no necklaces ; still let us not flatter ourselves, as the Gentiles do, by thinking that God only created us and that he does not now look down upon his creatures. How far more expedient and prudent is it to suppose that everything was provided then by God and placed in the world, in order that there should now be the means of testing his servants' discipline and that the liberty to use should serve as a proof of continence. Do not wise masters offer and permit some things to their servants on purpose, so that they may find out whether

and how they use their permission, whether they do so
with honesty and moderation ?   How much more praiseworthy is the servant who refrains altogether and even
fears his master's indulgence !   So it is that the apostle
says :   *All things are lawful, but all are not expedient.*
How much more easily will he dread what is unlawful
who has a respectful fear of what is lawful !

What motives have you for appearing in elaborate attire
seeing that you have naught to do with the occasions that
call for outward show ?   You do not go the round of the
temples, nor want to be present at public spectacles, nor
have you any acquaintance with the Gentiles' festivals. It
is because of these gatherings, for the sake of seeing and
being seen, that all the pomps of dress are exhibited ;
either to help in the business of wantonness or else to
swell foolish pride.   Your only reason for appearing in
public is a serious one. Either some sick brother has to be
visited, or sacrifice offered, or the word of God dispensed.
Any one of these duties is a grave and sober business,
requiring no extraordinary attire, and calling neither for
elaboration nor wantonness in dress.   If friendships
among the Gentiles and social obligations call you forth,
why not go to them clad in your own armour ?   The more
so, indeed, since you are visiting strangers to the faith.
Let there be a difference between the handmaids of God
and the handmaids of the Devil. Be an example to them.
Let them be edified in you. As the apostle says : *Let God
be magnified in your body*.   And it is by chastity that
God is magnified in a mortal body ; and, of course, by
attire suitable to chastity.

Perhaps some women will say : " We fear lest the Holy
Name be blasphemed in our case, if we make any changes
in our old style and dress."   Let us not, then, forsooth,
abolish our old vices !   Let us cling to the same character,
if we must cling to the same outward appearance as of
yore !   Then truly there will be no fear of the heathen
blaspheming !   It is a splendid blasphemy that says :

" From the day she became a Christian she appears abroad in poorer dress." Will you be afraid to seem poorer, now that you have become more rich ; fouler now that you have become more clean ? Is it according to the Gentiles' pleasure or according to the pleasure of God that Christians ought to walk ?

Let us only wish that we may not give cause for just blaspheming. How much greater reason for blasphemy is it if you, who are called priestesses of chastity, should appear in public decked out and painted after the fashion of the unchaste. What mark would then distinguish the unhappy victims of public lust as your inferiors ? Some laws in the past did forbid them to wear the insignia of a wife and matron, but now the daily increasing depravity of the age has put them so closely on an equality with respectable women that the difficulty is to distinguish them.

And yet even the Scriptures imply that meretricious aids to beauty are always closely connected with the bodily prostitution to which they are appropriate. The great city which sits upon the Seven Hills and rules over very many waters has earned from the Lord the name of " harlot ". And what dress enforces the comparison of that name ? Why, she sits *in purple, and scarlet, and gold, and precious stones*. How accursed are the things without which she could not be described as a harlot and accursed. It was because Thamar had painted and adorned herself that Judah thought her to be a prostitute, and she was so disguised by her attire—the quality of her dress giving the false impression that she was a harlot—that he judged her to be one and addressed and bargained with her as such. From this we learn that every care must be taken to avoid immodest company and suspicions. Why should the purity of a chaste mind be marred by a neighbour's suspicions ? Why should what I hate be hoped for in me ? Why does not my dress proclaim my character, so that my spirit may not be wounded through my ears

by shameless proposals ?   Granted that it be lawful to
assume the garb of a chaste woman ; it is certainly unlawful
to dress as though one were unchaste.

Perchance some woman will say : " To me it is not
necessary to be approved by men ; I do not require
men's testimony ;   God is the inspector of the heart."
We all know that ; but we must remember also that the
same God has said by his apostle : *Let your honesty be
manifest in the sight of men.* Why so, unless that malice
may have no access to you and that you may be an example
and witness to the evil ? What else do the words mean :
Let your works shine forth ? Why does the Lord call us
the light of the world ?   Why has he compared us to a
city set upon a hill, if we do not shine in the darkness and
stand out from among those who are sunken down ?   If
you hide your lamp beneath a bushel, you must of necessity
be left in darkness, and many will run against you. The
things that make us the luminaries of the world are these—
our good works. That which is good, provided it be full
and true, loves not darkness ; it rejoices in being seen and
exults over pointing fingers. For Christian chastity it is
not enough to be ; it wishes also to be seen. So great ought
to be its plenitude that it overflows from the mind to the
dress and bursts out from the conscience to the outward
appearance, from the outside gazing, as it were, upon its
furniture designed to hold the faith safe for ever. Such
delicacies, then, which can by their softness and effeminacy
unman the manliness of faith, must be discarded. The arm
that has been wont to wear a bracelet will scarce endure
to be benumbed to the rigour of a prisoner's chains. The
leg that has rejoiced in a jewelled garter will hardly suffer
itself to be squeezed in the stocks. I fear that the neck on
which coils of pearls and emeralds have rested will never
give a place to the executioner's sword. Therefore, blessed
sisters, let us practise hardships now, and we shall not
feel them ; let us abandon luxuries, and we shall not regret
them.   Let us stand ready to face any violence, having

nothing that we fear to leave behind. These things are but fetters that retard our hopes. Let us cast away earthly ornaments, if we desire heavenly. Love not gold ; for it is gold that brands all the sins of the people of Israel. You ought to hate that which brought your fathers to ruin and was adored by them who were forsaking God. Even then gold was food for fire.

It is in iron, not in gold, that Christians always, and now more than ever, pass their days. The stole of martyrdom is to-day prepared for us. We are waiting for the angels to carry us to heaven. Go forth to meet them arrayed in the cosmetics and adornments of the prophets and apostles. Draw your whiteness from simplicity, your rosy hues from chastity. Paint your eyes with modesty and your lips with silence. Fix in your ears the words of God and fasten on your necks the yoke of Christ. Bow your head before your husbands, and you will be sufficiently adorned. Busy your hands with wool ; keep your feet at home ; and then you will please more than if you were arrayed in gold. Clothe yourselves with the silk of honesty, the fine linen of righteousness, and the purple of chastity. Thus painted you will have God for your lover.

Men of Carthage, ever princes of Africa, noble in
antiquity, happy in modernity, I rejoice that the times go
so well with you now that you find both pleasure and leisure
to criticize modes of dress. These are the piping times of
peace and plenty. Blessings shower down upon us from
the empire and from the skies. Still, you do not dress now
as you did in the old days when you wore your tunics.
They were known everywhere for the carefulness of their
weaving, the harmony of their colour, and the proportion-
ment of their size. They were not baggy across the legs,
nor immodest between the knees, nor stingy to the arms,
nor tight to the hands. They had not even the shadow of
a girdle arranged to divide the folds, but stood firm upon
their wearers in four-square symmetry. Over the tunic
an oblong cloak was worn, thrown back on either side to
rest on the shoulders, and meeting closely round the neck
in the grip of a buckle. Its counterpart to-day is the robe
worn by the priests of Aesculapius, now your patron god.
So, too, your sister city used to dress, and wherever else
in Africa there are traces of Tyre.

When the urn of worldly fortune shifted the lots and
God favoured the Romans, your sister city of her own
choice hastened to change, and, as far as dress went, had
greeted Scipio before he landed, precocious in her
Romanizing. It was not, however, until after the happy
issue of all your wrongs, whereby you were saved from
senility but not deposed from eminence—after Gracchus
and his foul omens, after Lepidus and his rough jests,
after Pompey and his three altars, and Cæsar and his long
delays—it was not until at last Statilius Taurus built
your walls again and Sentius Saturninus solemnly

inaugurated them, that to you, I say, beneath the smiling
eye of concord, the toga was presented. Ah, what a circuit
it has taken, from Pelassians to Lydians and from Lydians
to Romans! And now, descending from the shoulders of
the sublimer race, it embraces the Carthaginians! Henceforth you find your tunic too long, and it must hang controlled by a girdle. Your cloak has changed to a smooth
toga and you prop up its redundancy by gathering it fold
on fold. As for the cloak, which used to be worn by all
classes among you, whatever other garment social position,
or rank, or season imposes, that at least is both forgotten
and derided.

For my own part, remembering incidents in the past,
I am not surprised. Take the case of the ram—not the
animal which Laberius calls " *Back-twisted-horned, wool-
skinned, drag-testicled* "—but the wooden engine which
serves in the army to break down walls. Never before had
it been poised by any man until great Carthage, as we are
told, " *keenest in war's pursuits,*" first equipped it for the
oscillatory work of swinging battery, modelling the power
of its engine upon the choleric fury of the head-avenging
beast. But when our country's last hour had come and the
ram, turned Roman, was doing deeds of daring against
the walls that were once his own, the Carthaginians
forthwith stood gaping at it, as though it were a new and
foreign invention :—

" *So far doth time's long age avail to change.*"
And so, in short, it is that the cloak also is not recognized
to-day.

Draw we now our material from some other source,
lest in the midst of Romans our Punicity be left to smart
and blush. To change her garb is surely the usual business
of Nature. It is a function which the world itself, on which
we press, is all the time discharging. Anaximander must
consider the bearing of this, if he thinks there are more
worlds than one ; and so must anyone who imagines there
is another universe among the Meropes, as Silenus prates

in Midas' ears, fit recipients for an even taller tale. Nay
even if Plato judges that a world exists of which our world is
but the image, that one also, like this, must have to undergo
change. If it is a world, it will be composed of substances
different in kind and different in their working, according
to the form of that which is the world here : for it will not
be a world if it is not just like the world we know.

Things which being diverse yet tend to unity are made
diverse by demutation, while the discord of their diversity
is harmonized by the changes they undergo. So it is by
mutation that every world will exist, its corporate structure
being the result of these diversities and its final blending
the result of these changes. At all events this caravanserai
of ours is altogether versiform—a fact plain to all eyes,
even to those that are kept shut or are as blind as Homer's.
Day and night come round in turns. The sun varies by
his yearly stopping places, the moon by her monthly
phases. The stars, each one distinct amid the blended
mass, now sink in heaven and now rise again. The circuit
of the heaven is now bright with clear sky, now blurred
with clouds : there is a downfall of rain and hail clattering
with it ; then a few sprinkled drops ; and then brilliant
sunshine.

The sea, too, has an ill repute for constancy ; at one
time, as the breezes equably sway, its tranquillity gives it
an honest look and the gentle waves a temperate mien ;
and then of a sudden it is tossing restlessly with billows
mountain high. So, too, if you survey the earth, that loves
to suit her vestments to the season, you would be almost
ready to deny she was the same : remembering her in
green, you now behold her golden, and ere long will see
her, too, in white. Of the rest of her adornments also,
what is there that is not subject to continual change—
the shoulder blades of her mountains by erosion, the
veins of her fountains by disappearance, the pathways of
her rivers by alluvial deposits. There was a time withal
when her whole orb was changed, completely covered by

water ; and to this day sea-shells and spiral horns sojourn
as strangers on the mountains, eager to prove for Plato's
sake that once the hill tops floated. But she swam free
again and changed back to her former shape, another
world but yet the same.

Even now the earth's dress suffers local mutation when
some particular spot is damaged. Among her islands,
Delos is no more and Samos is a heap of sand ; and so
the Sibyl's prophecy is proved true. In the Atlantic you
will seek in vain for the land that equalled Libya or Asia
in size. Long ago the side of Italy was cut away to its
centre by the shattering force of the Adriatic and
Tyrrhenian seas, and from its remnants Sicily was made.
There, too, the stroke of severance, hurling back from the
straits the contentious unions of the mains, endowed the
sea with a novel vice, the vice not of spewing out wrecks
but of swallowing them whole.

Even continents are affected by climate or by their own
mass. Look at Palestine. Where the Jordan rules the
boundary line, behold a vast waste, an orphaned country,
and useless fields. Yet once there were cities here, and a
numerous population, and the soil yielded its fruits.
Afterwards by the judgment of God impiety earned fiery
rain as its reward. Now Sodom's day is over ; Gomorrha
is no more ; all is ashes ; and the neighbouring sea no
less than the land knows a living death. Such another
cloud as that in Etruria consumed with flames the ancient
city of Volsinii and by the destruction of Pompeii taught
Campania what to expect from her mountains. Heaven
save us from such ruin ! May Asia have no fear of the soil's
voracity, and may Africa tremble no more before an
opening chasm, expiated by the treacherous absorption of
a single host !

Many other disasters of this kind have altered the look
of the world and changed particular sites. The licence
of war, too, has been very great. But it is as tedious to tell
these sad stories as to recount the vicissitudes of

kingdoms and their constant changes, from Ninus, the son
of Belus, onwards ; if indeed Ninus was the first man to
sit on a throne, as the ancient profane writers assert.
Generally speaking, among you heathen the pen goes no
further back. With the Assyrians, it may be, the history
of recorded time begins to open. We Christians, however,
who are in the habit of reading God's own records, are
masters of the subject from the very nativity of the world.

I prefer for the moment to deal with joyful events,
inasmuch as they, too, are the result of change. Whatever
the sea has washed away, the heaven burned down, the
earth undermined, and the sword shorn off, by the turn
of compensation's wheel comes back again at some other
time. In early days the earth over most of her circum-
ference was empty and devoid of inhabitants ; and if
any particular race had seized upon any district, it existed
for itself alone. And so at last understanding that all her
surface needed care, and that in one place there was an
over-abundance of men, and that in another they failed
her, she took thought to weed them out and scatter them,
so that, from grafts and settings as it were, peoples from
peoples and cities from cities might be planted over
every portion of her orb. From such races as had a
redundancy of men transmigrations took place in swarms.
The Scythian exuberance fertilizes Persia ; the Phœnicians
belch into Africa ; the Phrygians give birth to Rome ;
the seed of the Chaldæans is led out into Egypt, and afterwards, transferred from that land, becomes the Jewish
race. So, too, the children of Hercules under Temenus
stretch out and occupy the Peloponnese. So, too, the
Ionians in the train of Neleus furnish Asia with new cities.
So, too, the Corinthians with Archias fortify Syracuse.

But antiquity is but an empty name to-day, when our
own progress is before our eyes. How great a portion of
the world has our present age reshaped ! How many
cities has the triple strength of our existing rulers planted
or increased or restored ! While God looks with favour

upon our three emperors in one, how many populations
have been transferred, how many nations vanquished,
how many orders in the state restored to their former
splendour, how many barbarians shut out from our lands !
In truth, the world is now the empire's farm, and well is
it cultivated. The aconite of enmity is uprooted ; the
cactus and the bramble of clandestine intimacy wholly
destroyed ; the earth surpasses in delights the orchard
of Alcinous and the rose garden of Midas. Praising, therefore, the world in its mutations, why do you criticize
man ?

Beasts change their form instead of their garments.
And yet the peacock has a robe of feathers, and of the
choicest. In the bloom of his neck richer than any purple,
in the effulgence of his back more golden than any fringe,
in the sweep of his tail more flowing than any train,
many-coloured, diverse-coloured, versi-coloured, never
himself but ever another, yet ever himself when another ;
in a word, as mutable as he is movable. The serpent too,
deserves mention, though he is not in the same class as
the peacock. He, too, completely changes what has been
allotted him—his skin and his age. When he feels old age
creeping on him, he squeezes himself in a narrow space,
and crawls into his hole and out of his skin simultaneously.
Clean shorn on the spot he leaves his slough behind him
as he crosses the threshold again, and then and there
uncoils himself a new creature. With his scales his years,
too, are thrown off. The hyena, if you were to watch him,
is of an annual sex ; he is masculine and feminine in
alternate years. I say nothing now of the stag ; for
he is the arbitrator of his own life, and when he thinks the
time has come he eats a serpent, and by the venom's
force is brought back languorous to youth.

There is withal

> " *A tardigrade, field-dwelling quadruped,*
> *Humble and rough.*"

The tortoise of Pacuvius, you think ? Not so. There is

G

another beastling whom the versicle fits : in size he is one of the moderate exceedingly, but he has a grand name. If, without previously knowing him, you were to hear tell of a chameleon, you would shiver, and expect some enormous monster with a lion's head. But when you come across him, usually in a vineyard, his whole bulk sheltered beneath a vine leaf, you will laugh straightway at the egregious audacity of his name, for there is not a drop of wet in his body. Other creatures far smaller than he is have something of moisture within ; but the chameleon is a living pellicule. His headkin begins straight from his spine, for neck he has none. Thus reflection for him is a hard matter, but in circumspection his eyes are swift emissaries, nay, they are revolving points of light. Dull and weary, he scarcely rises from the ground, but drags as he moves forward with bewildered gait, rather making a show than actually taking a step. Ever fasting yet never fainting, he feeds agape and ruminates like a bellows, his food wind. Still though the chameleon can do nothing else, he is able to change himself completely. For, whereas his proper colour is one, he takes the hue of anything that approaches him. To the chameleon alone it has been granted—as our common saying has it—to sport with his own hide.

Much had to be said to pave the way before we should arrive at Man. Whatever beginning you assign to him, he certainly came from his maker's mould naked and undressed ; and it was only later that without waiting for permission he prematurely possessed himself of wisdom. Then at once he hastened to hide that part of his newly made body which modesty up till that time had not required to be concealed, and covered himself for the moment with fig leaves. Subsequently, on being driven out from the place of his birth because he had sinned, he went skin-clad into the world' like a convict to the mines.

But these are mysteries, not for universal knowledge. Let us take something now from your store, a tale that the

Egyptians tell which Alexander has set out for his mother's reading. It is a story of the days of Osiris when Ammon, rich in sheep, made his way to him from Libya and Mercury joined their company. They say that the god, delighted with the softness of a ram which he chanced to stroke, flayed a little lamb and made a further trial with its fleece. The pliancy of the material invited him to go on, and gradually by assiduous traction he drew out a thread and from it wove the first piece of cloth. You, yourselves, however, have generally preferred to assign to Minerva the management of wool and the structure of the loom ; although Arachne had an even more industrious workshop than hers.

Henceforth material has been abundant ; and I am not going to speak of the sheep of Miletus and Selge and Altinum, nor of those for which Tarentum and Bætica are famous, whose colours are provided by nature. Now even trees give you cloth, and the grass of flax, losing its greenness, turns white in the washing. Nor has it been enough for you to plant and sow a tunic : you have pushed your luck further and to-day fish for raiment. Even the sea yields you fleeces, inasmuch as the more expensive shell fish are of a mossy wooliness and furnish a kind of hair. Furthermore, it is no secret that the vermicle we call a silkworm produces ready for use the threads which, by drawing them through the air, she stretches even more skilfully than a spider's dial web, and after stretching devours. Therefore, if you kill her, the fibre you will unroll from her will be something that was once alive.

The ingenuities of the tailor's art complementary to this abundant store of material have promulgated various forms of garment. Their first object was to cover man, and here Necessity led the way. But soon Ostentation followed in her wake, and their purpose then became to adorn man and to puff him up withal. Of these forms of dress, some are worn by particular nations and are not common to the rest of mankind ; others, on the other hand, are worn universally as being useful to all. To this latter class belongs our Cloak ; for though it is especially Greek, in speech it has by this time found a home in Latium. With the word the garment came in. Indeed, the very man who once drove all Greeks from Rome and then in his old age learned their alphabet and speech, that self-same Cato in the year of his prætorship bared his shoulder, and by his cloak-like dress showed that he favoured the Greeks as much as anyone.

If Romanism is universal salvation, why is it that in some discreditable ways you people are so very Greek ? In provinces trained for better things, provinces fitted by nature for struggling with the land, whence, if not from Greece, have men borrowed the decrepit fashions of the wrestling-school and the ceaseless labours they involve, their rubbing with mud, their rolling in dust, and their dry dietary ? Whence comes the trick that some of our Numidians use, who with their long locks made longer with horsehair plumes bid the barber shave their faces close and' leave only their crown unshorn ? Whence comes it that among a shaggy and hirsute race the resin works such havoc on the armpits and the tweezers take such plunder from the chin ? 'Tis strange, portentous strange, these Greek customs without the Greek cloak ! To the cloak belongs all this Asiatic mode ! What have Europe and Libya to do with such smooth refinements when they know not how to dress ? And what sort of thing is it, forsooth, to practice Greek depilation and to scorn Greek attire ?

To alter one's dress is culpable just in so far as it is nature, and not merely habit, that suffers the change. There is a considerable difference between the sanctity of religion and the respect paid to time. Let Habit keep her word with Time : Nature owes faith to God. It was to Nature, therefore, that the Thessalian hero gave a shock by turning into a virgin, he who had been reared upon the marrow of wild beasts—he was called Achilles, because he had never sucked a warm breast and therefore always was a-chill—and trained in a stony school with a rock-like sylvan monster for tutor. If it were the case of a child, you could be patient and bear with a mother's anxiety ; but he already had hair between his legs, he had already secretly given proof of his virility to some one, when he consented to wear a woman's dress, to put up his hair, to powder his face, to consult the mirror, and to bedizen his neck ; effeminated even as to his ear by ear-ring holes, as his bust at Sigeum still shows. Obviously he turned soldier afterwards ; necessity gave him back his sex. The trumpet had sounded battle ; nor were weapons far to seek. " The steel itself," says the poet, " draws the warrior to it." Else if, after that incentive, he had persevered in his maidenhood, he might have won a husband. Here, then, is mutation indeed. A monster, I call him, a double monster : from man to woman, and then from woman to man. The truth ought not to have been denied and the deception ought not to have been confessed. Both kinds of change were bad : the first was opposed to nature, the second contrary to self-preservation.

Bad was it when maternal fears transfigured a man's dress ; but greater far the shame when the change was due to lust. And yet you worship him for whom you ought to blush, the Club-arrow-skin bearer, who bartered all the glory of his name for a woman's attire. Such power was given to his Lydian wanton, that Hercules prostituted himself in Omphale's shape and Omphale in Hercules'. Where, then, were Diomede and his bloodstained mangers ? Where Busiris and his funereal altars ? Where Geryon, the three in one ? The old stains of blood left upon his arrows by the Hydra and the Centaurs were now removed with pumice-stone and sponge, while wantonness exultingly proclaimed that after transfixing monsters their points might sew together chaplets of flowers. No sober woman or heroine of repute would have ventured her shoulders beneath the hide of that monstrous beast, for fear the lion's roughness would chafe her tender neck. She would have insisted that it should be smoothed down by long softening and deodorized ; and that in Omphale's house, I hope, was brought about with ointments of balsam and fenugreek : I suppose, too, that the mane submitted to the comb. So the lion's gaping jaws were filled by the lady's ringlets, his teeth concealed beneath the shadow of her kiss-curls ; his whole outraged visage would have roared at the insult, if it had been able. Nemea surely groaned aloud—if that place has any presiding genius—for when she looked about her she saw that she had lost her lion. What sort of figure the great Hercules cut in Omphale's silk chemise has now been inferentially depicted by this description of Omphale in Hercules' lion skin.

Consider, too, the boxer Cleomachus who formerly rivalled the Tirynthian hero in strength. At Olympia, by a miraculous metamorphosis he passed from the male to the female sex, and while till then he had been bruised without, he was now bruised within his body. Well does he deserve a chaplet among Novius' *Fullers*, and right deservedly has his tale been told by the farce-writer Lentulus in his *Catinensians*. Of course, he had to cover with bracelets the marks left on his arms by the boxing-gloves, and replace his thick woollen vest with a shift of transparent gauze. Of Physco and Sardanapalus I must be silent ; whom, but for their eminence in lust, no one would recognize as kings. I must be silent; for I fear lest even they mutter something about certain of your Emperors equally shameless as themselves. Nor would I have a cynic philosopher's firmness point out to us a Cæsar who is a second Nero, fouler than was Physco and more effeminate than Sardanapalus.

Not less warmly does the force of vain glory work for mutation of dress, even where manhood is preserved. There is heat in all emotion ; but when by windy bellows it is blown up to emotionalism, you get at once a blaze

and a conflagration of glory. This was the fuel, look you,
that fired the mighty king, master of all things save desire
for fame. He had conquered the Persians, but he was
conquered by the Persian garb. Doffing the knightly
mail of victory, he degraded himself into the trousers of
his conquered foe. He bared his chest, that still showed
the marks of his iron breastplate, by covering it with a
transparent texture, and while it yet panted and quivered
with the work of war he put out its fire with an airy silken
robe. Great Alexander did not swell enough in spirit
until he had also an inflated garb to delight his vanity.

So much, then for the Macedonian ; and I believe that
even philosophers to-day affect something of the same
kind. I hear talk of philosophizing in purple. If a
philosopher wears purple, why not gilded slippers as well ?
You are not in the proper Greek fashion if you sport a
Tyrian gown without gold shoes. Some one will say,
" There was once a philosopher who wore a silk robe and
bronze sandals." That is true ; and it was quite in keeping
for Empedocles to have cymbals on his feet ; he wished
their clatter to increase the effect of his Bacchanalian garb.
But if at that time Diogenes had been barking from his
tub, he would not have been satisfied with rubbing his
muddy feet upon him, as he did to Plato's sumptuous
couch. He would have carried him down entire to the
sanctuary of the sewer nymphs, so that, madly thinking
himself a god, he might greet his sister divinities before
he spoke to men.

Such garments then as overstep the bounds of nature
and modesty will only meet with their deserts if we fix
them with a scornful glance, point at them with a mocking
finger, and expose them to ridicule with a shake of the head.
If a man wears a dainty robe, such as Menander affected,
trailing effeminately on the ground, he should hear applied
to himself the comedian's line : " *What a madman with
his trailing gown, the waster !* " For now that the frown of
a censor's vigilance has long ago been smoothed away so

far as serious notice is concerned, all the world offers to
our gaze freedmen dressed as knights, branded slaves as
gentlemen, and rogues as honest folk ; the ploughman
looks like a city clerk, the cheap-jack like a lawyer, and
the clodhopper like a guardsman ; pimps, pugilists, and
undertakers, all go to the same tailor as you do.

Turn now to women. The sight to which Cæcina
Severus once called the Senate's serious attention, matrons
appearing in public without the matron's robe, is now a
commonplace. And yet by a decree of the augur Lentulus
any woman who thus cashiered herself was liable to the
same punishment as for illegal debauchery : for the
disuse of the garment which revealed and guarded a
respectable woman's position was designedly encouraged
by some females as being a hindrance to their playing the
part of prostitutes. But to-day women act as their own
pimps and that they may be the more readily accosted
they have foresworn their long dresses, and modest
chemises, and bonnets with rattling ornaments ; yes,
and even the very litters and sedan-chairs in which they
used to preserve a domestic privacy in public.

But while one puts out the light that is properly hers,
another kindles one to which she has no claim. Look at
the common whores, with whom the mob's lust does its
trafficking ; look at the female votaries of Lesbian vice.
'Twere better certainly to withdraw your eyes from the
shame of chastity thus publicly slaughtered ; but still
take a sidelong glance, and to the outward view they will
seem respectable mothers of families. Observe the madam
who presides over some brothel sink, how she airs her
silken gown, how she consoles with necklaces the neck
that is more filthy even than her haunt, how with
bracelets—the prizes of a man's bravery which even
matrons should not lightly wear—she decks the hands that
are privy to every sort of shameful deed, how upon her
impure leg she fits a pure white shoe. Observe, too, those
fashions that falsely claim religion as the reason of their

strangeness. Some have themselves initiated into the
mysteries of Ceres merely for the sake of the white dress,
and the distinction of the fillet, and the privilege of wearing
the close cap. Others have the opposite hankering for
dark raiment and a black wool head-covering, and so they
throw off all restraint of reason in Bellona's temple. To
others, again, Saturn recommends himself ; for then they
can put on a purple tunic with extra-broad stripe and cast
over their shoulders a shawl of Galatian scarlet. Yes, even
our cloak, if it be arranged with particular care and worn
with slippers in the Greek way, may serve to flatter
Æsculapius.

Under these conditions you may indeed cast upon it
a reproachful eye and accuse it of being guilty of
superstition, albeit superstition of a simple and unaffected
kind. But when it garbs our Christian wisdom which
renounces superstitions and their vanities, then our cloak
is indeed an august robe, superior to all the vestments in
which you array your gods and goddesses ; a priestly
ornament, surpassing all your tiaras and tufted plumes.
Cast down your eyes, I urge you, and for the moment
reverence the cloak as marking the renunciation of your
past errors.

You may say, " Must we, then, give up the toga for the
cloak ? " Why not ? If it were a case of giving up a
diadem and sceptre, did not Anacharsis do that when he
preferred philosophy to the Scythian throne ? Even though
there be no miraculous signs of your change for the better,
there are some things which the cloak will do for you.
Consider first the simplicity of its use ; it needs no
tedious arrangement. Accordingly, there is no necessity
for an expert to arrange its folds from the top a day
beforehand, to draw them down into pleats, and to put
the whole structure of their massed boss under the guardian-
ship of pincers, while next morning he comes back and
gathers up your tunic in a girdle—it were better to have
it woven of a moderate length—and after scrutinizing

the boss again and rearranging anything that has gone
wrong, pulls the left side of the toga forward and draws
back from the shoulders the circle where the folds end and
the hollow begins, finally leaving the right shoulder free
and heaping the cloth upon the left with another similar
set of folds reserved for the back.

The final result is more burden than dress. I will
challenge you to say what you really think. What is the
first sensation a toga gives you ? Do you feel yourself
dressed or loaded ? Are you wearing a garment or carrying
a pack ? If you say there is no discomfort, I will come
home with you and see what you hasten to do as soon as
you get indoors. There is really no garment whose removal
so congratulates a man as does the toga's. Of shoes I
say nothing now, implements of torture most appropriate
to the toga, an unclean and an unreal protection for the
feet. Whether it be hot or cold who would not better go
with stiff feet bare than bear the constriction of a tight
shoe. A mighty protection for the tread have the Venetian
shoe factories provided with their effeminate boots !

But than the cloak nothing is more simple, even if it
be double, like that which Crates used to wear. It offers
no obstacle to the process of dressing : its one business is
to cover your body loosely. You can do that in one fling
without any superhuman effort ; and it covers every part
of a man at once. The shoulder it leaves either bare or
covered ; but in either case it fits close to it without being
oppressive or tight. It does not have to trouble about the
possible treachery of its folds ; it keeps itself straight and
makes its own readjustments without difficulty. Even
when you take it off, it has not to be put on a hanger for
the next day. If you wear a shirt under it, the torture of
a girdle is superfluous. If anything in the way of shoeing
is required, sandals are the cleanest wear ; they leave the
feet more exposed and are certainly more manly than
shoes.

So much for the moment on the cloak's behalf, in so far

as you have defamed it by name. Now it challenges you
in its own person on the ground of its function withal.
" I owe nothing," says cloak, " to forum or polling
booth or senate house : I keep no obsequious vigil, I
rush to seize no platform, I haunt no general's head-
quarters : I am not rank with the water of the market-
place nor do I stand in rank as a suppliant by the law
courts : I wear out no benches, I upset no laws, I bark
not in any court : I am neither judge nor soldier nor
monarch : I have withdrawn from the populace. My only
business is with myself : no other care have I save that
I care for naught. One can enjoy a better life in seclusion
than in publicity. ' A life of indolence ! ' you will say
with a sneer, ' Men ought to live for their country and
empire and estate.' Nay, those sentiments are out of
date. No one is born for other people : he is destined to
die and that concerns himself. Even you give the title of
' sage ' to such folk as Epicurus and Zeno, and all their
quietist teacherhood, who have consecrated quietude as
the unique and supreme form of pleasure.

" Still to some extent even to me it will be allowed to
confer benefit on the public. From every curbstone and
altar it is my wont to prescribe physic for morals—physic
more successful in giving health to public affairs and states
and empires than any effort of yours. Nay—to take off
the gloves against you—your civilians' togas have done
more harm to the state than your soldiers' coats-of-mail.
I for my part flatter no vices, I give no quarter to lethargy
and sloth. I cauterize the foolish love of show which led
Cicero to pay four thousand for a table of citron-wood,
and Asinius Gallus to spend twice as much on a tray of
the same material from Mauretania. Gad, what a price
these gentry set on a few spots in wood !

" I put my iron, too, to such pride as Sulla's, that had
silver platters made weighing a hundred pounds. Although
I fear that even their weight would seem insignificant
to-day, when a Drusillanus, one of the Emperor Claudius'

slaves, constructs a dish that weighs five hundred. A dish like this, of course, is quite necessary for the tables we have mentioned : it had a special workshop built for it, and it ought to have had a special dining room as well. Likewise I plunge my scalpel into the cruelty that induced Vedius Pollio to throw slaves into his fish-ponds for his lampreys to devour. Delighted with this new form of savagery, he kept these monsters, toothless, clawless, and hornless, as though they belonged to the land, and found a pleasure in forcing fish to be wild-beasts, cooking them of course directly after their meal, so that their flesh might give him something of the taste of his slaves' bodies.

" Then I will operate on gluttony : such gluttony as the orator Hortensius indulged when he started a new fashion and had the heart to kill a peacock for food ; or Aufidius Lurco, who first corrupted joints with stuffing and by means of forcemeat gave them a flavour that was not their own ; or Asinius Celer, who for one mullet for dinner paid fifty pounds ; or the actor Aesopus, who set aside in his pantry an equally extravagant dish of game, one composed of song birds and pretty warblers, which had cost him hard on a thousand pounds ; or, lastly, Aesopus' son, who after this titbit could still hunger for something more expensive : fearing, I suppose, that his meal might seem beggarly compared with his father's, he took a set of pearls, whose mere name made them precious, and swallowed them down. As for people like Nero and Apicius and Rufus, I say nothing of them. I will administer a purge to the foulness of a Scaurus, the gambling of a Curius, and the drunkenness of an Antony. Remember that all these, whom I have chosen from many like them, were men of the toga : you will not easily find their like among the company of the cloak. What, indeed, save the cloak's wise words can heal by poultice and suppuration the festering sores of the state ?

" ' With such words,' says my opponent, ' you have urged me to conviction ; and words are the wisest of medicines.' Nay, even though my tongue were mute, stilled by lack of words or checked by bashfulness—for life itself is satisfied by a wordless philosophy—my very cut speaks for me. A philosopher is heard all the time that he is seen. My very approach puts vice to the blush. Who does not suffer when he sees the rival he fears? Who can bear to look with his eyes on one from whom his inner thoughts shrink? Great is the cloak's service; seeing that the very idea of me brings a blush to the cheeks of vice. Philosophy may well reflect on the help I give her, but she is not my only associate. I have in my company other arts of public utility. I supply vestment to the primary schoolmaster who teaches the shape of the letters and explains their sounds and sets forth the elements of arithmetic. I clothe the grammarian, the rhetorician, the sophist, the physician, the timebeater in the theatre, the astrologer, and the fortune-teller who watches the flight of birds. All the liberal arts are kept covered by my four corners. ' True,' you say, ' but all these rank lower than the knights of Rome.' Yet remember that your gladiators' trainers and all their ignominious following wear the toga when they march out into the arena. That, of course, will be the indignity you mean when you say ' Give up the toga for the cloak ! ' "

This, then, is the cloak's speech. And I for my part confer upon the cloak full fellowship with God's own sect and God's own teaching. Rejoice, cloak, and exult ! A higher wisdom now has deigned to take thee and thou hast begun to be a Christian's vesture.

CYPRIAN

CAIUS CAECILIUS CYPRIANUS, also called Thascius, was a native of North Africa born in the early years of the third century A.D. Neither the exact date nor the place of his birth are known, but he came of a pagan family possessed of very considerable wealth. After an early manhood of some licence he studied law, and soon was famous in Carthage as the most eminent master of forensic eloquence. In the year 245, however, he was converted to Christianity by a presbyter Caecilius, whose name he took, and selling his property for the benefit of the poor he gave up his great practice as an advocate and entered the Church of Carthage as a simple novice. His baptism probably took place on Easter Day, 246, and passing rapidly through the lower ranks of the ecclesiastical hierarchy as deacon and presbyter, on the death of Donatus he was by the voice of the people unanimously called to the Bishopric. Five of the senior presbyters dissented, and Cyprian at first declined the office : but the people would not be denied, and early in 249 he was ordained.

Soon after his appointment the persecution of Decius began, so that Cyprian was compelled to go into hiding and direct the affairs of his church from a distant retreat. This was certainly the wisest course, but it led to two difficulties. A certain number of rebellious presbyters set themselves up against him during his absence, and on his return he found a distinct spirit of arrogance among the " *confessors* ", those Christians who had refused to bow to the persecution and by confessing Christ publicly had incurred an imminent risk of death. An even more serious problem was presented by the " *lapsi* ", men who had fallen away from the faith during the persecution and were seeking to be readmitted to the Church. On this

question there were acute differences of opinion both at
Carthage and at Rome, where they led eventually to the
Novatianist schism, and it is now generally recognized
that Cyprian's counsels of moderation were justified.
He was perhaps less happy in the controversy with Stephen,
Bishop of Rome, on the subject of the validity of baptism
conferred by heretics ; but this dispute was brought to
an end by the edict of Valerian 257 announcing a fresh
persecution. Cyprian as head of the church was summoned
before the Proconsul at Carthage, and by him was banished
to Curubis, a little town 50 miles away. There he stayed
for a year, and then, the Roman government thinking
sterner measures necessary, he was recalled for martyrdom
and beheaded by the public executioner at Carthage
14th September, 258.

Cyprian is greater as a man than as a writer. His favourite
author was Tertullian, of whose treatises he made a daily
study. " Da magistrum " he would cry—" Now for
my teacher "—and plunge into the reading of one of the
master's works. But his own compositions, though clear
and elegant, show little of that racy eloquence which marks
Tertullian's style. His Latin is the Latin of Cicero, as
taught in the schools, equable and temperate, but lacking
in savour and personality. He is easier to read than
Tertullian, but from a literary point of view not so worth
reading. For Cyprian the subject matter is more important
than the language : he is a man of action rather than a
man of letters, and nearly everything he writes has a close
relation to some practical problem of church administration.
He is, first and foremost, a Bishop in charge of a flock
whom he must guide and inspire with his own spirit
of ardent faith and loving charity. As an eloquent French
writer says : " A whole people lived on his word ; each one
of his sermons, each one of his discourses was a real act,
right up to that last hour in which, for reply to the
Proconsul, he discovered a still more eloquent silence, and
placed in a resolute ' No ' his whole soul." (E. Havet.)

Cyprian's writings, nevertheless, in spite of his multifarious activities, are fairly extensive, and fill some eight hundred pages in Hartel's Vienna edition. About half their bulk consists of letters, written in his episcopal capacity either to the African bishops and to subordinate ministers in his own diocese or to the church of Rome and to the two Roman bishops of his time, Cornelius and Stephen. They are largely concerned with details of church management, the ordination of deacons and presbyters and the excommunication of schismatics and heretics; and mingled with these are letters of fervent exhortation to martyrdom and loving congratulation on the faithful endurance of suffering. Among the subjects of wider importance the three most prominent are, as might be expected, the proper treatment of the "lapsed", the validity of heretic baptism, and the best methods of stamping out schism. Occasionally, moreover, we obtain a glimpse into the inner working of a Christian community. One correspondent, for example, asks Cyprian whether an actor, retired from the stage but still giving dramatic lessons, should be allowed church membership; Cyprian answers in the negative. "The credit of the church must not be polluted by so disgraceful and infamous contagion. The man must give up his teaching, and if he has no money you must send him to us at Carthage and we will support him." Another writer puts the case of some women who have professed virginity but have been discovered with men in suspicious circumstances: Cyprian replies: "Virgins must not be allowed to live with men, much less to sleep with them; for in the past to my sorrow many have been corrupted by dangerous conjunctions of this kind. In the case of these women, they should be examined and if found intact receive a severe admonition but be allowed to remain in the church."

Apart from the letters, a fair selection of Cyprian's works may be made by taking the three treatises, "*Ad Donatum*," a monologue on the world and its vanities, "*On those who*

H

lapsed from the faith," and " *On the unity of the Catholic Church* ", the first important for its literary merits, the second for its historical information, the third for its doctrinal teaching. This is not to say that his other writings will not well repay study. The treatises " *On the dress of Virgins* ", " *On the Lord's Prayer,* " and " *On Patience* " are a milder treatment of subjects already handled by Tertullian, but by their very contrast of style they are interesting ; while the two essays " *On Envy* " and " *On Mortality* " are beautiful examples of church oratory. The three treatises mentioned first, however, are of special significance, and two of them are given here in full together with an extract from the third.

The " *Ad Donatum* " is sometimes wrongly classed with the letters ; but it is in fact a dramatic monologue and one of the earliest of Cyprian's writings. There is in it a much greater care than usual for the beauties of style, and much more of literary artifice. The introduction is faintly reminiscent of the opening of Plato's *Phaedrus*, and in the elaborate descriptions of the theatre, the arena, and the law-courts, the influence of Juvenal is manifest. But the piece is valuable, both for the insight it gives us into the conditions of society in Cyprian's time, and even more for its plain statement of one of Cyprian's two great discoveries, the doctrine that man is not definitely evil and that human nature can be perfectly remoulded by divine grace.

Cyprian's other discovery, the realization that the Church ran far greater danger from internal schism than it did from pagan persecution, is embodied in the " *On the Unity of the Catholic Church* ", an impassioned plea, supported by constant scriptural quotations, for unity within the church and obedience to episcopal control. The treatise has had immense influence, and is of very great historical importance. Of the arguments that have been drawn from Cyprian as to the supremacy of one particular bishop, and of the very difficult question of text interpolation, this is not the place to speak.

The World and its Vanities: A Monologue

You do well to remind me of my promise, dear Donatus, for not only do I remember it, but this is certainly the appropriate time for its fulfilment, when the vintage season invites the mind to unbend in repose, and to accept the annual and appointed truce that the weary year affords. The place, moreover, is in harmony with the day, and the villa's picturesque aspect accords with the gentle breezes of a mild autumn in soothing and cheering the senses. Here it will be delightful to pass the day in talk, and by studious discourse train our inmost hearts in the divine precepts. Let us make our way to yonder bower, so that no profane intruder may interrupt our converse nor the heedless clatter of the noisy household deafen our ears. The neighbouring thickets ensure us a safe retreat, where the vagrant trailings of the vine shoots, creeping in pendent mazes over their reed supports, have made for us with their leafy shelter a vine colonnade. Here we can well pour our earnest thoughts into one another's ears, and while we gratify our eyes with the picturesque view of trees and vines, we may instruct our minds by what we hear, and feed them on what we see. Not but what I know that your only pleasure, your only interest, at this moment is in our discourse. You despise the prospect before you with its alluring charms, and have fixed your eyes upon me, a rapt listener in face, in mind, and in ardent affection.

And yet what will be the character or value of anything that my mind is likely to impart to yours ? The narrow mediocrity of my humble powers produces very thin crops and is never weighed down by heavy ears ripening to the abundance of a copious harvest. Nevertheless, with such

faculties as I have, I will set about the matter; for the
subject of my discourse is a strong assistance. In courts
of law and in political debates men may display the riches
of their eloquence in voluble ambition; but when we
raise our voice to speak of the Lord God, a chaste sincerity
of speech is sufficient, relying on facts rather than on the
resources of rhetoric for the conviction of faith. In short,
the words that you will hear from me will be weighty
rather than eloquent: they will not be adorned with
learned talk to charm a popular audience, but by their
sheer truth and simplicity they will be fitted to proclaim
the divine mercy. Take what was felt before it was learnt,
what was not accumulated by long study during the lapse
of years, but was drawn swiftly in one draught from the
spring of ripening grace.

When I lay in darkness and blind night, wavering,
tossed on the billows of this stormy world, uncertain of
my wandering steps, ignorant of my way in life, and a
stranger to the light of truth, I used to think it a
very difficult matter that a man could possibly be born
anew. The divine indulgence had made me the promise
for my salvation, but considering my character at that
time it seemed to me very doubtful if anyone could be
quickened to new life by baptism in saving water, and,
putting off what he had been, should be himself changed
in heart and soul, although retaining all his bodily structure.
" How," I would say, " is so great a change possible ?
How can we so suddenly divest ourselves of what was
either born with us and has hardened by long use in our
material nature or else was acquired by us and has become
inveterate by lapse of time ? These things go deep, and
are now radically engrained within us. When does a man
learn thrift who has grown accustomed to splendid
banquets and magnificent feasts ? When does a man
descend to ordinary simple garb who has always been
conspicuous in costly robes glittering with gold and purple ?
He who has once felt the charm of power and office can

never be a commoner again, inglorious and unknown. He who has lived attended by serried bands of clients and honoured by the close concourse of their officious train regards it as a punishment when he is alone. Things do not change, and it is inevitable that wine should always entice, pride inflate, passion inflame, greed disquiet, cruelty sting, ambition delight, and lust drive headlong to ruin ; their allurements are eternal and will never let go their hold."

These were my constant thoughts. I myself was held in bondage by the manifold errors of my previous life, from which I thought I could not possibly get free, and so I was inclined to acquiesce in my clinging vices. Despairing of better things, I used to indulge my sins, regarding them as familiar servants devoted to my pleasure. But when, by the help of the water of new birth, the stains of the past were washed away and a clear light from above poured into my purified heart ; when, through the Spirit drawn from heaven, a second birth made me into a new man ; then in wondrous fashion the things that had been uncertain began to seem clear, hidden things were revealed, dark things made light, what before had appeared difficult now explained itself, what had been thought impossible now became capable of achievement. I was able to realize that what had lived in thraldom to sin, being earthly and born of the flesh, had now begun to be of God and was animated by the Holy Spirit. I am sure that you know and recollect as well as I do what was taken from us and what was given to us by that death of sin and birth of virtue. You know it of yourself, and I need not tell you.

Boasting of one's own glory is offensive ; but this is not a question of boasting but of gratitude, since we do not ascribe it to the virtue of man but declare it to be the gift of God. That we sin not now is the beginning of faith's work ; that we sinned before was the result of human error. All our power is of God : of God, I repeat. From

Him we have life, from Him we have strength, by power
derived and conceived from Him while still in this world
we recognize beforehand the signs of things yet to come.
Only let fear be the guardian of innocence, that the Lord
who of His mercy has shone upon our hearts with access
of celestial grace may be welcomed in the hostelry of a
mind rejoicing in righteous sacrifice, and that the
assurance we have gained may not breed carelessness, so
that our old enemy creep upon us again.

If you keep to the way of innocence and righteousness,
not allowing your feet to falter or slip, if you depend on
God with all your strength and all your heart, and be
indeed what you have begun to be, then, as your spiritual
grace increases, so will opportunity also be offered to you.
The dispensation of God's gift follows not the fashion of
earthly benefits : with it there is no measure nor stint.
The spirit flowing generously forth is checked by no
limitations, is confined by no encircling barriers within
a definite bounded space : it gushes out perpetually with
exuberant stream. Only let our heart be athirst and open
to welcome it. The more capacious the faith we bring, the
more abundant grace shall we draw from that fountain.

From the Spirit, in sober chastity, in purity of speech
and integrity of mind, we derive power for the healing
of the sick to counteract the venom of poisons, to restore
health of mind, and purge away the stains of madness, to
bid peace to those who are at enmity, repose to the violent
and gentleness to the unruly. By the spirit's help we can
deal with the foul vagrant demons who have taken refuge
in the bodies of men whom they purpose to destroy ;
forcing them by stern threats to avow themselves, compelling them with heavy blows to come out, stretching
them on the rack while they struggle, howl, and groan
beneath the severity of their punishment, beating them
with whips, and burning them with fire. Though the eye
cannot see the work is done within : the strokes are hidden,
but the punishment is plain. So true is it that inasmuch as

we have made a beginning the gift of the Spirit avails itself of its opportunity, but inasmuch as we have not changed our corporeal members our fleshy vision is blinded by the world's darkness. How great is the empire of the mind, how wonderful its strength that not only is it itself saved from the world's dangerous contact and kept pure and clean, undefiled by the attacks of the Enemy, but even grows firmer and more powerful every day, so that it can crush beneath its masterful dominion all the hosts of our aggressive Adversary !

That the truth of the divine gift may be more clearly revealed and the signs thereof made plain, I will give you the light of knowledge, and wiping away the murk of sin I will bring daylight to the darkness of this blind world. Imagine yourself for a moment to be transported to the high peak of some lofty mountain, and gaze down thence upon the aspect of all that lies beneath you. Turn your eyes this way and that, and while you yourself are free from all earthly contacts, look at the storms that vex our wave-swept sphere. Then will you feel compassion for the world and in self recollection with gratitude to God rejoice with increased gladness that you have escaped from it. Consider the high roads barred by robbers, and the seas beset by pirates, consider the strife of camps in every land with all the horror of bloodshed. The whole world reeks with mutual carnage, and murder which is a crime when done by one man is called a virtue when it is committed wholesale. Impunity is claimed for wrongdoing, not on the ground of innocence, but because of the magnitude of the sin.

If now you turn your eyes and gaze upon our cities you will behold a concourse more saddening than any solitude. The gladiatorial games are being prepared, that the sight of blood may gladden the lust of cruel eyes. Bodies are crammed with rich food to fill men with marrow, and strong limbs are loaded with a mass of brawny muscles, so that the wretches, fattened for punishment, may cost the more to kill. Man is slaughtered to give pleasure to man. It is for murder that they use their training, their experience and their skill. Not only is wickedness done, but it is taught to others. What can be imagined more savage and barbarous ? Men are trained to commit murders, and murders bring them fame. What madness is it, pray, when people uncondemned by a judge, in the prime of life, comely in appearance and clad in costly garments, offer themselves to the wild beasts ? Living men, they deck themselves for a voluntary death : wretched men, they even make a boast of their misfortune. It is not crime but frenzy that brings them to battle with the lions. Fathers look on at their sons fighting ; brothers and sisters sit close by in the crowded seats ; and though the extravagant grandeur of the show puts up the price of admission, a mother, oh, shame ! pays the increase to be present at her own sorrow. In looking at scenes so impious and hellish as these men seem not to realize that with their eyes at least they are parricides.

Turn your face next to the pollution, not less abominable, of another kind of spectacle. In the theatres, too, you will see things that will make you ashamed and indignant. The business of the tragic buskin is to relate in verse the crimes of the past. The ancient horrors of parricide and incest are unfolded before us in action framed to the likeness of truth. The ages pass, but any sin that was formerly committed is not allowed to be forgotten. Each generation is reminded by what it hears that whatever has once been done can be done again. Crimes never die out by the lapse of ages, wickedness is never blotted out by time, villainy is never buried in oblivion. Things which have ceased to be done become examples for wrong-doing to-day. The mimes are our instructors in infamy, and each spectator delights to see repeated on the stage what he has done at home, or to hear what he may do on his return. Adultery is learnt while it is seen : the mischief authorized by the state serves as a pandar to vice :

and the matron, who perchance went to the play a modest
woman, returns from it a harlot. What a stain upon a
man's character is it, what a stimulus to lust, what food
for immorality, to be polluted by the sight of the actor's
gestures, to look on while the laws of nature are broken
and pathics submit openly to the foulest shame ! Males
are made female, their bodies softened and by lewdness
robbed of strength, until all the glory and vigour of their
sex has gone. The more an actor forces man to be woman,
the more pleasure he gives. His offence is his glory :
the greater the scandal, the greater his renown. The
audience gazes at him—oh, abomination !—and are
delighted with what they see. And what cannot such
a creature suggest ?   He inflames men's passions, he
flatters their emotions, he overpowers conscience, honesty,
and fortitude. To pave the way of ruin for men, the
blandishments of vice are supported by the authority of
heaven. The actors set before us the harlotries of Venus,
the adulterous passion of Mars : they show us their great
Jupiter, supreme in vice as in power, with the fire of his
thunderbolts ardent for earthly amours, now turning white
in a swan's plumage, now pouring down in golden rain,
now rushing with his eagles' help to ravish some blooming
youth.   Ask yourself if those who look on at such
performances can be untainted and really chaste. They
take pattern, poor wretches, by the gods they worship,
and make their religion an excuse for sin.

Oh, if on your high watch-tower you could pierce men's
secret retreats, if you could open their chambers' barred
doors and reveal their hidden mysteries to the conscious
eye, then would you see deeds of shame committed which
no one without a front of brass could bear to behold, you
would see things which it is a crime even to look upon,
things done in a fit of vicious madness, things which the
doers deny and then hasten to repeat. In their mad lust
men fall on men, and do what can give even them no
pleasure. Either I err from the truth, or else it is people

of this sort who accuse others, bespattering the foul with their own foulness and thinking—as if conscience were not sufficient—that thus they have thrown off the burden of their guilt. In public they arraign the sins which in secret they commit, sitting in judgement while they themselves are criminals. They condemn abroad that which they do at home, and make a crime in others of that wherein they themselves delight. Their audacity indeed is fitly mated with their vice, and their lack of shame suits exactly with their lack of decency. I beg you not to wonder at the things that persons of this kind say : in their mouths sins of speech are comparatively unimportant.

The high roads, then, are beset with snares and battle rages manifold over all the world. The arena runs red with blood, the theatre is degrading ; and exposed for sale in brothels or hidden in private houses, we meet the abominations of lust, abominations whose guilt is but fostered by secrecy. But perhaps you may think that the law-courts are immune from all this, that they are not exposed to the provocation of wrong, nor polluted by contact with vice. Turn your gaze in that direction : you will find more abominations there, and you will be glad to look away. Though the laws are engraved on the Twelve Tables and the statutes published on plates of brass, yet in the midst of the laws wrongs are done and in the face of the statutes crimes are committed. Innocence is defended there, but it is not preserved. The fury of disputants rages in turn ; men break the peace although they wear a peaceful garb ; and the forum echoes with the madness of strife. There close at hand is the spear, the sword, the executioner : there is the nail that tears, the rack that stretches, the fire that burns—more tortures for one poor human body than it has limbs. And who is there here to help ? Your patron ? He is but a fraud and a broken reed. The judge ? He sells his verdict. The man who sits to punish crimes commits them, and the judge becomes a criminal that the accused may perish though

innocent. Wrongdoing everywhere is rife, and sin takes
on a multitude of shapes as its deadly poison works on
dishonest minds.   One man palms off an alleged will,
another commits the capital offence of forgery ; by one
trick children are cheated of their inheritance, by another
strangers are endowed with their estates ; enemies make
their charges, false accusers attack, and witnesses slander.
Everywhere hired eloquence with venal impudence
undertakes to bring false accusations, and in the meantime the guilty do not even perish with the innocent.
The laws excite no dread : no one cares for judge or
jury : when money can secure acquittal, why be afraid ?
It is a crime now among the guilty to be innocent : whoever
does not imitate the wicked is an offence to them. Law has
come to terms with crime, and to-day it allows anything
that is commonly done. What integrity, what sense of
shame can you find in a place where there is no one to
condemn the wicked and you only meet those who ought
themselves to be condemned ?

I may seem perhaps to be picking out the worst cases,
and in my destructive zeal to be directing your eyes only
to such things as must offend the gaze of an upright
conscience by their gloomy and repellent aspect. Well,
I will now show you the things which the world in its
ignorance deems to be good ; and among them also you
will find much from which you should shrink. In the state
honours which you deem so enviable, in the rods of office,
in the abundance of wealth, in military command, in the
glory of the magistrate's purple robe, and in the emperor's
autocratic power, in all these there lurks a venom of
flattering mischief and an appearance of smiling wickedness, joyful indeed for the moment, but treacherous with
the snares of hidden calamity. It is like some poison with
whose baleful juices sweetness has been mingled in subtle
craft, so that the potion, its savour thus disguised, seems
to be but a harmless draught : but when you have drunk
it up the death you have swallowed leaps quick upon you.

Look at yon man, glittering in his purple, who fancies himself so notable in his brilliant dress. With what baseness has he purchased that splendour ! What haughty arrogance in the past has he endured ! What proud doors has he besieged with his morning greetings ! How often, packed in a wedged mass of clients, has he walked before the scornful footsteps of the great, in order that a similar train later on might attend and precede him too with salutations, a train subservient not to his person but to his power ; for his only claim to reverence lies in the rods of his office ! And mark now his degrading end. When his time-serving flatterers leave him and his sycophants, turning traitor, insult him, unprotected now by his rank ; then the havoc he has wrought upon his squandered property smites his conscience, then he realizes his losses, then he sees that all his fortune has gone in buying the people's favour and in praying with vain entreaties for popular support. Foolishly indeed is money wasted on the disappointing pleasures of a show : the people get nothing substantial from it and the magistrate himself is ruined.

As for those whom you consider rich, who add forest to forest, and driving the poor from their demesne stretch out their fields into space without any limits, who possess masses of gold and silver, piled up heaps and buried stores of money—these men even in the midst of their wealth are troubled by doubt and tortured by anxiety. They tremble lest robbers should despoil or assassins attack, or lest the envy of some wealthier neighbour should turn hostile and disturb them with malicious law-suits. Eating and sleeping the rich man knows no security. At his dinner table he sighs, though he be drinking from a jewelled cup, and when his soft couch enfolds his body, languid with feasting, in its deep bosom, he lies wakeful in the midst of the down. He does not see, poor wretch, that his life is but a gilded torture, that he is bound fast by his wealth, and that his money owns him rather than he owns it. Alas, for the abominable blindness of human minds and the deep darkness of their senseless greed. He might disburden himself and find relief from his load ; but he prefers to brood over the wealth that is throttling him, and clings obstinately to the hoards that are his punishment. He never thinks of sharing with the poor or of showing generosity to his dependents. Such people call it their money which they guard anxiously like a stranger kept under lock and key, and from which neither their friends nor their children nor themselves derive any benefit ; but their ownership merely amounts to this— they keep other people out ! They say, too—strange contrariety of language—" these are my goods ", and can do nothing but make a bad use of them.

Do you think that those men at least are safe and know a firm security amid their great possessions and chaplets of honour, who live in the glittering splendour of a royal palace and are surrounded ever by a watchful guard of armed men ? Nay, they have more to fear than anyone. He who is dreaded is compelled to dread. High place exacts its penalty from the potentate, though he be hedged about with minions and though a numerous retinue protect his sacred person on every side. Even as he does not allow his subjects to be secure, so inevitably he has no security himself. The power that makes men terrible is a terror first to its possessors ; it smiles and frowns ; it flatters and deceives ; it lifts up and casts down. Ruin is like an usurer ; the greater the sum of dignity and office the greater is the interest in penalties which a man has to pay.

The one sure and certain peace, the one solid and un-shakeable security is for a man to withdraw himself from the storms of this distracting world and to find a firm anchorage in the harbour of salvation. Let him lift up his eyes from earth to heaven, and being admitted to God's gift and in mind now very close to his God, let him boast that all those things which other men in mortal life think lofty and grand now lie altogether beneath his consciousness. He who is greater than the world can seek or want nothing from the world. How firm, how unshaken is that guard, how heavenly the protection with its perennial blessings, to be released from the world's entangling snares and to be cleansed from the dregs of earth in the light of eternal immortality! Avaunt now the treacherous dangers wherewith the Enemy in his malice once assailed us! We are constrained to have more love for what we shall be, by being allowed to know and to condemn what we were. For this there is no need of bribes in money or service: man's highest dignity and power is not won by elaborate effort: it is God's free gift, easy for all to win. Even as the sun shines spontaneously and the fountain flows, as the day gives light and the rain yields moisture, so does the heavenly spirit pour itself upon us. When the soul gazing to heaven has recognized its Maker, it rises higher than the sun and far transcends all the powers of this earth. Then, indeed, it begins to be that which it believes itself to be.

Do you, then, whom the heavenly warfare has enrolled in the Spirit's camp, observe a discipline uncorrupted and sober in the virtues of religion. Be constant in reading and in prayer. Now speak with God, now let God speak with you. Let Him instruct you in His precepts and direct you. The man whom He has made rich no one shall make poor. There can be no lack for him whose heart has once been filled with the food of heaven. Ceilings panelled in gold and mansions decked with facings of costly marble will seem mean to you when once you realize that it is your own self that needs rather attention and care, and that the dwelling of your body, in which God abides as in a temple and which the Holy Spirit has begun to make his home, is of more importance than any house. Let us paint this abode with the colours of innocence, let us lighten it with the light of righteousness. This will never fall into decay with the passing of years, this will not lose its beauty as the paint upon its walls fades and its gold

tarnishes. Artificial charms are short-lived, and such
things as contain not the reality of possession afford no
sure confidence to their possessors. But this remains in
a beauty perpetually vivid, in unsullied honour and in
lasting splendour. It cannot be destroyed or quenched ;
it can only be fashioned to a fairer perfection when the
body returns.

This for the moment then briefly, dearest Donatus.
For although your kind and courteous patience, your firm
and well-balanced mind and your assured faith delight
in salutary conversation, and nothing is so pleasant to your
ears as what is pleasant to you in the Lord—still some
moderation in words must be observed, especially as we
are neighbours now and can often talk together. Since
this is a quiet holiday, and a time of leisure, let us spend
in gladness what remains of the day now that the sun is
sloping towards the evening, and let not even the hour of
repast be without its gift of heavenly grace. Let the sound
of psalms be heard at our sober meal ; and as your memory
is good and your voice tuneful, do you, as is your wont,
undertake that duty. Your friends will relish your good
cheer all the more, if we have something spiritual to listen
to, and the sweetness of religious melody charms our ears.

Since the Lord warns us, and says :—" *Ye are the salt of the earth,*" and since He bids us be simple to harmlessness and yet with simplicity to be prudent, what else, beloved brethren, befits us than to show foresight, and with anxious hearts vigilantly to perceive and beware of the treachery of our cunning enemy, that we, who have put on in Christ the wisdom of God the Father, may not seem to lack wisdom in regard for our salvation? It is not persecution alone that we ought to fear, nor those forces which advance to undermine and cast down God's servants by open methods of attack. Caution is comparatively easy when danger is obvious, and when the adversary declares himself the mind is prepared beforehand for a conflict. There is more need to fear and beware of the enemy when he creeps upon us secretly, when he beguiles us by a show of peace, and steals forward by those hidden approaches which have given him the name of " Serpent ". Such is ever his craft, such his dark and guileful artifice for entrapping man. Thus from the beginning of the world at once did he deceive, and by lying words of flattery ensnare a soul careless in its simple credulity. Thus did he try to tempt the Lord himself, as though he could creep again upon Him unawares, and secretly approach Him. But then he was recognized and beaten back, brought to the dust in that he was detected and unmasked.

From this an example has been given us, to shun the way of the old man, and to stand in the footprints of conquering Christ, so that we may not a second time through carelessness be brought into the snare of death, but foreseeing our danger receive the gift of immortality. And yet how can we possess immortality, unless we keep those commands of Christ whereby death is conquered and overcome ?   He Himself warns us and says, " *If thou wilt enter into life, keep my commands.*"   And again : " *If you do what I command you, I name you now not servants but friends.*"   These men are they whom He calls strong and steadfast, these He says are founded upon a firm foundation of rock, these stand square against all the storms and tempests of the world in firm and unshaken solidity. " *Whosoever,*" says He, " *heareth my words and doeth them, I will liken him to a wise man, who built his house upon a rock : the rain descended, the floods drew near, the winds came, and beat upon that house : and it fell not.   For it was founded upon a rock.*"   Therefore we ought to stand in His words, to learn what He taught, to do what He did. How can a man say that he believes in Christ, when he does not do Christ's precepts ?   By what road will he attain to the reward of faith, who does not faithfully keep his commandment ?   He must of necessity waver and wander, blown by the spirit of error like dust that is caught in the wind, and for all his walking he will never come to salvation, since he does not hold to salvation's true and only way.

Moreover, we must avoid all pitfalls, not only those which are clear and visible, but also those which by a clever and subtle deceit escape our notice.   What in fact is cleverer and more subtle than our adversary ?   It is true that he was unmasked and brought low by the coming of Christ, when light shone out for the nations and a saving brightness for the salvation of men, so that the deaf heard the gracious words of the Spirit, the blind opened their eyes to the Lord, the sick became strong again with an everlasting health, the lame ran to church, and the dumb prayed aloud in a clear voice. But the tempter when he saw his idols abandoned by a people of believers and his homes and temples deserted, devised a fresh plan to deceive us, and trapped the unwary by borrowing the very title of the Christian Church.   He invented heresies and schisms, that by their aid he might overthrow the faith, corrupt the truth, and destroy our unity. Those whom he cannot keep in the blind folly of their old way he circumvents and beguiles by the error of a new path. Out of the bosom of the Church he snatches men, and when they think that they have come near to the light and have escaped the darkness of this world, he again overwhelms their ignorance in night. The result is that though these men do not keep to the gospel of Christ and to his law and worship, they still call themselves Christians. Walking in darkness they think that they have the light, thanks to the persuasive deceptions of the devil, who, as the apostle says, transforms himself into an angel of light and equips his ministers as the ministers of righteousness, claiming that night is day and ruin is salvation, and making despair put on the guise of hope, treachery the garment of loyalty, Antichrist the name of Christ. Thus, while they feign things like the truth, by their subtlety they make truth void. That, my beloved brethren, is what becomes of us when we do not go back to the beginning and seek the fountain-head of truth nor keep the doctrine of the Heavenly Master.

If you were to weigh and consider all this there would be no need of a long treatise or of arguments. For a convincing proof of the truth of this is easily found. The Lord saith unto Peter : " *And I say unto thee that thou art Peter, and upon this rock I will build my church and the gates of hell shall not prevail against it. And I will give unto thee the keys of the kingdom of heaven and whatsoever thou shalt bind on earth shall be bound in heaven, and whatsoever thou shalt loose on earth shall be loosed in heaven.*" And again after His resurrection, He says : " *Feed my sheep.*" Upon him alone He builds His church, and into his care He gives His sheep to be fed. And while after His resurrection He gives equal power to all the apostles and says : " *As my Father hath sent me even so I send you . . . Receive ye the Holy Ghost. Whose soever sins ye remit, they are remitted unto them ; and whose soever sins ye retain, they are retained.*" Still, in order to make clear the general unity, by His own authority He caused that same unity to be traced back to one man. It is granted that the other apostles were even as Peter was, having an equal share with him of honour and power, but the beginning proceeds from unity. The primacy is given to Peter that it may be shown that the Church is one and the See of Christ is one. All are pastors, but the flock is one, and it is fed by all the pastors in perfect agreement, in order that the unity of Christ's church may be demonstrated. It is this one Church to which the Holy Spirit refers in the Song of Songs, speaking with the voice of the Lord and saying : " *My dove, my undefiled, is but one. She is the only one of her mother, elect of her that bore her.*" He that holds not this unity of the Church, does he think that he holds the true faith ? He who resists the Church and contends with it, who abandons the throne of Peter on which the Church is founded, is he confident that he is within the Church ? Does not the blessed apostle Paul teach this and prove the doctrine of unity, when he says : " *There is one body and one Spirit, one hope of your calling, one Lord, one faith, one baptism, one God.*"

It is our duty to hold fast this unity and to justify it, especially those of us who are bishops of the Church, that we may show that the episcopate itself also is one and indivisible. Let no man deceive the brethren with false doctrine or destroy faith in the truth by disloyally tampering with it. The episcopate is one, and a part of it is held by each of us, making a complete whole. The Church is one, but with rich exuberance it spreads far and wide among men. Even so there are many rays of the sun, but one sunlight ; many branches of a tree, but one trunk firmly grounded in a sound root ; and when many streams flow from one spring, although its unity seems to be scattered abroad in the very abundance of the water that flows, yet that unity is preserved in the source. Try to remove one ray of the sun from the whole : the unity of sunlight suffers

no division. Break off a branch from a tree : the broken
branch will not bud. Cut off a stream from its source :
it will dry up. So also the Church of Christ pours forth
its light and spreads its rays throughout the whole world ;
yet it is one light that is everywhere poured forth and the
unity of the whole is not destroyed. Or, again, its
inexhaustible fertility puts forth branches over the whole
world ; and like a mighty river it spreads its streams
far and wide. But one is the head, one the source, one the
mother of abundant and continuous fertility. From her
womb we are sprung and reared on her milk, by her breath
we are quickened.

The bride of Christ cannot admit of adultery, she is
pure and chaste. She knows but one home, and with
unbroken chastity she guards one sacred chamber. She
it is who preserves us for God, who offers to the Kingdom
of God the sons whom she has borne. He that separates
himself from the church and makes an adulterous union,
he is cut off from the promises of the church, nor shall he
who has deserted the church of Christ attain to the rewards
of Christ ; he is a stranger, an outsider, an enemy. He
cannot have God as a father who has not the church as his
mother. There was no escape for any who remained
outside the ark of Noah ; and even so he who is outside
the Church cannot escape. Our Lord Himself tells us :
" *He that is not with me is against me ; and he that gathereth
not with me scattereth abroad.*" He that breaketh the peace
and harmony of Christ is an enemy of Christ. He that
gathereth outside the Church, scattereth the Church of
Christ. Our Lord says " *I and My Father are one.*" And
again it is written of the Father, the Son, and the Holy
Spirit " *And these three are one.*" How could anyone
believe that this unity, coming as it does from the
unchangeableness of God and bound together by the
heavenly sacraments, could ever be sundered or split
apart by the schism of conflicting opinions ? He who
holds not this unity holds not the law of God nor

yet the faith of the Father and the Son neither life nor salvation.

This sacrament of unity, this bond of concord inseparably cohering is set forth to us when in the Gospel the coat of the Lord Jesus Christ is not divided nor cut. The men draw lots for Christ's garment, as to who should put on Christ, and the winner receives the entire robe for his own, uninjured and undivided. Holy Scripture speaks, saying, " *But as for his coat, because above it was not sewed but woven all in one piece, they said to each other ' Let us not rend but cast lots whose it shall be.' "* That garment bore an unity coming from above, coming, that is, from heaven and from the Father ; nor could it at all be rent by the receiver and possessor ; it kept inseparably a whole and substantial integrity. He cannot possess the robe of Christ who rends and divides the Church of Christ. On the other hand, when at Solomon's death his kingdom and people were divided the prophet Abijah meeting King Jeroboam in the field rent his mantle into twelve pieces and said : " *Take ten parts for thyself ; for thus saith the Lord ' Behold I rend the kingdom from Solomon's hand and I will give thee ten sceptres ; two sceptres shall be his for my servant David's sake and for Jerusalem, the city I have chosen that there I may set my name.' "* When the twelve tribes of Israel were rent asunder, the prophet Abijah rent his mantle. But because Christ's people cannot be rent, His coat woven and united throughout is not divided by those who possess it. Undivided, closely fastened, firmly connected it signifies the united concord of our people, we who put on Christ. By the sacrament and sign of His garment He has declared the unity of His church.

Who, then, is so wicked and faithless, so maddened by the frenzy of discord that he can believe it possible to rend the unity of God, the garment of the Lord, the church of Christ ? Who would dare to attempt it ? He Himself in His Gospel warns us and teaches, saying, " *And there shall be one flock and one shepherd.*" Do you suppose that in one place there can be many shepherds and many flocks? The Apostle Paul presses this same unity also upon us, when he exhorts and beseeches us in these words: "*I beseech you, brethren, by the name of Our Lord Jesus Christ, that you agree together in speech, and have no schisms among you: be ye joined together in the same feeling and the same judgement.*" And again he says: "*Bearing with one another in love, doing your best to preserve the unity of the Spirit in the harmony of peace.*" Do you think that you can stand firm and live if you secede from the Church and build for yourself other homes and a different dwelling place. The message was given to Rahab, in whose person the Church was prefigured, "*Thou shalt bring together to thee thy father and thy mother and thy brethren and all thy father's house: they shall come to thy house, and whosoever shall pass out beyond the door of thy house, his blood shall be on his own head.*" The sacrament of the passover also in the law of Exodus has but a single injunction: that the lamb, prefiguring Christ, which is then slain, shall be eaten in one house. God speaks, saying: "*In one house shall it be consumed: ye shall not send its flesh abroad from that house.*" The flesh of Christ and that which is holy of the Lord cannot be sent abroad, and there is no other house for believers save the one church. This home, this resting place of concord, the Holy Spirit shows to us and announces in the Psalms, saying, "*God who maketh men to dwell of one mind in a house.*" In the house of God, in the Church of Christ the dwellers are of one mind and endure to the end in concord and simplicity.

Therefore it was that the Holy Spirit came in the form of a dove, a simple and joyous creature, not bitter with gall, not savage in its bite, not fierce with rending talons. Doves love to find a resting place with men; they cling to association with one house; when they have young they bring them forth together; when they go abroad they keep close in their flight; they spend their lives in mutual and friendly intercourse ; they recognize the harmony of peace by the kisses of their beaks ; in all things they fulfil the law of unanimity. This is the simplicity that we should know in our church, this is the charity to which we should attain. The love of our brotherhood should take example from the doves ; our gentleness and meekness should be like the lambs and sheep. What part in a Christian breast has the fierceness of wolves, the rage of dogs, the deadly poison of serpents, and the bloody cruelty of wild beasts ? We may be thankful when such men as these are separated from the Church, so that they cannot prey upon Christ's doves and sheep, or infect them with the contagion of their cruelty and venom. Bitterness cannot combine or enter into union with sweetness, darkness with light, rain with fine weather, war with peace, barrenness with fertility, drought with running springs, tempest with tranquillity. Let no man think that the good can leave the church. The wind does not carry away the wheat, nor does the storm bring down the tree that has a firm solid root. It is the light stubble that is tossed by the tempest, the weak trees that are overthrown by the onrush of the hurricane. These are they whom the Apostle John smites with a curse, saying : "*They went forth from us, but they were not of us. If they had been of us, with us they would have stayed.*"

Hence it is that heresies have arisen so often and still arise to-day. A perverted spirit has no peace, and faithless discord cannot maintain unity. Every man has freedom of choice and God allows and permits these things to be so that the test of truth may prove our hearts and understandings, and the faith of those that pass her test shine forth unharmed in the clear light. The Holy Spirit warns us by the Apostle's mouth, and says : "*Heresies must be, that those who have been proved may be known among you.*" Thus the faithful are proved and the faithless are unmasked ; thus even here, before the day of judgement, the souls of the just and the unjust are already divided, the straw is separated from the wheat. These are they who without divine order preside of their own accord at some convention of rash strangers, who appoint themselves prelates without any law of ordination, who take to themselves the name of bishop though no one has given them a bishopric. The Holy Spirit in the Psalms brands them as men who sit in the seat of pestilence, plague spots, and abominations of the faith, deceiving with a serpent's lips, crafty to corrupt the truth, vomiting deadly poisons from their pestiferous tongues, whose speech is as a creeping cancer and their conversation pours a mortal venom into each man's heart and breast.

Against people of this kind the Lord cries, from them he restrains and recalls his erring people, saying : "*Hearken not to the speech of false prophets, for the visions of their hearts deceive them. They speak, but their words do not come from the Lord's mouth. They say to those who cast away the word of God : ' You, and all who walk according to their own wishes, shall have peace ; no evil shall come upon you, all ye who walk in the error of your hearts. I have not spoken to them, it is of themselves that they prophecy. If they had stood firm in my substance and had heard my words and taught my people, I would have turned them from their evil thoughts.*" And these same men, the Lord again brands and marks, when he says : "*They have left me, the fountain of the water of life, and have dug for themselves broken cisterns which cannot carry water.*" There can be no baptism save one ; and yet these men think that they can baptize. They have deserted the fountain of life ; and yet they promise the grace of the living water of salvation. With them men are not washed clean but rather made foul, sins are not purged away but rather increased. Their new birth brings forth sons not to God but to the devil. Born in falsehood they can not hold the promises of truth : begotten of faithlessness they lose the grace of faith. They cannot attain to the reward of peace, for they have broken the Lord's peace in the madness of discord.

Let not men deceive themselves by a vain interpretation, in that the Lord said : " *Wherever two or three are gathered in my name there am I with them.*" Corrupters of the gospel and false interpreters take the last words and omit the previous ones, remembering one part and cunningly suppressing the other ; and as they themselves are cut off from the church, so they cut in twain the meaning of one passage. The Lord was urging his disciples to be peaceful and to be of one mind : " *I tell you,*" He said, " *that if two of you agree on earth on something you shall ask, it shall be given you by my Father who is in heaven. For wherever two or three are gathered in my name, there am I with them.*" Thereby He shows that most importance is attached not to the number of suppliants, but to their unanimity. "*If two of you,*" He said, " *agree on earth.*" Unanimity He put first ; peaceful concord He made a prerequisite ; He taught us faithfully and firmly to agree together. How can that man agree with anyone who does not agree with the body of the Church itself, and with our whole brother-hood ? How can two or three be gathered in Christ's name, when it is certain that they are separated from Christ and from His gospel ? We did not leave them ; they left us. Heresies and schisms have arisen by their setting up of other conventicles, and they have abandoned the one source and fountain head of truth.

Concerning His church the Lord speaks, and to those men He speaks who are in His church. If they are in accord together, if they follow His commands and admonitions, though there be but two or three gathered, yet if they be unanimous in their prayer, though they be but two or three, they may possibly obtain from God's majesty that which they seek. " *Wherever two or three are,*" He says, " *there am I with them.*" He means that He is with the simple and the peaceful, with men who fear God and keep God's precepts. With these, though they be but two or three, He said He was, even as He was with the three youths in the furnace of fire. Because those youths trusted simply in God and were of one mind among themselves, even when they were shut about by the encircling flames He saved them from death by the dew of the Spirit ; just as He came in person to aid the two apostles shut up in prison, because they were simple and of one mind together, and breaking their prison bars set them again in the market place, that they might declare to the multitude the word which they faithfully preached. When, therefore, among His precepts He sets the words : " *Where two or three are, there I am with them,*" He does not divide men from the church, since He Himself ordained and made the church. He rather reproaches the faithless for their discord and by His word recommends peace to the faithful, showing that He is with two or three who pray with one mind rather than with very many if they be at variance, and that more can be obtained by the concordant prayer of a few than by the discordant pleading of a multitude.

So when He gave the law of prayer, He added, saying " *When you stand at prayer, forgive all that you have against anyone, that your Father also who is in heaven may forgive you your trespasses.*" And he calls away from the altar anyone who comes to the sacrifice in strife and bids him first make peace with his brother, and then return with peace and offer his gift to God. God paid no heed to Cain's gifts ; for he could not have God at peace with him who by reason of his quarrelsome jealousy had not peace with his brother. What peace then do the enemies of their brethren promise to themselves ? What sacrifices do those who are rivals of the priests think that they celebrate ? Do they imagine that Christ is with them when they are gathered together, they who are gathered outside the church of Christ ?

Even if such men met death confessing the name of Christ, their stain is not washed away even by blood. The guilt of discord is inexpiable, too grave to be purged even by suffering. He cannot be a martyr who is not in the church ; he cannot attain to the kingdom who has deserted her that in that kingdom shall reign. Christ gave us peace ; he bade us live in concord and be of one mind ; he commanded that the bonds of love and charity be kept unbroken and intact. He then who has not kept brotherly love cannot show himself a martyr. Paul the apostle teaches this and bears witness, saying : " *And though I have faith, so that I can move mountains, but have not love, I am nothing. And though I give all my goods to feed the poor, and surrender my body to be burned, but have not love, I avail nothing. Love is magnanimous ; love is kind ; love envieth not ; love acteth not vainly, is not puffed up, is not easily provoked, thinketh no evil, loveth all things, believeth all things, hopeth all things, endureth all things. Love will never fail.*" He says, " *Love will never fail,*" for she will ever be in the kingdom, in the unity of a brotherhood firmly joined to herself. Discord cannot attain to the kingdom of heaven, the prize promised by Christ, who said : " *This is my commandment, that ye love one another even as I have loved you.*" That prize he cannot win who by perfidious dissension has marred the love of Christ. He who has not charity has not God.

The word of the blessed Apostle John is this : " *God,*" he says, " *is love : he that dwelleth in love dwelleth in God, and God dwelleth in him.*" They cannot dwell with God who have refused to be of one mind in God's church. Although they be burned, given up to flame and fire ; although they lay down their lives, thrown to the wild beasts, their death will not be the crown of faith, but the punishment of faithlessness ; it will not be the glorious end of religious courage, but the destruction of despair. Such an one may be killed, but he cannot be crowned. He professes himself to be a Christian in the same way as the devil often feigns to be Christ. The Lord Himself has forewarned us, saying : " *Many men will come in my name, saying, ' I am Christ, and they will deceive many.*" As the devil is not Christ, though he uses a false name ;

so that man cannot appear as a Christian who does not abide in His gospel and the truth of the faith.

To prophesy and cast out devils and perform great deeds upon earth is certainly a sublime and wonderful thing ; but a man does not obtain the kingdom of heaven, though he be found doing all these things, unless he walks in the observance of the straight and just way.　The Lord gives warning and says : " *Many shall say to me in that day,* ' *Lord, Lord, have we not prophesied in Thy name, cast out devils in Thy name, and in Thy name done great deeds ?* ' *And then I shall say to them,* ' *Depart from me, ye who are workers of iniquity*.' "　There is need of righteousness that a man may deserve well of God the Judge : we must obey His precepts and warnings that our services may receive their reward.　The Lord in His gospel, directing in a brief summary the way of our hope and faith, says : " *The Lord thy God is one God : and thou shalt love the Lord thy God with all thy heart and with all thy soul and with all thy strength. This is the first commandment and the second is like unto it : thou shalt love thy neighbour as thyself. On these two commandments hang all the law and the prophets.*"　By His instruction He taught us love and at the same time unity, including in two precepts the law and all the prophets.　But what unity does that man observe, what love does he guard or consider who, mad with the frenzy of discord, divides the church, destroys the faith, disturbs the peace, scatters charity, and profanes the sacrament ?

This evil, my faithful brethren, began long ago, but to-day the dangerous losses caused by it have increased and the venomous plague of perverse heresies and schisms has started to shoot out and flourish more than ever before. So it must be in this period of the world's decline, even as the Holy Spirit warns us speaking by the mouth of the apostle.　" *In the last days,*" says he, " *times of trouble will come and men will be self-lovers, proud, boastful, ambitious, blasphemers, disobedient to their parents, ungrateful, undutiful,*

*without love and without loyalty, false-accusers, incontinent,
merciless, not loving the good, treacherous, wanton ; puffed
up with folly, lovers of pleasure rather than of God, having
a false semblance of religion but denying its true power. Of
these men are they who creep into houses and take foolish
women captive, loaded with sins and led away by all sorts of
desires, ever learning and never attaining to a knowledge of
the truth. Even as Jannes and Mambres withstood Moses,
so do these men withstand the truth : but they shall not
avail, for their folly shall be made plain to all men, as those
others' was also.*" All that was foretold in the past is now
being fulfilled and both by men and time is it approved,
for the end of the world draws near. As our adversary grows
more and more fierce, error deceives, folly puffs up, envy
inflames, ambition blinds, impiety depraves, pride inflates,
discord angers, and wrath hurries headlong down.

But let not the rash and excessive faithlessness of many
move or disturb us. Let it rather strengthen our belief in
the truth of what we have been told. As some men have
begun to be of this kind, because this was predicted
before, so let the rest of the brethren beware of them,
because that, too, has been predicted and the Lord has
instructed us, saying : " *Beware : behold I have told you
all things.*" Avoid, I beseech you, men of this kind and
keep their mischievous talk from your side and from your
ears, as if it were a deadly contagion. For it is written :
" *Hedge thine ears about with thorns and refuse to listen to
a mischievous tongue.*" And again : " *Evil communications
corrupt good manners.*" From such men the Lord by
his teaching warns us to depart. " *They are blind,*" He
says, " *leaders of the blind, and if the blind lead the blind they
shall both fall into the ditch.*" Such a man must be shunned
and avoided, and so must all who have separated themselves from the church. A man of this kind is perverse,
a self-condemned sinner. Does he think that he has Christ
who acts in opposition to Christ's priests and separates
himself from the company of His clergy and people ?

He is carrying arms against the Church and fighting against God's appointment. An enemy of the altar, a rebel against Christ's sacrifice, faithless instead of having faith, profane instead of having religion, a disobedient servant, an undutiful son, an unfriendly brother, despising the bishops and deserting the priests of God, he dares to set up another altar, to make another and unlawful prayer and to profane the truth of the Lord's offering by false sacrifices, not knowing that he who strives against the ordinance of God is punished for his reckless temerity by the vengeance of heaven.

So it was that Korah, Dathan, and Abiram, who tried to claim for themselves the privilege of sacrificing in opposition to Moses and Aaron the priest, paid an immediate penalty for their attempts. The earth broke its fastenings and gaped open in a deep gulf, and the cleft in the receding ground swallowed up the men alive as they stood. Nor did the wrath of angry God strike the ringleaders alone ; two hundred and fifty of their comrades, who had joined in their madness and mingled in their reckless crime were consumed in swift vengeance by the fire that the Lord sent forth ; to admonish others plainly and to show that these wicked men were working against God when they tried by their mortal will to over-throw God's ordinance. Thus also King Azziah, when he took the censer and violently claimed the right of sacrifice against God's law and refused to yield to the priest Azariah, was confounded by the divine wrath and branded upon his forehead with the white spot of leprosy ; marked by the offended Lord in that part of the body where they are sealed who deserve well of the Lord. The sons of Aaron, too, who placed upon the altar strange fire which the Lord had not commanded, were at once extinguished before the eyes of the avenging Lord.

It is such men as these whom they imitate and follow, who, scorning God's tradition, seek after strange doctrines and bring forward teachings of men's appointment. The

Lord upbraids and rebukes them in his Gospel, saying : " *Ye reject the command of God, in order that you may set up your own tradition.*" This is a worse crime than that which the backsliders seem to have committed, and yet these latter come forward as penitents and making full atonement pray God to forgive them their sin. They seek after and entreat the church ; the others fight against her. In their case there may have been necessity ; with the others there is a fixed wish to do wrong. The backslider has only injured himself ; the heretic and schismatic draws many others into his own errors. In the first case, one soul is lost ; in the other the souls of thousands are endangered. The backslider knows that he has sinned and is filled with bitter regret ; the heretic proud in his error and self satisfied even in wrong-doing, separates sons from their mother, tempts sheep from their shepherd, upsets the sacraments of God ; and while the backslider has sinned but once, he goes on sinning every day. Lastly, the backslider, if he afterwards attains to martyrdom, may possibly receive the promises of the kingdom ; the heretic, since he is outside the church at his death, can never win the church's reward.

Let not anyone, beloved brethren, wonder that some even of the confessors proceed to this extremity of guilt and induce others to join them in their grave and heinous offence. Confession does not make a man immune from the devil's snares nor while he is still in this world does it give him perpetual security against the world's temptations, its perils, its onsets, and its attacks. Otherwise we should never see in confessors those subsequent frauds and fornications and adulteries which now with sighs and sorrow in some we witness. Whoever the confessor is, he is not greater or dearer to God than Solomon, who, so long as he walked in the Lord's ways, kept the grace he had won from the Lord, but when he abandoned the Lord's way, he lost His grace also. Therefore is it written : " *Hold fast that which thou hast, lest another receive thy crown."* The Lord certainly would not threaten that the crown of righteousness might be taken away, were it not that when righteousness departs the crown inevitably must depart with it.

Confession does not at once earn the crown ; it is rather the beginning of glory. It is not the final stage of praise but rather the first step in honour. It is written : *" He that endureth even to the end shall be saved "* : and anything before the end is merely a step whereby we mount to the summit of salvation, not a terminus where the full result of the ascent is already reached. A man is a confessor : yes, but after confession his danger is the greater, since he has definitely challenged the Adversary. He is a confessor : yes, but he ought the more for that to stand on the side of the Lord's gospel, since by the gospel he has obtained glory from the Lord. *" To whom much is given, of him much is required : to whom more dignity is ascribed, from him more service is exacted."* Let no man perish by a confessor's example ; let no man from a confessor's ways learn unrighteousness, arrogance and faithlessness. A man is a confessor : then let him be humble and quiet ; let him in all his doings be modest and disciplined, so that he who is called a confessor of Christ may imitate Christ whom he confesses. Since He says : *" Whosoever exalteth himself shall be abased, and he who humbleth himself shall be exalted "* ; and since He Himself has been exalted by the Father, inasmuch as He, the word the strength and the wisdom of God the Father, humbled Himself on earth, how can he love arrogance who by His own law enjoined humility upon us and as the reward of humility received from the Father the highest of all names ? A man is a confessor of Christ : yes, but only if the majesty and dignity of Christ be not afterwards blasphemed by him. Let not the tongue that has confessed Christ be slanderous or turbulent, let it not be heard clamouring with abuse and disputation, let it not after words of praise shoot forth serpent's venom against the brethren and against God's priests. If a confessor shall subsequently show himself blameworthy and deserving of rebuke ; if he shall have wasted his confession by evil conversation ; if he shall have stained his life with scandalous vice ; if, finally, forsaking the church where he has been a confessor and severing the concord of unity he shall have exchanged his first faith for a subsequent faithlessness, then he may not flatter himself that by his confession he has been, as it were, picked out to receive the reward of glory. Nay, from the very fact of confession his deserving of punishment has become the greater.

The Lord chose Judas among the apostles, and yet afterwards Judas betrayed the Lord. But not on that account did the faith and firmness of the apostles fail because the traitor Judas fell away from their company. So also now the holiness and dignity of confessors is not diminished because the faith of some among them is broken. The blessed apostle in his epistle speaks, saying : " *What if some of them fall away from the faith ? Shall their faithlessness make God's faith void ? God forbid : for God is true, and every man is a liar.*" The greater and better part of the confessors stand firm in the strength of their faith and in the truth of the law and the Lord's discipline. They do not secede from the peace of the church who remember that by God's favour they have obtained grace in the church. Indeed by this they gain a higher praise for their faith, in that they separate themselves from the faithlessness of those who have been joined with them in the fellowship of confession and have withdrawn from the infection of their guilt. Illuminated by the true light of the gospel, shining in the pure clear radiance of the Lord's day, they are as praiseworthy in maintaining the peace of Christ as they have been victorious in fighting against the devil.

It is my earnest desire, beloved brethren, and it is the object of all my consultations and exhortations, that if it

K

be possible, none of the brethren should perish and that
our Mother may have the joy of enfolding in her bosom
the one body of an harmonious people. But if wholesome
counsel cannot recall to the way of salvation certain ringleaders of schisms, and authors of dissensions who persist
in their blind and obstinate madness, do you at least
liberate yourselves from the snares of their deceits. It
matters not whether you were beguiled by your simplicity,
or led on by error, or deceived by some cunning and mis-
leading craft : free your wandering steps to-day
from errors, and recognize the straight way of the heavenly
road.

These are the words of the apostle testifying : " *We bid
you in the name of our Lord Jesus Christ, withdraw yourselves from all brethren that walk disorderly and not after
the tradition that they have received from us.*" And again
he says : " *Let no man deceive you with vain words ; because
of these things the wrath of God cometh upon the sons of
contumacy. Be ye therefore not partakers with them.*" We
must withdraw, nay, rather, we must flee, from these
delinquents, lest, while we join with those who walk in
sin and take the path of error and wickedness, we also
wandering from the true way should be found guilty of
a like offence with them. God is one, Christ is one, His
church is one, the faith is one, His people is one joined
in a solid unity of body by the cement of concord. Unity
cannot be severed, nor can one body be separated by
breaking up its structure or torn into bits, its flesh lacerated
and wrenched apart. That which has left the shelter of
the womb cannot live and breathe by itself ; in its severed
state it loses the basis of its existence.

The Holy Spirit warns us and says : " *What man is he
that desireth to live and would fain see good days ? Refrain
thy tongue from evil and thy lips that they speak no guile.
Eschew evil and do good ; seek peace and ensue it.*" The
son of peace ought to seek peace and ensue it. He who
knows and loves the bond of charity ought to refrain his

tongue from the evil of dissension. Among His divine commands and saving teachings the Lord, now very near to His passion, added this one, saying: "*Peace I send among you : to you I give my peace.*" He gave this to us as an inheritance : all the gifts and rewards of His promise to us he made dependent on our maintaining peace. If we are Christ's legatees, let us abide in the peace of Christ ; if we are sons of God it is our duty to be peacemakers. "*Blessed are the peacemakers,*" says He, "*for they shall be called the sons of God.*" It behoves the sons of God to be peacemakers, gentle in heart, simple in speech, harmonious in affection, faithfully joined one to the other in the bonds of unanimity.

This unanimity prevailed formerly under the guidance of the apostles, and the infant church keeping the Lord's commandments held fast to Christian charity. Scripture proves this when it says : "*The multitude of those who believed were of one heart and of one soul.*" And again : "*These all continued with one mind in prayer with the women and with Mary the mother of Jesus and with his brethren.*" Therefore when they prayed their prayers were effectual ; therefore they could with confidence obtain whatever they asked from the Lord's mercy.

But amongst us unanimity has diminished, even as the liberality of our charitable offerings has grown less. Formerly men would sell their houses and farms, and, laying up for themselves treasures in heaven, would offer to the apostles the price of them to be distributed for the use of the needy. But now we do not even give the tenths of our estate, and while the Lord bids us sell, we prefer to buy and to increase our property. Thus has the vigour of faith decayed among us : thus has the strength of believers grown faint. Therefore the Lord looking to our times, says in His Gospel : "*When the Son of Man cometh, think you that He shall find faith on the earth?*" We see that what he foretold is coming to pass. There is now no faith in the fear of God, in the law of righteousness, in love, and in work. No man in his thoughts has fear of the future, no man considers the day of the Lord, the wrath of God, the punishments that will fall upon unbelievers and the eternal torments decreed for the faithless. What our conscience would fear if it believed it now fears not at all because it lacks belief. But if it believed it would take heed : and if it took heed it would escape.

Let us use all our strength, beloved brethren, to arouse ourselves. Let us break the sleep of our ancient lethargy and be wakeful to observe and to do the Lord's precepts. Let us be such as He Himself bade us to be, saying : "*Let your loins be girt and your lamps burning and ye yourselves like unto men that wait for their Lord when He shall come from the wedding, that when He cometh and knocketh they may open to Him. Blessed are those servants whom their Lord when He cometh shall find watching.*" We ought to be ready girt, lest when the day of setting forth comes it finds us hindered by burdens and entanglements. Let our light shine forth brightly in good works so that of itself it may lead us from the night of this world to the daylight of eternal clarity. Let us always with anxious caution be awaiting the sudden coming of the Lord, that when He knocks our faith may be on the watch ready to receive the reward of vigilance from the Lord. If these commands be observed, if these warnings and precepts be kept, we cannot be caught asleep by the devil's guile ; as watchful servants we shall reign with Christ in his Kingdom.

SELECTION FROM *THE LAPSED*

The Punishment of Apostasy

(De Lapsis §§ 23–29)

Hear my words and hearken to what I say. Why are your ears deaf, why will they not listen to the saving counsels that I give ? Why are your eyes blind and will not see the way of repentance that I show you ? Why does your mind, isolated and distracted, not perceive the life-giving remedies contained in the Holy Scriptures which we both learn and teach ? Those who have but little belief in the future should at least be moved by things happening in our own day. All around us we see the tortures of those who have denied their faith and we mourn for their sad end. They cannot go unpunished even in this world, although the day of judgement is not yet come. Meanwhile, certain are chastised that others may be corrected. The torments of a few are examples for all.

One of these persons ascended the Capitol with the deliberate intention of denying Christ. As soon as he had done so, he was struck dumb, so that the tongue which had committed the crime received also the punishment, and he could not even pray for mercy. There was another, a woman, who was at the baths—consoling herself, one may suppose, for the loss of the grace of the bath of salvation—and there seized by an unclean spirit she devoured her own tongue with which she had spoken the guilty words or tasted the forbidden food. Then when she had swallowed this abominable fare the disease that had affected her mouth attacked her vitals. She became . her own executioner and could not long survive the agonies in the stomach and the bowel and finally died.

I was myself present on the occasion of another punishment and can testify to its accuracy. A father and a mother were fleeing from the persecution and unable in their terror to make any other provision for their little girl left her in charge of a nurse. She at once brought the child to the magistrates. The little girl was not old enough to eat meat, but before an idol surrounded by many people the magistrates gave her to eat bread dipped in wine— which was serious enough, for it had been left over from previous sacrifices. Later the mother received her daughter back ; but the child was as little able to tell her mother of the deed she had done as to understand or prevent it when it took place. Thus the mother remained in complete ignorance until one day she brought her to church when I was administering the Holy Sacrament. But the child, now among the faithful, showed great impatience at my prayers and exhortations and at one moment would burst into floods of tears and at another threw herself about in great mental agitation as though undergoing torture. By such indications as she could give her young uneducated mind was trying to confess her consciousness of guilt. But when at the end of the service the deacon began to offer the cup to those present and her turn came with the rest, she turned her face away at the presence of the divine majesty and resolutely shut her lips refusing the cup. The deacon, however, persisted in spite of this refusal and forced some of the wine from the cup between her lips. Immediately there were hiccoughs and vomitings. The Eucharist could not remain in a mouth or a body that had been defiled, and the wine sanctified in the blood of the Lord burst out of her unclean stomach. Such is the power and majesty of God ; by His light the secrets of the darkness were laid bare, and the unknown crime did not escape the vigilance of God's priest.

I have mentioned a story of a child who was too young to tell what another had done to her ; but there was another girl much older, indeed almost adult, who crept

into one of our services. She took the sacrament and behold
it was not bread but a sword ! For when she swallowed it,
it was like some deadly poison inside her and she began
to writhe and to be suffocated. So under the lash of her
own crime, not under the persecution, she suffered death
in agonies of throbbings and tremors. Her crime and
her guilty conscience were not long unpunished or
unknown. She had deceived men but in God she found
punishment.

Moreover, a certain woman tried to open with polluted
hands a box which contained the remains of the Holy
Sacrament ; a flame shot out and so terrified her that she
dared not touch the contents. Another who, also polluted
with idolatry, had the presumption secretly to receive the
sacrament along with the others when the priest was
officiating, found himself unable to make his lips touch the
sacred bread, and when he opened his hands saw that he
was carrying a little heap of ashes. By this one example
it is shown that God departs from him who denies Him
and that no man receives benefit from the sacrament unless
he deserves it ; for when God's holy presence is removed
the saving Grace is changed to ashes.

How many are filled each day with unclean spirits !
How many are driven out of their senses and racked with
fits of insanity ! There is no need to describe the fate
of each one, for in all the manifold disasters of the world
the ways of chastising sins are as many in number as the
sinners. Let each one therefore consider not what fate
some other has met, but what fate he himself deserves,
and if his punishment has been delayed for a time, let
him not think that he has escaped it. For he whose
punishment an angry God has reserved to Himself ought
to be all the more fearful.

Those again who without actually defiling their hands
with unclean sacrifices have been guilty of receiving
certificates to that effect, ought not to delude themselves
that they will escape punishment. For, indeed their act

is that of a renegade, of a Christian who denies that he ever was a Christian. What another has certainly done he has admitted having done himself also. It is written " *Ye cannot serve two masters,*" and he has served an earthly master and obeyed his commands, hearkening more to the orders of man than to the voice of God. Whether he will be able to hold his head higher among men by this means it is his own business to find out; but God's justice at any rate he will never escape or avoid; for the Holy Spirit says in the Psalms : " *Thine eyes saw my unwrought substance and all men shall be written in thy book,*" and again : " *For man looketh on the outward appearance but God looketh on the heart.*" And God himself warns and admonishes us in the words : " *And all the churches shall know that I am he which searcheth the reins and the hearts.*" He seeth that which is secret and hidden, and beholdeth that which is unseen; nor can any escape the eye of Him that saith : " *I am a God nigh at hand, and not a God afar off. Shall anyone hide himself in secret places, and I not see him?* " God sees the minds and hearts of each of us and will judge us not by our deeds alone but also by our words and our thoughts; and with this intent He is looking into all our minds and all the desires that lie deep down in the secret places of our souls.

How much deeper is their faith and greater their fear of God who though greatly tempted have not fallen into the error of sacrificing to idols or claiming to have done so. Their guilty thoughts they lay before God's priests in all frankness and repentance; so that they render their conscience clear, throw a weight from off their minds, and, however slight and trivial the wounds on their souls, obtain the saving health from above. They know that it is written : " *God is not mocked.*" God cannot be mocked and deluded, cannot be deceived by any clever cheating. Nay, all the more guilty is the man who thinking God is made after the pattern of man, expects to escape the penalty of his sin by keeping it secret. In his own gospel Christ says : " *Whosoever therefore shall be ashamed of me . . . of him also shall the Son of Man be ashamed.*" And can he deem himself a Christian who is ashamed and afraid to be a Christian ? How can he be with Christ who blushes or fears to belong to Christ ? It may be that his sin is lessened because he has not looked upon idols nor profaned the holiness of our faith before the eyes of a mocking crowd, nor befouled his hands with unclean sacrifices, nor soiled his lips with accursed meats. All this makes his fault less, but does not make his conscience clear. He can the more easily come by pardon for his sin, but he is not innocent of sin. Let such a man not be weary in repentance and in beseeching God for mercy, lest by failing to make amends for a lesser fault he find it has grown into a serious error.

Therefore my brethren I beseech you each one to confess his faults while he is yet on earth, while the confession is yet open to him and the atonement and remission which is in the hands of his priests is still valid in the eyes of the Lord. Let us turn to God with our whole minds and with unfeigned grief express our repentance and ask pity of God. For it is to God that the soul must bow, to God shall your tears be pleasing and on Him all your hope shall rest. He Himself tells us how we ought to pray : " *Return ye to me with all your heart,*" saith the Lord, " *and with fasting and with weeping and with mourning. And rend your heart and not your garments.*" Let us return to the Lord with our whole heart, and by fasting and weeping and mourning, as He bids us Himself, let us appease His wrath.

ARNOBIUS

AS the traveller follows the road from Carthage to Cirta, along the valley of the little river Mesdag, he sees a great mass of stone frowning down upon him. It is the strongest positon in all modern Tunis, and to-day, left in lonely solitude, is known as El Kef, " The Rock." But in Roman times there was a flourishing town upon these heights, one of a dozen settlements within fifty miles of Carthage, which commanded all the Medjerda country, Colonia Julia Veneria, sometimes called simply Sicca, " Drytown." It had been one of Masinissa's royal cities and after the Battle of Muthul submitted at once to the Romans, who took over its great Phœnician temple of Astarte and dedicating it afresh to Venus gave the place its new name. Here the Astarte-Venus cult had its chief centre in Roman Africa, and in its temple the maidens of the town, including even those of good family, would publicly prostitute themselves in order to collect a marriage portion. Religion was made to serve the purposes of lust, and it may reasonably be supposed that the whole atmosphere of the town was alien and hostile to the spirit of Christianity.

In Sicca Arnobius was born and there for many years during the latter half of the third century he practised as a teacher of rhetoric, winning some notoriety because of his violent attacks on the little Christian community which had planted itself in this unfavourable soil. Of his life before he was sixty little is known, but in his sixtieth year he at last saw the error of his ways and came over as a convert from paganism. We have no information as regards the circumstances of his conversion, or why it was that he changed his beliefs so late in life ; but there are some indications that his tardy repentance was looked upon with suspicion. According to the story in Jerome the bishop of the diocese required from Arnobius a definite proof of sincerity, and it was in reply to this challenge that the treatise, *Against the Heathen* was written. There are difficulties in the tale, for this, his one surviving work, seems to bear the marks of long and careful composition ; and while part of it plainly dates from the second half of the third century A.D., there are passages in the later book which appear to refer to the great persecution under Diocletian 303.

But these questions of date are of minor importance : it will be better to examine the *Adversus Nationes* itself, and note the features which give it value and interest. It is divided into seven books, and falls into two main divisions. In the first part Arnobius is apologetic, and at some length shows the folly and injustice of the belief, commonly held by the Romans, that the calamities of the state were due to the impiety of the Christians. The Christians, it is true, says Arnobius, do not build temples to the gods nor do they offer sacrifice. But the fact is that sacrifices are unnecessary, and that the Roman gods are a delusion. The proof of this last statement involves a fierce assault upon the Graeco-Roman theological system, and this occupies all the later part of his work.

The method of attack used by Arnobius is two-fold, an ironical criticism of the absurdities of pagan ritual and a downright statement of the scandals of pagan mythology : and it is perhaps not surprising that in his hands the second of these methods is the more convincing. That his irony has a very blunt edge and is altogether an inferior weapon is not wholly his fault, for the Latin language, like the English, lacks those finer shades of meaning in which the ironical mind delights. Greek and French supply a much more suitable medium as Lucian and Voltaire discovered. Moreover, Arnobius' natural tendency is to be diffuse, and he gets most of his best effects by a lavish use of all the stock Latin devices of alliteration, apostrophe, and assonance. He was a professional rhetorician before he became a Christian, and when he likes he can be exceedingly verbose. For example, he will take a simple statement—" Right and left are relative terms "—and then by dint of repetition and prolix amplification swell it out into half a page of writing. Such a method is well enough in its way, but it is not suited to the ironical style.

Arnobius, indeed, is sadly lacking in delicacy, and some of the stories he repeats are so revolting that they are scarcely found in ancient literature, except in his pages, and were doubtless passed on by word of mouth as part of the more obscure mysteries. His own excuse for relating them is that his duty as an advocate defending the Christian religion compels him to rake up all details, however unsavoury, which are damaging to the other side ; although he recognizes the fact that it is difficult to touch filth without being defiled. It may be considered however that even the most zealous advocacy scarcely justifies the repetition of the story of Acdestis and Attis which comes early in the Fifth Book, or the brutal narrative of Jupiter's attack upon Ceres, which fills the next chapters. These two passages are merely an accumulation of horror upon horror ; and for most readers the milder and more concise criticism of divine immorality in the Fourth Book will be sufficient.

THE GODS OF THE ROMANS

(Adv. Nat. iv, 1–10, 20–28)

I would fain ask you a question, you Romans above all, who are lords and princes of the world. Do you consider that Piety, Harmony, Safety, Honour, Virtue, Felicity, and other names of the same sort, to whom we see you build up altars and splendid shrines, have a divine power and pass their time in the realms of heaven ? Or, as is usually said, have you put them in the class of gods, merely because we wish and pray that such blessings may fall to our lot ? If you think that they are but empty names devoid of substance and yet give them a consecrated place in the heavenly realm, you will have to consider whether this is only a childish frolic or whether it does not tend to make a mock of your other deities, seeing that you add to their number vain and empty words and endow those words with equal power. But if in your definite judgement you hold them to be gods and honour them with temple and festal couches, we pray you to instruct our ignorance by what method and in what way Victory, Peace, Equity and the other names mentioned above can be understood to be divinities and to belong to the assembly of the immortals.

Perhaps you would deny us the ordinary feelings of men ; but we Christians do not perceive or recognize that any of these names has divine power or is contained by an outward form corresponding to itself. We think that Virtue is the virtue of the virile, Safety the safety of the safe, Honour the honour of the honoured, Victory the victory of the victorious, Harmony the harmony of the harmonious, Piety the piety of the pious, Memory the memory of those who remember, and Felicity the felicity of those who live a felicitous life without exciting any enmities. That our statement is correct will be easily recognized by a consideration of the opposite qualities ; infelicity, discord, forgetfulness, injustice, impiety, poor spirits, and weak health. As all these things are human accidents and depend on men's actions and chance emotions, so their opposites, named after kinder qualities, must necessarily also depend on acts and from our conception of such acts these invented names derive their origin.

As for the bands of gods, gods of quite another stamp from this, whom you bring on to the stage, we really do not know whether you are acting seriously and believe in their existence, or are only mocking us with idle fictions and giving rein to your wanton imagination. There is a goddess Luperca, for example, as you tell us, so named on Varro's authority because the fierce wolf was merciful to the exposed infants. Did that goddess then come into existence not by the force of nature, but by the issue of events ? Was it only after the savage beast restrained its cruel teeth that she began herself to exist and took her significant name. If she was a goddess long before the birth of Romulus and his brother, tell us what was her name and her title. Prestana was so called, as you assert, because in throwing the javelin Quirinus had precedence over all men in strength. The goddess Panda, or Pantica, obtained her designation because Titus Tatius was permitted to expand and widen a road that he might occupy the Capitoline Hill. Before these things happened then, did these deities not exist ? If Romulus had not won the Palatine by his javelin cast, and if the Sabine king had been unable to take the Tarpeian rock, would there be no Pantica and no Praestana ? If you say that they existed before there was a reason for their names, I repeat my previous question. What were they called originally ? Tell us that.

Pellonia is a goddess strong and mighty to expel enemies. If you do not mind, tell us whose enemies. Two sides meet and fighting hand to hand at close quarters decide the issue ; one side is hostile to the one, the other to the other. Whom then will Pellonia expel, since both will be fighting ; and in whose favour will she incline, since she should give to both parties the strength and support of her name ? If she did that of course, I mean if she gave both sides her vote and good will, she would destroy the meaning of her name, which implies the expulsion of one of the two.

You will say, perhaps, that Pellonia is solely a Roman goddess ; she is on the side of the Quirites alone, and is ever ready to help them with gracious assistance. I wish, indeed, that it were so, for I like the name; but it is a very dubious question. Consider. Do the Romans possess a private property in gods, who have nothing to do with other nations ? How can they be gods, if they do not extend their divine power impartially to all peoples everywhere ? Moreover, tell me, pray, where was your Pellonia long ago, when the national honour was brought beneath the yoke at the Caudine Forks ? Where was she when at Trasimene the rivers ran with blood, and when the plains of Diomede at Cannae were piled high with Roman corpses ? Where was she at a thousand other defeats and at countless other disastrous battles ? Was she asleep and snoring, or had she learned the rogue's lesson and deserted to the enemies' camp ?

The sinister gods and goddesses preside over the left-hand regions only, and are the enemies of the right-hand faction. What sense or reason such a statement has we cannot understand ; and we are confident that you also could not justify it in the light of ordinary intelligence. To start with, the world in itself has neither left nor right, top nor bottom, before nor behind. Whatever is round and bounded on all sides by the convexity of a solid sphere has no beginning and no end : and where there is no end or beginning there cannot be any part bearing those names.

So when we say—This is the right side and that the left—
we do not refer to the way in which the world lies, for that
is everywhere very much the same, but merely to our own
place and position, we being so formed that we speak of
some things as being on our right hand, and of others as
being on our left. And yet the things we call left and right
have no continuance or fixity in relation to ourselves ;
they take their figuration from the sides of our body, just
as chance and the accident of the moment have placed us.
If I look towards the rising sun, the north pole and the
north are on my left hand. If then I look northwards,
the west will be on my left hand, although when I was
looking east it was behind my back. If next I turn my eyes
to the western region, there is another change, and it is
the south wind and the south that are now said to be on
my left. Finally, if the needs of the moment turn me to
the south, this last change of position gives the left side to
the east. It is obvious therefore that right and left are not
made so by nature : they depend on position and circumstance according to the way our body is placed in respect
to surrounding objects. And this being so, how can there
possibly be gods of the left, since it is clear that the same
regions are now left, now right ? And what harm has the
right done to the immortal gods that it should have no
deities to preside over it, although it is declared to be
fortunate and attended ever by lucky omens ?

Lateranus, the Brick God, is, as you say, the divinity of
hearths and their guardian spirit ; and he got his name
from the fact that men build fire places of this kind with
unbaked bricks. Well, suppose a hearth is made of tiles
or any other material, will it not have a guardian spirit ?
Will this Lateranus of yours, whoever he be, give up his
guardian duties because his realm and kingdom has not
been made of clay bricks ? Morover, this god who has
received the charge of presiding over hearths, what are
the things which he has to do ? He runs about men's
kitchens, spying and testing with what kinds of wood the

L

heat in his fires is produced. He keeps the casseroles in good condition, so that they may not split in pieces overcome by the violence of the flames. He takes care that the various flavours of food, each with its own particular attractiveness, reach the palate unspoilt. He acts the part of a taster, and tries whether the sauces have been rightly prepared. Is it not a disgrace, nay, to speak more truly, is it not an insult, and an impiety to bring on pretended deities for this sort of work ; not to do them reverence with befitting honours, but to appoint them to menial occupations of a scandalous kind ?

You have a military Venus—have you not ?—who presides over the debauchery of youths and the vices rife in a soldiers' camp. Among the mob of your divinities is there not one Perfica, the Finisher, whose task it is to bring the foul delights of lust to their end with uninterrupted pleasure ? Is there not another Pertunda, the Borer, who stands by the marriage bed when husbands labour in a virgin field ? Have you not also Tutunus, a second Priapus, upon whose huge member and rigid phallus you think it lucky for your matrons to ride ? If facts have no power to make you understand the truth, can you not see from their very names that such gods as these are the products of deluded imaginations, the creatures of idle superstition ? Puta, the Pruner, you say, presides over the pruning of trees ; Peta the Seeker, presides over men's petitions ; Nemestrinus, the Forester, is the god of woods ; Patellana and Patella the Disclosers, are set over things that either are, or will be, brought to light. Nodutus, the Knotter, is so called because he is the god who brings the sown grain up to a knotted stalk ; Noduterensis is the goddess who looks after the treading out of the ears. The goddess Upibilia sets you right if your lose your way ; parents bereft of their children are under the care of Orbona ; and people near to death under that of Naenia. Ossipago, the Bone-fixer, as they call her, gives firmness and solidity to the bones of young children ; Mellonia is the strong divinity who holds sway over bees, carefully guarding the sweetness of their honey.

Tell me, please (and may Peta, Puta, and Patella graciously favour you), if there were no bees at all on earth, would there be no goddess Mellonia ? If the human race were born without bones, like some worms, would Ossipago, the bone solidifier, have no name of her own ? I should very much like to know whether you think that the gods come first in nature, time, and duration, or if you give precedence over them to men and trees and crops etcetera. Everyone knows that the gods precede all other things by countless ages and generations, and you yourselves acknowledge it. Since then that is so, how in the nature of things could they have taken their names, which are earlier in point of time, from things which were created afterwards ? How could they as gods have been charged with the care of things that had not as yet been produced and assigned for men's use ? Were the gods for a long time without names ? Was it only after things began to be born and spring up on earth that you deigned to give them these titles and appellations ? How could you have known what name to give to each, since you were wholly ignorant of their existence ? And seeing that you were equally unaware which of them had any power and over what thing he should be placed to suit his divine might, how could you possibly have discovered that there were definite powers inherent in them ?

" Well," you may say to us, " do you give it as your judgement that these gods exist nowhere in the world, and are merely the creation of unreal opinions ? " We are not alone in saying so : truth and reason are with us and the general feeling of all mankind. Who is there that believes that there are Gods of Gain and that they preside over the getting of it, seeing that it frequently comes from the foulest sources and always is at other people's expense ? Who thinks that there is a God of Prurience and a Goddess of Desire set over those lusts which wanton obscenity follows by a thousand methods and which wisdom bids us utterly to avoid ?   Who can believe that there are Threshold Gods and Goddesses who look after doors and perform a janitor's duties, when every day we see the thresholds both of temples and of private houses destroyed, while a brothel's infamous entry stays undisturbed ? Who thinks that the Limi watch over obliquities, that Saturn presides at the sowing of seed, that Montinus is the guardian of hills, and that Murcida is the patron of the slothful ?   Who, finally, can credit the divinity of Money, whom your literature declares to be the greatest god of all, she who gives to men the golden ring of knighthood, the front seats at games and shows, the highest place of honour, the dignity of office, and what the indolent love most—secure and opulent idleness ?

If special guardians have been appointed to watch over bones, thresholds, honey, and other things of that sort— we have touched cursorily on some and to avoid tedium have omitted the rest—we might by a similar reasoning introduce a thousand other gods whose duty it would be to protect and guard innumerable things.   Why should there be a god in charge of honey only ?   Why should there not be one also for marrows, turnips, marjoram, cress, figs, beet, and cabbages ?   Why should the bones alone have earned protection, and not the nails, the hair, and the other parts of our body which are hidden away and regarded with shame, although they are exposed to very many dangers and stand more in need of the gods' care and attention than do our bones ?   If you say that these parts too perform their functions under the watchful care of divinities, there will begin to be as many gods as there are things ; and if you declare that there are definite things for which presiding deities care, it will be hard to explain why this divine watchfulness does not protect all things alike.

(*Having thus demonstrated the absurdity of two sorts of Roman gods—the vaguely abstract like Pietas and the minutely concrete like Mellonia—Arnobius next considers the nature of the Greek divinities whose worship the Romans had made part of their state religion. He first expatiates on the confusion on mythology caused by the plurality of certain deities and illustrates his point by an imaginary, and somewhat tedious, conversation between the three Minervas. He then returns to an argument which he has already used in the Third Book, and after showing the harm done by attributing to the gods the physical attributes of men, proceeds to examine the moral character of Jupiter and the other Olympians as revealed in pagan literature.)*

But you, on the contrary, forgetful of their majesty and grandeur, attribute to the gods nativities and ascribe to them births, which men of refined taste regard with feelings of execration and horror. From Ops his mother, you say, and from his father Saturn, Diespiter with his brothers was born. Do the gods then have wives ? Do they look for a suitable match and then enter into the marriage bond ? Do they accept the obligations of the bridal couch by prescription, by breaking bread, and by a fictitious sale ? Have they maidens whom they woo ; have they promised brides ; have they wives betrothed to them on settled conditions ? What are we to say about their wedding ceremonies ? You tell us that in the past some of your gods celebrated their nuptials and entertained joyous throngs ; that goddesses took part in the sport, and when they were not permitted a share in the ribaldry of the marriage songs, they threw the whole feast into confusion and sowed the seeds of destruction and danger for men in the next generation.

In the case of the minor gods the foulness of such pollution would be less noticeable ; but when we think of the great ruler of the heavens, the father of gods and men, who by one frown or nod shakes all the skies and makes them tremble, how could he ever have come to being from man and woman ? Unless both sexes, joined close together, had been dissolved in obscene delights, would

Jupiter, the most mighty, not exist, and up to this day would the divinities have no king and heaven stand without a master ?   And yet why should we be surprised that you say he was delivered from a woman's womb, seeing that your authors tell us that he had a foster-mother and that he only maintained the life that had been given him by nourishment drawn from a stranger's breast ?   What say you, sirs ?   I will repeat my question. Did the god who makes the thunder roar and the lightning flicker, who hurls the thunderbolt, and draws together the dreadful clouds, did he suck milk from the breast, did he utter wailing cries, did he crawl on all fours, was he persuaded by the sound of a rattle to cease his tiresome sobbing, and was he laid to rest in a soft cradle and lulled to sleep with baby talk ?   O devout claim !   How manifestly does it assert the majesty of your gods and their awful grandeur ! Is it thus, pray, with you that the exalted powers of heaven come to birth ?   Are your gods produced by the same methods of generation as those whereby pigs, asses, dogs, and all the unclean flood of beasts upon this earth is conceived and begotten ?

Not satisfied with having attributed these unions to the venerable Saturn, you declare that the ruler of the world himself begot children in a fashion even more shameful than that in which he was brought to light. From Hyperiona, you say, and from Jove, who wields the thunderbolt, the golden and most ardent Sun was born. From Latona and the same, the Delian archer and Diana huntress in the woods. From Leda and he same, those called in Greek Dioscori. From Alcmena, and the same, the famous Hercules of Thebes whose arms were a club and a lion's skin. From Semele and Jove himself came Liber, who is also called Bromus, and was born a second time from his father's thigh. From Jove again and from Maia, Mercury eloquent in speech and bearer of the harmless serpents. Can any worse insult be put upon your Jove, or is there anything which can more effectually

destroy and ruin the authority of heaven's ruler than this
belief of yours that he yielded on occasion to lustful
pleasures and that his heart burned with hot desire for
a woman's charms?   What had the son of Saturn to
do with strange nuptials?   Did not Juno suffice him?
Could he not have appeased the fury of his desires with
the queen of heaven, commended as she was by her high
nobility, her beauty, the majesty of her countenance,
and the snowy marble whiteness of her arms?   Was he
not content with one wife that like a wanton youth he
must sport with concubines, mistresses, and courtezans,
and scatter his incontinence abroad, a god salacious in his
old age, by constant change renewing his flagging appetite
for pleasure?   What say you, impious ones?   What
vile thoughts do you invent about your Jove? Do you not
clearly realize with what disgrace you brand him, of
what crimes you make him the author, what stains of
vice, what enormity of scandal you heap upon him?

Though men are prone to lust and by the infirmity of
their nature inclined to yield to the allurements of pleasure,
they still punish adultery by the laws and visit with the
capital penalty those whom they find to have possessed
themselves of another's rights by forcing the marriage bed.
But the greatest of kings, according to you, did not know
how base and infamous is the character of a seducer and
an adulterer ; and he who, as the story goes, sees all our
doings, good or bad, was himself so lost to reason that he
did not see what was his own fitting course. This mis-
handling might perhaps be bearable if you mated him with
persons who were at least his equals and set him up only
as the paramour of the immortal goddesses. But what
beauty, pray, or grace could there be in human bodies,
to attract and captivate the eyes of Jove? Skin, flesh,
mucus, and all the filth that is hidden in the intestines,
stuff which not only the piercing gaze of a Lynceus must
shudder at, but which would make any man turn away
merely by thinking of it. O glorious reward of sin, O fit

and precious joy, for which great Jove became a swan and a bull, and did beget white eggs!

If you will open your mind's eye and see the real truth without any wish for private gratification, you will find that the causes of all the miseries by which, as you say, the human race has long been afflicted, flow from beliefs of this kind which in the past you held about your gods and which you have refused to amend even when the truth is set before your eyes. What have we Christians ever imagined about those gods that was unbecoming, what shameful tales concerning them have we ever put forth, that we should bear the odium of being responsible for the troubles of mankind and the diminution of the world's prosperity? Is it we who say that certain gods, as though they were storks or pigeons, were produced from eggs. Do we say that the white beauty of Cytherean Venus took shape and substance from the sea foam and from the severed genitals of Cœlus? Do we say that Saturn was imprisoned for killing his father and that on fixed days his chains were loosened and he was relieved of their weight? Is it our story that Jove was saved from death by the help of the Curetes, and that he drove his father from his kingdom and by force and fraud obtained a sovereignty that was not rightly his? Our tale that the old god, when driven out, lay hid in the land of the Itali and as a reward for being protected from his son gave their country the name of Latium? Do we say that Jove himself contracted an incestuous marriage with his own sister, and that when invited by Lycaon to his table he dined unwittingly upon his host's son in mistake for pork? That Vulcan limping on one foot worked at a smithy in the island of Lemnos? That Aesculapius, as the Boeotian Pindar tells, was transfixed by a thunderbolt because of his greed and avarice? That Apollo having become rich by the ambiguity of his oracle deceived the very kings whose gifts and treasures had made him wealthy? Did we ever publish it abroad that Mercury is a thief, and that Laverna is one also, with him presiding over secret frauds ?   Is the writer Myrtilus one of us, who declares that the Muses were the handmaids of Megaclon, daughter of Macareus ?

Who was it said that Venus was a courtezan whom a certain King of Cyprus named Cinyras deified ?   Who declared that the Palladium was formed from the remains of Pelops ?   Was it not you ?   Who said that Mars was a Spartan warrior ?   Was it not your writer Epicharmus ? Who wrote that he was born in the land of Thrace ?   Was it not the Athenian Sophocles, and did not every audience agree with him ?   Who says that he was imprisoned in Arcadia for thirteen months ?   Was it not Homer, son of the river Meles ? Who said that dogs were sacrificed to him by the Carians and asses by the Scythians ?   Was it not Apollodorus especially, and other writers as well ?   Who described him as taken captive by an entangling snare while he wantoned in another's bed ?   Was it not you, in your books and on your stage ?   Did we ever write that the gods served as hireling slaves ; Hercules, for example, to Omphale at Sardis for lust and wantonness ; Apollo of Delos to Admetus ; Jove's brother, in company with his nephew, the Pythian god, to Laomedon of Troy ; Minerva, who holds the candle for secret lovers and trims its wick ?   Is he not one of your bards, the poet who made Mars and Venus to be wounded by mortal hands ?   Is not Panyassis one of you, who relates that father Dis and queen Juno were wounded by Hercules ?   Do not the writings of your Polemo assert that Pallas the warrior maid was cruelly used by Ornytus, beaten and covered with blood ?   Does not Sosibius declare that all Hercules got from the sons of Hippocöon was the pain and anguish of the wound they dealt him ?   Is it recorded on our authority that Jove was committed to the grave in the island of Crete ?   Do we say that the twin brethren, Castor and Pollux, united in their cradle were buried in the land of Sparta and Lacedaemon ?   Is the writer, called Patrocles

of Thurii on the first page of his book, one of us, who says
that the tomb of Saturn is in Sicily and that his remains
now rest there ? Is Plutarch reckoned as one of our party,
who related that Hercules after the havoc caused by
epilepsy was reduced to ashes on the top of Mount
Oeta ?

What shall I say of the lustful passion for women, which,
as your writers and literature tell us, fired the hearts of the
holy gods ? Is it by us that the King of the Sea is asserted
in the heat of his frenzied desire to have stolen the maidenhood of his Amphitrites, Hippothöes, Amymones,
Melanippes, and Alopes ? That the spotless Apollo,
Latona's son, most chaste and pure, in the fervour of
reckless love, took his Arsinöes, Aethusas, Hypsipyles,
Marpessas, Zeuxippes, Prothoes, and Daphnes, and
Steropes ? Is the tale told in our poems of how old Saturn,
his matted locks this long time gray and now cool with the
weight of years, was caught by his wife with a paramour,
and to escape her put on animal shape and flew away
neighing loudly in a horse's form ? Have you not brought
scandal even upon Jove himself, the ruler of the world,
saying that by endless metamorphoses and mean deceptions
he disguised the fire of his wanton passion ? Have we
ever written of him that to carry out his lustful stratagems
he changed himself now into gold, now into a sportive
satyr, then again into a serpent, a bird, and a bull, and, to
pass beyond all limits of disgrace, into a tiny little ant,
that he might, forsooth, make Clitor's daughter the mother
of Myrmidon in Thessaly ? Who made him lie awake with
Alcmena for nine successive nights ? Was it not you ?
Who made him desert his post in heaven and slothfully
abandon himself to his lusts ? Was it not you ? You certainly ascribe to him no mean favours, but you would have
your god Hercules born to surpass and transcend his
father's powers in such matters. Jove had to labour for
nine nights to fashion, mould, and shape one son : but
your holy god Hercules in one night taught the fifty

daughters of Thestius to lay aside the name of virgin, and to take the burdens which mothers must bear.

Moreover, not content with attributing love of women to the gods, you say also that they lusted after men. One of them is enamoured of Hylas ; another spends his days with Hyacinthus ; this one burns with longing for Pelops ; that one sighs even more ardently for Chrysippus, Catamitus is carried off to heaven to be a minion and cup-bearer ; Fabius is branded with a mark upon his soft buttocks, so that he may be known as Jove's own barn-door fowl. And are your male gods alone wanton, while the female sex has preserved its purity ? Nay, is it not laid down in your literature that Tithonus was loved by Aurora, that the Moon was enamoured of Endymion, Aegina of Aeacus, Thetis of Achilles' father, Proserpine of Adonis, her mother Ceres of some ploughboy Iasion, and that Venus herself after having Vulcan, Phæthon, and Mars, came to the bed of Aeneas and so by him became the mother of the Aeneadæ and founder of the might of Rome ?

When, therefore, you impute such portentous acts of vice and profligacy, not to one god only but without exception to all the race of the immortals in whom you believe, how can you dare to say without blushing that we are impious or that you are pious ? The wrong you do to the gods by repeating scandalous tales to their discredit more than counterbalances any honour and respect you pay them in the way of ritual and ceremonial observance. Either all these tales are false which you bring forward, to the injury of their individual credit and reputation ; and then we have in them an adequate reason why the gods should utterly destroy the race of men. Or if they are true and certain and unshadowed by any suspicion of doubt, then the conclusion of the whole matter is this ; however unwilling you may be to consent, we must believe your gods to be not of heavenly but of earthly birth.

Where there are weddings, marriages, births, foster-mothers, artifices, and weaknesses ; where there is liberty and slavery ; where there are wounds, blood, and carnage ; where there are lusts, desires and carnal pleasures ; where there is every sort of passion arising from restless emotions—there inevitably can there be nothing divine : for what belongs only to a fleeting race and to the frailty of earth can never find a place in a higher nature. If a man once perceives and recognizes the true nature of divine power, will he ever believe that a god had generative members, and was deprived of them by a shameful operation ; or that he frequently swallowed his own children and was punished by being put in chains ; or that he engaged in civil war against his father and deprived him of his regal place ; or that filled with fear of one younger than himself he turned tail in flight, and like a runaway slave or exile hid himself in distant solitudes ? Who, I say, can believe that a god took his place at men's tables, was put to death because of his greed, deceived his suppliants with ambiguous oracles, excelled in thievish tricks, committed adultery, served as a slave, fell in love, and yielded to the allurements of impure desires by every form of lust ? And yet you assert that all these things both were and are in your gods ; and you leave no aspect of vice, wickedness, and error without bringing it forward in your naughty imaginations as a reproach against the gods. Either then you must seek out some other divinities to whom these tales shall not apply—for they are only applicable to a human and earthly race—or if these are the only gods, whose names and characters you have declared, by your beliefs you do away with them. For all the stories that you tell relate only to men.

LACTANTIUS

LUCIUS CAECILIUS FIRMIANUS, better known by the familiar name of Lactantius, was born, a pagan, about the year 250, and probably in Africa, where he was a pupil of Arnobius. He studied rhetoric, became professor at Nicomedia, and there was converted to Christianity. The great persecution of 303 deprived him of his professorial chair, and although he escaped death he had for some time to endure the most painful hardships of poverty. Then, with the recognition of Christianity as the state religion, there came for him another change of fortune. He was appointed by Constantine as tutor to his young son, Crispus, spent his latter years in comparative affluence, and finally died at Trèves in extreme old age.

There is a long list of writings by Lactantius given in Jerome's catalogue, but most of them are now lost. Of the four books that remain the earliest in date is " *De Opificio Dei* ", " *God's Handiwork*," a defence of Providence and God's dealings with man. The two last are the treatise " *De Ira Dei* ", " *God's Anger*," and, closely connected with this in thought, the historical pamphlet " *De Mortibus Persecutorum*," " *The Deaths of our Persecutors*," a vivid narrative of the vengeance taken by God on all those Roman Emperors, from Nero onwards, who had persecuted the Christian Church. This is a very striking work, and for sheer horror it would be hard to surpass the description of Galerius' fate, when the tyrant eaten alive by worms roared aloud like a bull in his agony, and " the stench of his body filled not only the palace but the whole city."

There is, however, grave doubt as to the authorship of " *The Persecutors* ". If Lactantius wrote it, he threw aside here the bland and somewhat insipid style from which perhaps he takes his name, and on this occasion dipped his pen in gall rather than in milk. In any case it is from a book of a very different sort that he gained his title of the " Christian Cicero ". The " *Institutiones Divinae* ", dedicated to " the mighty Constantine, the first of Roman princes to repudiate error and to acknowledge the majesty of the one and only true God ", is one of the great doctrinal treatises of the Catholic Church, and in the vast mass of patristic literature it is still among the most widely read volumes. Nor is its fame undeserved, for it contains not only a critical history of ancient religion but also a practical code of morals, and a system of philosophy based on the divine working of Providence framed to supersede all those Pagan systems which at the beginning of the fourth century still held pride of place. It is long, carefully written in Ciceronian style, and divided into seven books, the first three a destructive criticism of Pagan religion and philosophy, the last four a constructive effort to establish a rule of life upon the maxim—" In philosophy is religion, in religion philosophy."

The first two books, following Arnobius, deal with the various pagan cults, which are shown to be both immoral and absurd, a partial exception being made in favour of the Sibyls in whom Lactantius seems seriously to believe. In the third book the claims of ancient philosophy are demolished, and in the next two the foundations of the new Christian system are laid. The sixth book " *On true religion* " is the keystone of the whole work and in its course Lactantius succeeds in establishing firmly the main principles of Christian morality. He has not the vigour of Tertullian, the learning of Jerome, the sensitiveness of Augustine. He is, indeed, in some ways a person of limited perceptions. But his limitations have their value. Standing nearer to the ordinary man, he is more fitted than a greater mind would be to act as guide and counsellor in the common business of living, and the precepts of conduct that he lays down had a considerable influence in later ages. It is interesting to notice how far his teaching diverges both from the habits of Paganism and from the usages of modern life, and the chapters that follow on the pleasures of the senses, forming about a quarter of the sixth book, give a fair idea of his method.

The Pleasures of the Senses

(Div. Inst., vi, 20–23)

I have still to utter a warning against the pleasures of the five senses ; but I shall be brief, for the measure of my book itself now demands moderation. All these pleasures, since they are faulty and fraught with death, ought to be overcome and subdued by virtue ; or, as I said just now in treating of the affections, be at least compelled to keep in their proper place. The rest of the animal creation have no perception of any pleasure, save that of generation. They use their senses therefore according to the necessities of their nature. They see things in order to seek what they need for the preservation of life. They hear each others' cries and distinguish them, in order that they may assemble together in herds. Things useful as food they either discover by smell or perceive by taste : things that are useless they refuse or reject, measuring the business of eating and drinking by the fullness of their stomach. But upon man the foresight of the most wise Creator bestowed the gift of pleasure, which is both infinite in extent and also liable to degenerate into vice ; inasmuch as he set virtue too before him, to strive continually with pleasure as with a domestic foe. Cicero in the *Cato Major* says : " Debauchery, adultery, vice of every kind, is stimulated by no allurements so much as by those of pleasure. Nature or some god has given to man nothing more excellent than the understanding and to this divine benefit and gift nothing is so hostile as pleasure." When lust is master there is no place for temperance, nor can virtue exist where pleasure reigns supreme. God meant the opposite, and gave men virtue in order that it might subdue and conquer pleasure. If pleasure seeks to pass beyond its allotted bounds, virtue should confine it within the prescribed limits and not allow it to beguile man with its delights and bring him captive beneath its sway, to pay the penalty of everlasting death.

The pleasure of the eyes is various and manifold, arising from the sight of things, wherewith men have to do, delectable either by nature or by reason of their workmanship. Upon it philosophers have most rightly put their veto, declaring that it is a far finer thing, and one more worthy of a human being, to gaze upon the vault of heaven than upon a vaulted ceiling. The bright garden of the skies, they say, with its flower-beds of twinkling stars, is more wonderful than any picture or statue or jewelled ornament. Most eloquently do they urge us to despise earthly sights and to enjoy the spectacle of the firmament. But still they themselves do not despise the public spectacles of the circus; nay, they take pleasure in them, and gladly lend them their presence. And yet these exhibitions are among the greatest incentives to vice and the most powerful agents of corruption. They ought to be prohibited; they contribute nothing to men's happiness and do a great deal of harm. He who counts it a pleasure to see a man slain, even though he has been deservedly condemned to death, is polluting his own conscience just as much as if he were a spectator and sharer in a secret murder. They call them " sports " forsooth, sports in which human blood is shed. So far have they lost all feeling of humanity that they think it a sport to put men to death, themselves worse criminals than the poor wretches whose bloodshed gives them pleasure.

Can they be just and pious, I ask, who seeing men beg for mercy as they crouch beneath the deadly sword, not only suffer them to be put to death but even demand their execution and vote against all pity with ruthless inhumanity? Wounds will not satisfy them nor bloodshed

M

appease their cruelty. When a man has been struck down to the ground they bid his assailant to deal another wound, and are not content until the corpse has been hacked to pieces. No tricks of shamming dead for them : they are enraged with both combatants unless one of the two is quickly killed, and in their thirst for human blood they hate anything that may check its flow. To satisfy their eyes as soon as possible they clamour at once for a fresh pair : use and custom have robbed them of humanity. They do not spare even the innocent : the cruelty they have learned by watching criminals butchered they vent upon all men alike.

It is not fitting then that those who strive to keep to the path of justice should act as partners and sharers in these public murders. When God says : " Thou shalt not kill," He not only prohibits individual violence, a thing which the law of the state forbids, but He warns us against doing some acts which are held permissible by men. A just man therefore may not enlist as a soldier : he is already serving in the army of justice. Nor may he accuse any one on a capital charge : it makes no difference whether you kill a man with a word or with a dagger ; it is the act of killing that is prohibited. In this one of God's precepts no exception at all can be made : it is always a crime to cause a man's death ; for it is God's will that his creature should be held sacred.

Let no one think then that it is permissible to strangle new-born babes. It is the greatest impiety. God breathes souls into them for life and not for death. But men, lest there be any crime wherewith they do not stain their hands, deprive these innocent and simple souls of the life which was not their gift. You may expect men forsooth to be careful of another's blood, when they do not spare their own ! Such folk are villainous and unjust ; there can be no dispute about words. And what of those whom a false piety drives to expose their babes rather than kill them ? They cannot be considered innocent, when they

offer their own offspring as a prey to dogs and in so far
as they themselves are concerned kill them more cruelly
than if they had strangled them. Who can hesitate to call
that father heartless who depends upon the compassion of
other men ? Even if his wish be granted and the child
finds someone to rear it, he is surely consigning his own
offspring either to slavery or to the brothel. But who does
not know, who does not understand, what things are able,
or even are wont, to happen in the case of both sexes
when mistakes are thus made possible ? The case of
Oedipus with its confusion of two fold crime is a warning
to us. It is therefore as wicked to expose as to kill a child.
But you say such unnatural murderers complain of their
scanty resources and allege that they have not the means
to rear more children. As though forsooth wealth was
under the control of its owners, and God did not every day
make poor men out of rich and rich men out of poor.
Therefore if any man from poverty be unable to rear
children, he had better abstain from intercourse with
his wife than mar the work of God with his impious
hands.

If, then, it is in no way permissible to commit a murder,
it is also not allowed us to be present at a murder. The
blood that is shed to give the people pleasure in the circus
is a stain upon our conscience. And the corruption of the
stage is perhaps even more contaminating. The plots
of comedies deal with the seduction of virgins or the amours
of harlots ; and the more eloquent the authors of these
scandalous inventions are, the more easily do they beguile
us by the elegance of their sentiments, the more readily
do their rhythmical and polished lines remain in the
memory of their audience. So, too, the stories of tragedy
set before our eyes the parricides and incests of wicked
kings and give to crime a tragic presentation. As for the
shameless movements of the actors, what other effect
have they than to teach and incite men to lust ? These
fellows with their wanton gestures play the whore, their

soft, strengthless bodies made to take on a woman's gait, and a woman's dress. And what shall I say of the mimes who make a public profession of corruption ? They teach men the tricks of adultery by representing them on the stage, and by pretence train to reality. What are young men and maidens to do, when they see these things done without shame and gladly beheld by all ? They are in any case reminded of what is possible, and the fires of lust, which from the eyes draw their chief nutriment, are kindled within them. Each spectator according to sex sees him or herself as part of these pictures : by smiling they approve and when they return to their bedrooms they take with them the corruption and the infection of vice. And not only is this the case with boys who ought not to be inured prematurely to sin ; it is true also of old men, whose age renders such faults especially unbecoming.

What else does the frequentation of the circus mean but folly, levity, madness ? Men's minds there are excited to frenzy with a speed equal to that of the chariots as they race. Those who come to see the spectacle are themselves a spectacle more surprising still, as they shout and caper and leap into the air. All such performances then should be avoided, not only to prevent vice sinking into our hearts, which should be tranquil and peaceful, but also that the habit of pleasure may not beguile us and turn us aside from God and good works. The celebrations of the games are festivals in honour of gods, since, indeed, they were instituted to commemorate their birthdays or the dedication of new temples. Wild beast shows were first given in honour of Saturn : stage performances in honour of Bacchus ; games in the circus in honour of Neptune. Gradually, however, the other gods also received the same mark of respect, and separate games were dedicated to their divinities, as Sisinnius Capito explains in his book *The Public Games*. If any man therefore attends a performance which has a religious origin and motive, he has departed from the worship of God and joined the side of those deities whose birthdays and feasts he has celebrated.

The pleasure of the ears is derived from the sweetness of voices and musical strains ; and it is as fraught with possibilities of vice as the delight of the eyes whereof we have spoken. Who would not think that man a worthless voluptuary who could give a theatrical performance in his house? And it makes no difference whether you practise luxury alone at home or with the people in the theatre. But as regards these public shows we have already spoken : there remains one victory that we must win : we must not be captivated by those things that touch our innermost feelings. Anything that lacks words, the sweet sounds of the air, for example, or of musical instruments, can be easily disregarded ; they do not cling to us and cannot be put into writing. But a well-composed poem, or a speech beguiling with its sweetness, captivates men's minds and works upon them as it wills. So when men of letters turn to God's religion, unless they have been grounded by some skilful teacher they are disinclined to believe. Accustomed to sweet sounding and polished speeches and poems, they despise the simple language of the divine writings and think that what is popular is mean. They require something that shall charm the senses. Anything pleasant easily persuades, and while it gives pleasure it fixes itself deeply in the heart. Cannot God then, who devised mind and voice and language, speak eloquently? Yea, indeed ; but he willed in his foresight that those things which are divine should be free from rhetorical tricks, in order that all men might understand what he spoke to all.

Therefore he who is anxious to gain the truth and does not wish to deceive himself voluntarily, must cast from him those hurtful and injurious pleasures which seek to bind the soul to themselves as pleasant food binds the body. True things must be preferred to false, eternal things to those that are fleeting, useful things to those that are pleasant. Let nothing be grateful to the sight save those acts which you see are acts of piety and righteousness. Let nothing be agreeable to the hearing save that which nurtures the soul and makes you a better man. And this latter sense especially ought not to be distorted to vice, seeing that it was given us in order that we might attain to knowledge of God. So if it is a pleasure to hear songs and music, let us make it our delight to sing and listen to the praises of God. This is true pleasure, the handmaid and companion of virtue. This is not frail and fleeting, as those pleasures are which men seek who, like cattle, are the slaves of their bodies. This lasts for ever and never fails to give delight. If anyone goes beyond its bounds and seeks from pleasure nothing else but pleasure itself, he is devising his own death. For as in virtue there is perpetual life, so in pleasure there is death. He who shall choose temporal things will forfeit the things eternal: he who shall prefer the things of earth will lose the things of heaven.

With regard to the pleasures of taste and smell, the two senses which affect the body alone, there is no point that needs discussion. Unless perchance anyone requires us to say that it is a disgrace to a wise and good man if he is the slave of his gullet and belly, or if he walks the street besmeared with unguents and garlanded with flowers : a man who acts thus is in any case a poor worthless fool, and the fragrance of virtue has never reached him. Perhaps someone may say : " Why were these things made, save for us to enjoy them ? " Nay, it has before been frequently remarked that virtue could never have come into existence if there had been nothing for virtue to overcome. When God made the universe, He arranged a contest between two things. The allurements of pleasures are the weapons of him whose one task it is to conquer virtue and keep men from righteousness. With these enticements and sweetnesses he tickles our souls ; for he knows that pleasure is the architect of death. As God calls man to life by the path of virtue and labour, so that other calls man to death by the path of pleasure and delight. And as men through apparent evils attain to real good, so through apparent goods they attain to real evil. Those enjoyments then are to be avoided, as though they were nets and snares; lest captivated by the softness of pleasure we should fall with our body, to which we have enslaved ourselves, under the dominion of Death.

I come now to the pleasure of touch, a sense which is indeed common to the whole body. But I do not think that I need speak here of ornaments or of fine clothes; my subject rather is wantonness, a vice which must be sternly repressed inasmuch as it is capable of doing prodigious mischief. When God devised the plan of having two sexes he gave them as attributes mutual desire and delight in union. And so of all living creatures he put the most burning passions in men's bodies, so that they might most eagerly rush into love of this kind, and their races thereby be propagated and multiplied. This passion and this impulse is found in man to be more vehement and more intense than in any other animal; either because God wished that mankind should surpass all other creatures in number, or else having given virtue to man alone he meant him in checking his pleasures to win the praise and glory of self-restraint. Our great adversary, therefore, knows how powerful is the strength of this passion, which, indeed, some people prefer to call a natural necessity, and tries to move it from the straight and honest path into ways of evil and perversity. He inspires men with illicit desires, so that love for other men's wives sullies the heart of those who might love their own wives without sin. He puts suggestive shapes before their eyes, he adds fuel to fire, and gives food to vice. Deep in the flesh he plunges his restless spur, inciting and enflaming a man's natural ardour, until he has him bound fast in his toils. And lest there should be any who from fear of punishment might refrain from what is not theirs, he has even established public brothels, publishing the shame of unfortunate women and making a mock both of those who do the deed and those who are compelled to suffer it.

The soul that was born for holiness he plunges in obscenities of this kind, as though in a pool of mud ; he destroys all modesty, he overwhelms all shame. He even joins male with male and devises abominable unions contrary to nature and contrary to God's law : so does he train men and equip them for every crime. What can be sacred to those men who take a poor helpless child and make him a victim to their foul lust ? No language can match the enormity of crimes like these. The only name that fits such folk is that of impious parricide ; the sex that God gave them for pleasure is not enough for them, they must indulge in profane wantonness with their own kind. But with them these are but trivial diversions and have a sort of respectability. What shall I say of those who pursue the abominations of their lust even to madness. I shrink from describing such deeds ; but what are we to think of those men who do not shrink from doing them ? Speak, I must, for these things happen ; there are some accursed madmen from whose disgusting caprices even the mouth is not immune. What words can indignation find fit to stigmatize such wickedness ? The greatness of the crime surpasses all that our tongues could say. Since then these are the works of lust, and these the misdeeds it produces, we must arm ourselves against it with the shield of virtue. Whosoever cannot bridle his carnal affections, let him keep them within the bounds of lawful wedlock, and then he will obtain that which he eagerly desires without falling into sin. What do these sons of perdition want ? Pleasure is the fruit of decent living ; if it is pleasure only that they crave, here is a just and lawful pleasure which no one forbids them.

If necessity constrains us to a bachelor's life, we must call in the help of virtue and let continence wrestle against desire. God has bidden us to refrain not only from other men's wives, but also from the common women of the town ; when two bodies are joined together, He says, they are made into one. So the man who plunges into filth must of necessity with filthiness be stained. The body, indeed, can be quickly washed clean : but the soul cannot escape the contagion of the body's shame, and only long years and many good works can purge it from that adhering foulness. Every one then should remember that the union of the two sexes is meant only for the purpose of procreation in a man's lifetime, and that the carnal affections are rendered legitimate by the production of children. We received our eyes from God not that we might enjoy the pleasure of fine spectacles, but that we might see to do the acts necessary for life ; and in the same way our genital organs were given us, as their name implies, in order that we might beget the next generation. This divine law we must devoutly obey. Let all who profess themselves to be God's disciples so order their ways and mode of life that they gain the power of self-mastery. For those who indulge in pleasure and give way to lust hand their soul over to their body and condemn it to death ; inasmuch as they make themselves their body's slaves, and over the body death has power. Let each and every one, then, to the best of his ability, mould his life to the ways of virtue, let him honour modesty, let him guard his chastity with all the strength of heart and soul : let him not merely obey the laws of the state ; let him be above all laws, as one who follows the law of God. If once he has accustomed himself to these good things he will be ashamed to turn aside to what is worse ; let him find his pleasure in things right and honourable, for they give to the good more delight than things perverse and dishonourable give to the evil.

I have not yet finished the tale of duties which chastity imposes on us. God has fixed the bounds of lawful desire not only within the walls of one house but also within the narrow limits of one bed. A man who has a wife must not

want another woman in addition, slave or free ; he must
be faithful to his marriage vow. The law of the state
imputes adultery to the wife alone, if she has another man :
the husband, even if he has several women, is held free
of guilt. With us it is not so. The divine law, when it
joins two people in marriage and makes of them one body,
gives them both equal rights : whosoever of the twain
shall break and sunder that union of bodies is held guilty
of adultery. For no other reason than this has God decreed
that all other creatures when pregnant should refuse the
male, but that a woman should still submit to her husband's
embrace. God saw that if women were unwilling, a man's
desires would drive him elsewhere, and he would lose
thereby the glory of chastity. Moreover, if a woman were
not able to do wrong she could not possess the virtue of
modesty. For who would say that a dumb creature is
modest because when pregnant it refuses the male. It
does so because if it allowed his approach it would bring
upon itself pain and danger. It is no credit therefore not
to do that which you cannot do. Modesty in human beings
is praised because it is not a matter of nature but of will.
So both spouses should keep their vows one to the other :
nay, more, the wife should be taught to behave herself
chastely by the example of continence that her husband
gives. It is unfair to demand something which you yourself cannot guarantee ; and unfairness like this affords
an obvious reason for adultery, since wives are unwilling
to keep their marriage vows when husbands do not show
them mutual affection. Never was there a wanton so lost
to all sense of shame that she did make this a reason for
her faults. " I am doing no wrong," she will say, " by
leaving the straight path : I am merely paying my husband
back." Quintilian expressed the exact truth when he
declared : " A fellow who does not keep away from other
men's wives will never be able to guard his own : the two
things are naturally connected." A husband who is busy
seducing other women has no time to give to the purity of

his own house ; and a wife who comes across such a partner
as this is roused to action by his example and thinks either
that she is merely taking pattern by him or that she is
avenging the wrongs he has done her.

Beware, then, of giving occasion for wrong-doing
by our own intemperance. Let husband and wife get
used to one another's ways and bear the yoke of marriage
equally. Let us see ourselves in our partner. For the law
of justice may be summed up in one rule : " Never do
to another what you would not have him do to you." These,
then, are God's precepts of continence ; and lest any
man should think that he can cheat the divine ordinances,
to prevent all subterfuge and opportunity for deceit we
will add this. A man is guilty of adultery if he marries a
divorced woman ; and so is he who divorces his wife,
save on the ground of misconduct, in order to marry again.
God does not will that the union of bodies should
be severed and broken. Moreover, we must avoid not only
adultery but even the thought thereof. Let no man look
upon his neighbour's wife and desire her in his heart.
The mind is guilty of adultery, even if it merely pictures
to itself a vision of carnal pleasure. For the mind
assuredly then is guilty of sin, and in thought is enjoying
the fruit of immoderate desire, a thing which in itself is
both criminal and wrong. For even if the body be free
from stain, no credit for modesty can be given, if the heart
is impure : nor must we think that chastity is really pure
when the conscience is sullied by fleshly desires. Let no
one think it hard to put a bridle on pleasure and to confine
its roving fancies within the bounds of modesty and chaste
living. It is our business to do more, and win over it a
complete victory. Very many men I know who have kept
their bodies virgin in happy purity, and there are many
who have found their highest joy in this heavenly mode of
life. God's precepts in this matter do not lay any binding
command upon us ; for the generation of human kind is
a necessity : they are merely permissive. For He knows

the compelling strength of carnal affection : it was His own endowment. If any man can do this, He says, he will have a glorious and incomparable reward. Continence is the pinnacle, as it were, and the consummation of all the virtues. If any man is able by trial and tribulation to attain thereto, masters and teachers will recognize his pre-eminence though he be but a pupil or a slave : he will celebrate his triumph on earth and by attaining to God's virtue will become like to God. This may seem a difficult task : but we are speaking of the man who will trample under foot all earthly things as he makes his way to heaven. Virtue consists in perception of God, and everything seems hard so long as you are unacquainted with Him. When you know Him, everything becomes easy. Through the Pass of Difficulty we must find our way out, we who are striving to attain to the Supreme Good.

AMBROSE

AURELIUS AMBROSIUS was born about 340 of a
Christian family among whose members was counted
at least one martyr the virgin Sotheris, put to death in the
Great Persecution under Diocletian. His father was
Pretorian Prefect in Gaul, and when he died at Trèves his
widow brought her three children to Rome. There the
young Ambrose, following in his father's footsteps, gained
a post on the staff of the Pretorian Prefect of Italy, and
after a short period of subordinate service was appointed
"consular" of the provinces of Liguria and Aemilia
and stationed at Milan. About a year after his arrival the
episcopal chair in that city fell vacant by the death of the
Arian bishop Auxentius ; and as there was good reason to
expect that the election of his successor would cause
disturbances similar to those which had occurred in Rome
between the partizans of Ursinus and Damasus, Ambrose
himself put in an appearance at the church where the
choice was to be made. He was admonishing the crowd to
orderly behaviour, his biographer Paulinus tells us,
" when a child suddenly cried out—' Ambrose Bishop '.
The people caught up the words and the disputing between
Arians and Catholics at once gave way to a marvellous and
incredible unanimity ". The choice was made on the spot
and the assembly dispersed amid universal rejoicings.

But while everyone else was satisfied, Ambrose himself
was at first very unwilling to accept the bishopric. He had
no canonical qualifications, and he regarded the honour
as both undeserved and too great for his capacities. "You
would have me begin to teach," he wrote to his people,
" before I have begun to learn." This plea proved
ineffectual, and Ambrose then resorted to more drastic
measures in order to convince men of his unfitness for

high office in the Church. For instance, he ordered criminals to be brought to his tribunal and cruelly tortured, so that the people might see how stern and relentless he could be. He ordered women of bad character to be introduced into his private house, so that he might be proved a man of immoral life. When both devices failed and the people cried : " We will take responsibility and bear all your sins," he fled into the country and hid in a lonely cottage. But his place of concealment was discovered and he was escorted back to the city in triumph. At last he gave way, was baptised, and seven days later became bishop.

The appointment was approved by the Emperor Valentinian, but fiercely resented by his Empress Justina who was an Arian devotee, and against her Ambrose soon found it necessary to use all his strength. In this struggle, as in most others, he was successful, and after Valentinian's death he gained such an ascendancy over his successor Gratian that the latter was ready to follow his guidance in all matters. For example, Gratian had begun his reign by according permission to heretics to follow their religion, without molestation. Under Ambrose's influence during the next year that permission was revoked, and a stern decree published forbidding all heretic assemblies. Even more important was Gratian's law " *qui mos* ", which enacted that all matters affecting religion in which clerics were litigants, as distinct from criminal cases (a distinction afterwards conveniently ignored), should not be tried by the civil courts, but by the bishop of the diocese. This, the beginning of the process whereby the clergy was put above the common law, was one of Ambrose's greatest triumphs.

His next victory was over the Arians. Two Illyrian bishops complained to the Emperor that they had been denounced as heretics and petitioned to be judged by a council of all the Catholic Bishops both from the Eastern and the Western sees. Ambrose by this time was supreme in the West, and although he was deeply indebted to Basil and Gregory of Nazianzus, he had no wish to see his authority questioned by the bishops of Constantinople and Jerusalem, Antioch and Alexandria. He therefore wrote for the young ruler a treatise on the true faith and induced him to leave the case to be judged by a council of the Western bishops alone. The synod met at Aquileia in 381, and after a debate which lasted from daybreak till one in the afternoon, the eloquence of Ambrose prevailed and the two offending prelates were deposed from their office.

Unfortunately Gratian was murdered in 383, and for some years Ambrose had a difficult course to steer. On the one side were the usurpers Maximus and the pagan Eugenius, whose soldiers threatened to stable their horses in Milan cathedral : on the other the empress Justina, guardian of the young emperor Valentinian II, who demanded full liberty of worship for her Arian protégés. Twice imperial troops beleaguered Ambrose and his followers in the Portian Basilica for several days, the bishop meanwhile composing for his patient congregation the great hymns " *Aeterne rerum conditor*," " *Iam surgit hora*," and " *Veni redemptor gentium*." But his troubles ended when Theodosius defeated and killed Maximus in 388, for with the new ruler he stepped almost at once into the same position as he had held with Gratian. Theodosius was an able and experienced monarch who had a great record of achievements in the East before he ever appeared in Italy ; but, as he himself said, Ambrose soon showed him the difference between an emperor and a bishop.

The first occasion was at Milan. Theodosius attending Ambrose's church, did not return after the offertory with the rest of the congregation to the nave but remained in the sanctuary. Ambrose at once by the medium of his archdeacon bade him withdraw from a part of the sacred edifice reserved for the clergy ; and Theodosius meekly

acquiesced.   The next time there was a more definite
contest of wills.   Some Christians in Mesopotamia at the
instigation of their bishop had burned a Jewish synagogue
and Theodosius ordered that it should be rebuilt at the
bishop's expense.   Ambrose, jealous of any secular inter-
ference in religious matters, insisted that this order should
be revoked, and when Theodosius hesitated he preached
openly against him and threatened that he would refuse
him the sacrament.   The menace was too much for the
Emperor, and the order was recalled.   The third incident
is one of the most famous events in history.   The people
of Thessalonica had murdered their governor and
Theodosius retaliated by a general massacre of the
population in which at least seven thousand defenceless
victims perished.   Ambrose was horrified at the ruthless
cruelty of such a vengeance and insisted in a private letter
to the Emperor that he must do penance before he could
receive the sacrament again.   According to one tradition
Theodosius attempted to enter the cathedral but Ambrose
barred his way, and an ancient column still stands in
Milan to-day marking the spot where bishop and
emperor met.   In any case, Theodosius was compelled
finally to submit, and removing the insignia of his rank
fell prostrate on the ground repeating the penitential
formula : " My soul cleaveth to the dust : quicken thou
me according to thy word."

With an emperor so amenable to the discipline of the
church, Ambrose had no great difficulty in imposing his
own will and in crushing both Arianism and Paganism.
Before the death of Theodosius both were forbidden by
law, and then in 397 Ambrose himself passed peacefully
away, happy in the knowledge that the victory of
Catholicism was assured.

This brief account may show the diversity and abundance
of Ambrose's gifts, and how successful he was as bishop,
diplomat, theologian, and administrator.   But when we
turn to his prose writings there is a certain feeling of

disappointment. It seems almost impossible for the same person to be both a great man of action and a great man of letters. Ambrose certainly was the first, but he is not so certainly the second. He was however a copious writer, or rather a copious preacher, whose addresses were written down and then published. These sermons of his and his allegorical interpretations of the Old Testament, are very voluminous, but they scarcely would appeal to modern readers. The doctrinal books " *On the Faith* " and " *On the Mysteries* ", have a considerable theological importance ; but from a literary standpoint we need only consider the hymns and the ethical treatises. Of these latter the most interesting are the essay on " *Clergymen's Duties* ", composed on the model of Cicero's " *De Officiis* ", from which two extracts are given here, and the three books *De Virginibus*, written to his sister, from which comes the story of the maiden of Antioch.

But though in considering Ambrose's prose some faintness of praise is justifiable, his hymns deserve and have usually gained unstinted admiration. Not only are they in themselves a real effort of original creation, but they have served also as an exemplar to all the hymn-writers of the Western church. Hilary had certainly endeavoured to write hymns before Ambrose, but those of his attempts that have been preserved must be pronounced to be failures. Ambrose in his simple eight stanza iambics invented a form that was exactly fitted for antiphonal singing, and we can still realize the effect produced by his melodies on their first hearers if we read Augustine's *Confessions* : " What tears did I shed over the hymns and canticles when the sweet sound of the music of Thy Church thrilled my soul. As the music flowed into my ears and Thy truth trickled into my heart, the tide of devotion swelled high within me, and the tears ran down and there was gladness in those tears."

Ambrose's hymns form the nucleus of what is still called the Ambrosian hymnary, but the genuine examples form

N

only a small part of the whole collection. A generous estimate would allow about twenty hymns as possibly his, but only five are certain; these five, vouched for either by Augustine or by Ambrose himself, are given here in Latin and English.

FIVE HYMNS

Iam surgit hora tertia
qua Christus ascendit crucem;
nil insolens mens cogitet,
intendat affectum precis.

Qui corde Christum suscipit
innoxium sensum gerit,
votisque praestat sedulis
sanctum mereri spiritum.

Haec hora qua finem dedit
diri veterno criminis
mortisque regnum diruit
culpamque ab aevo sustulit.

Hinc iam beata tempora
coepere Christi gratia:
fide replevit veritas
totum per orbem ecclesias.

Celso triumphi vertice
matri loquebatur suae:
en filius, mater, tuus;
apostole, en mater tua;

Praetenta nuptae foedera
alto docens mysterio,
ne virginis partus sacer
Matris pudorem laederet.

Cui fidem caelestibus
Jesus dedit miraculis,
nec credidit plebs impia:
qui credidit salvus erit.

Nos credimus natum Deum
partumque virginis sacrae,
peccata qui mundi tulit.
ad dexteram sedens Patris.

Behold the hour of tierce draws nigh
When Christ went to the cross to die.
Let no proud thoughts distract our mind
That shall in prayer its solace find.

The heart where Christ is all in all
Shall ne'er be led by sense in thrall,
But by continual prayer within
Its depths the Holy Ghost shall win.

This is the hour that once did send
To sin's old lethargy its end.
Death's realm His victory must own ;
The crimes of earth are overthrown.

From hence by grace of Christ began
A time of happiness for man ;
And on the churches from the sky
Was shed the faith of verity.

As on His triumph-cross He hung,
His mother to the apostle clung :—
" Mother, behold your son," He cried,
" And you, your mother at your side."

He would not have the virgin birth
Bring to His mother shame on earth,
And so He showed her vows as bride
Did but a sacred mystery hide.

Proof of His words at once was given
By wondrous portents in the heaven,
To unbelievers shown in vain :
The faithful hence salvation gain.

We know ourselves that God was born
Child of a virgin on that morn.
And with the Father sits to-day,
The sins of earth all swept away.

Veni, redemptor gentium ;
ostende partum virginis ;
miretur omne saeculum.
talis decet partus Deo.

Non ex virili semine
sed mystico spiramine
Verbum Dei factum est caro,
fructusque ventris floruit.

Alvus tumescit virginis,
claustrum pudoris permanet ;
vexilla virtutum micant,
versatur in templo Deus.

Procedit e thalamo suo,
pudoris aula regia,
geminae gigans substantiae,
alacris ut currat viam.

Egressus ejus a Patre,
regressus ejus ad Patrem ;
excursus usque ad inferos,
recursus ad sedem Dei.

Aequalis aeterno Patri,
carnis tropaeo accingere,
infirma nostri corporis
virtute firmans perpeti.

Praesepe iam fulget tuum
lumenque nox spirat novum,
quod nulla nox interpolet
fideque iugi luceat.

Gloria tibi, Domine,
qui natus es de virgine,
cum Patre et sancto Spiritu
in sempiterna saecula.

Come, O thou Saviour, Saviour mild,
And show to us the Virgin's child.
Let every age adoring fall ;
Such birth befits the Lord of all.

He was not sprung of mortal race
But by the Spirit's mystic grace
The Word of God in virgin birth
Took fleshly shape and bloomed on earth.

A virgin's womb the burden bears
And still untouched by man appears.
God joys to linger in that shrine
Where virtue's banners proudly shine.

Forth from his chamber goeth he,
That royal home of purity,
A giant in twofold substance one
Rejoicing now his race to run.

From God the Father he proceeds,
To God the Father back he speeds,
His course he runs to death and hell
Returning on God's throne to dwell.

O equal to the Father thou,
Gird on thy fleshly trophy now,
And give to our poor mortal frame
The deathless virtues of thy name.

Behold thy cradle glitters bright
And darkness gleams with new found light
Where shadows ne'er shall intervene
But faith eternal smile serene

All glory now to God in heaven,
And to the Virgin's Son be given :
And through all ages, as is meet,
Praise we the Holy Paraclete.

Deus creator omnium
polique rector, vestiens
diem decoro lumine
noctem soporis gratia.

Artus solutos ut quies
reddat laboris usui,
mentesque fessas allevet
luctusque solvat anxios.

Grates peracto iam die
et noctis exortu preces,
votis, reos ut adiuves,
hymnum canentes solvimus.

Te cordis ima concinant,
te vox canora concrepet,
te diligat castus amor,
te mens adoret sobria.

Ut cum profunda clauserit
diem caligo noctium,
fides tenebras nesciat
et nox fide reluceat.

Dormire mentem ne sinas,
dormire culpa noverit,
custos fides refrigerans
somni vaporem temperet.

Exuta sensu lubrico
te cordis alta somnient ;
nec hostis invidi dolo
pavor quietos suscitet.

Christum rogemus et Patrem,
Christi Patrisque Spiritum,
unum potens per omnia
fove precantes Trinitas.

God that all things did create
And the heavens dost moderate,
Who doth clothe the day with light,
With benefit of sleep the night,

Which may our weakened senses make
Able new toils to undertake,
And all our minds from anguish ease
And our distempered griefs appease.

Day sinks ; we thank thee for thy gift.
Night comes ; to thee again we lift
Our prayers and vows and hymns, that we
Against all ills defended be.

Thee let our inmost hearts acclaim,
Thee let our tuneful voices name,
To thee our chaste affections cling,
Thee sober reason own as king.

That so, when shadows round us creep
And all is hid in darkness deep
Faith may not know of gloom, and night
Borrow from faith's clear gleam new light.

Sleep not, O stedfast heart and will ;
Sleep rather all ye thoughts of ill.
Let faith allay the warm caress
Of slumber and its wantonness.

From snares of sense, Lord, keep me free
And let my heart dream but of thee.
Let not the jealous foe draw near
To vex my quiet rest with fear.

Call we the Father and the Son
And Holy Ghost : O Three in One.
Blest Trinity whom all obey,
Guard thou the souls that to thee pray.

Aeterne rerum conditor,
noctem diemque qui regis
et temporum das tempora
ut al leves fastidium ;

Praeco diei iam sonat,
noctis profundae pervigil,
nocturna lux viantibus,
a nocte noctem segregans.

Hoc excitatus lucifer
solvit polum caligine,
hoc omnis erronum chorus
vias nocendi deserit.

Hoc nauta vires colligit
pontique mitescunt freta,
hoc ipse, petra ecclesiae,
canente culpam diluit.

Surgamus ergo strenue,
gallus iacentes excitat
et somnolentos increpat,
gallus negantes arguit.

Gallo canente spes redit,
aegris saius refunditur,
mucro latronis conditur,
lapsis fides revertitur.

Iesu, labantes respice
et nos videndo corrige ;
si respicis, lapsus cadunt
fletuque culpa solvitur.

Tu lux refulge sensibus
mentisque somnum discute,
te nostra vox primum sonet
et ora solvamus tibi.

Eternal Lord the world that made,
Who hides the day in night's black shade,
And fixes hour on hour, that we
May never faint or weary be.

Hark to the herald of the morn,
Who vigil through the dark has borne,
Still separating night from night,
To travellers a pledge of light.

The day star hears, and at the call
Looses the sky from night's grim thrall,
While roaming bandits at the word
From mischief cease and sheathe the sword.

His ringing notes the sailors cheer,
The angry waves less wild appear ;
And he on whom the Church is built
When the cock crew confessed his guilt.

So let us rise in eager haste ;
The cock forbids us time to waste.
He stirs the laggards and doth show
Those that deny the sin they do.

The sick man on his bed of pain
When the cock crows has hope again,
And weaklings who have lost belief
Feel faith return and find relief.

O Jesus, help us as we stray.
Look down and guide us on our way.
Beneath thy gaze our wanderings cease.
And tears of grace bring sinners peace.

Shine on our senses with clear light
And from our hearts put sleep to flight.
To thee let us our first songs raise ;
And end our singing with thy praise.

Splendor paternae gloriae,
de luce lucem proferens,
lux lucis et fons luminis,
diem dies illuminans.

Verusque sol, illabere
micans nitore perpeti,
iubarque sancti spiritus
infunde nostris sensibus.

Votis vocemus et Patrem,
Patrem perennis gloriae,
Patrem potentis gratiae :
culpam releget lubricam.

Informet actus strenuos,
dentem retundat invidi,
casus secundet asperos,
donet gerendi gratiam.

Mentem gubernet et regat
casto fideli corpore,
fides calore ferveat,
fraudis venena nesciat.

Christusque nobis sit cibus,
potusque noster sit fides,
laeti bibamus sobriam
ebietatem spiritus.

Laetus dies hic transeat,
pudor sit ut diluculum,
fides velut meridies
crepusculum mens nesciat.

Aurora cursus provehit,
aurora totus prodeat
in Patre totus Filius,
et totus in Verbo Pater.

O splendour of God's glory bright,
O thou that bringest light from light,
O Light of light, lights living spring,
O Day, all days illumining.

O thou true Sun, on us descend,
Thou whose clear radiance knows no end,
And let the Holy Spirit's beam
Upon our mortal senses stream.

The Father, too, let us implore,
Father of glory, evermore,
Father of majesty and grace,
To banish sin and sin's disgrace.

O may he shape our acts aright
And blunt the tooth of envy's spite,
And make ill fortune turn to fair,
Giving us grace our pains to bear.

May he direct and guide our mind,
Our body chaste and faithful find,
Where only faith with fire shall glow
Nor of the traitor's poison know.

Lord Christ for us our food shall be,
Our drink the faith of verity,
The Spirit's wine that maketh whole
And mocking not exalts the soul.

O may this day in joy go hence ;
As unstained dawn our innocence,
As fiery noon our faith appear
And never feel the twilight drear.

Morn in her rosy car is borne.
Let Him come forth, our perfect morn.
The word in God the Father one,
The Father perfect in the Son.

SELECTION FROM *ON VIRGINS*

The Maiden of Antioch

(On Virgins, ii, 4)

There was lately at Antioch a virgin, who constantly avoided the public gaze ; but the more she shrank from men's eyes the more she kindled in them the flame of desire. People are all the more enamoured of beauty when it is talked of but not seen, for there are then two incentives to passion, the craving for love and the craving for knowledge. So long as nothing comes in the way to diminish their fancy, men judge the chance of pleasure to be greater even than it is, inasmuch as the eye does not judge by examination but the mind is inflamed by anticipation. This holy virgin therefore made public profession of perpetual chastity, hoping thus to destroy all hopes of ever possessing her. But though she thereby quenched the fires of the ungodly and received no more declarations of love, in their stead an information was laid against her before the magistrates.

Persecution soon followed. The maiden certainly was filled with fear, but she knew not how to escape. Determined not to fall into the hands of those who were plotting against her virtue, she steeled her heart for some deed of heroic courage, her chastity bidding her to expect the death which her religion forbade her to fear. The day of her crown arrived. Expectation was at its height. The maiden was brought before the court and defying danger made her double profession of religion and chastity. But when the judges saw the firmness of her avowal, her fear for her modesty, her readiness for torture, and her blushes at being looked at, they began to consider how under guise of sparing her virtue they might overcome her religious faith. Their idea was to take from her first her greatest possession, and then to snatch away what she had left. Accordingly, they ordered that she must either offer sacrifice or be exposed in a common brothel. After what fashion do men worship their gods who thus champion their cause ? How do the judges themselves live who pass such sentences as this ?

Thereupon the virgin, not hesitating about her religion but fearful of her chastity, began to reflect : " What am I to do ? I thought to die as a martyr to-day or to live as a virgin ; but they grudge me both crowns. The name of virgin has no meaning when you deny Him who was the founder of virginity. How can you be a virgin, if you worship a wanton ? How can you be a virgin, if you cherish adulterers ? How a virgin, if you seek love ? It is better to have a virgin mind than a virgin body. Both are good if both be possible ; but if both are not allowed, let me be chaste not to man but to God. Rahab was a harlot, but after she believed in God she found salvation. Judith adorned herself to please an adulterer, but as she did it for religion and not for love no one considered her a wanton. I have done well to remember her example. If she who trusted herself to religion saved both her chastity and her country, perhaps I by keeping my religion shall also keep my honour. If Judith had preferred chastity to religion, when her country had been lost she would have lost her chastity with it."

Therefore, instructed by these examples and also bearing in mind the Lord's words, where He says : " *Whosoever shall lose his life for my sake shall find it*," she wept and fell silent, so that no wanton ear might catch her speaking. She did not choose the wrong that threatened her virtue, but she utterly rejected the idea of doing wrong to Christ. Judge, then, whether bodily adultery was possible with her, when she kept such guard upon her very tongue.

For some time now I have been ashamed to proceed with my tale and have shrank from telling the shameful

story. Close your ears, virgins. God's maiden is taken to
the brothel. Now open your ears, virgins. Christ's virgin
may be set among prostitutes, but she suffers no con-
tamination. In every place alike she is God's virgin,
and God's temple. A brothel cannot injure chastity ;
chastity rather purifies the brothel's shame.

A crowd of wanton fornicators at once rushed to the
foul den. Listen holy virgins, to the martyrs' miraculous
deeds and forget the name of the place where they were
done. The dove was shut within ; the hawks clamoured
without, contending one with the other as to who should
first fall upon the prey. But the maiden lifted her hands
to heaven, as though she had come to a house of prayer,
not a haunt of vice, and cried : " Christ, Who didst tame
the fierce lions for the virgin Daniel, Thou canst also
tame the fierce minds of men. For the Hebrew children
fire became as water ; for the Jews, by Thy mercy and not
of its own nature, the sea stood up straight ; Susanna
kneeling down for punishment triumphed over her
lecherous accusers ; the right hand withered which
violated Thy temple gifts. Now it is Thy temple itself
that is being violated ; suffer not the sacrilege of impurity,
Thou who didst not suffer theft. Let Thy Name even
here be glorified, in that I who came for shame may depart
a virgin."

Scarcely had she finished her prayer when lo ! a man
burst in upon her, a soldier terrible of aspect. How must
the virgin have trembled before him to whom the trembling
people had already given way ! But she did not forget
what she had read. " Daniel," said she, " went to see
Susanna punished, and though the people had condemned her, he pronounced her innocent. A sheep may
be hidden under the guise of this wolf. Christ, who is
master of legions, has soldiers in his service. Or perchance
it is the executioner who has come for me. Fear not, my
soul, such an one makes martyrs. Thy faith, virgin, has
saved thee."

Then the soldier spoke : " I pray you, sister," said he,
" be not afraid. I came here as a brother, to save and not
to destroy. Save me and save yourself. I entered in the
guise of an adulterer, but, if you will, I shall go forth as a
martyr. Let us change dresses ; yours fits me, mine fits
you, both fit Christ ; your robe will make me a true soldier,
mine will make you a virgin. You will be well covered,
I shall be even better stripped, for the persecutors will
easily recognize me. Take the garment that will hide the
woman and give me that which will consecrate the martyr.
Put on my cloak, which will hide a virgin's limbs
and preserve her modesty. Press down this hat which
will cover your hair and shade your face. Those who visit
brothels are wont to look ashamed. Be sure not to look
back when once you are outside. Remember Lot's wife
whose very substance was changed because she looked
back at the impure, though with chaste eyes. Be not
afraid lest any part of the sacrifice fail. I offer the victim
to God for you, do you offer the soldier to Christ for me.
You have fought the good fight of chastity, whose wages
are everlasting life ; you possess the breastplate of
righteousness, which protects the body with a spiritual
defence ; you carry the shield of faith to ward off wounds,
and the helmet of salvation. For where Christ is, there is
our salvation's defence ; and as man is the woman's head,
so is Christ the virgin's."

While he was saying this he took off his cloak, the
garment which at first she had feared as being that of a
persecutor, and adulterer. The virgin held forward her
neck, the soldier his cloak. What a spectacle, what a
marvel of grace, this contest for martyrdom in a brothel !
Consider, too, the characters in the piece, a soldier and a
virgin, persons unlike in natural disposition but now alike
through God's mercy, that the saying might be fulfilled :
" *Then the wolves and the lambs shall feed together*." Behold,
the lamb and the wolf not only feed together, they are
sacrificed together. Why say more ? The maiden changed

o

her dress and flew from the snare, borne not by her own wings, but by the wings of the spirit. She left the brothel a virgin—never had the ages seen such a sight—but a virgin dedicated to Christ.

Meanwhile, those who were looking with their eyes, yet saw not, began to rage like robbers for booty or wolves for a lamb. One more shameless than the others went in. But when he realized the state of the matter he said : " What is this ? A maiden entered, but now it is a man I see. This is not the old fable of a hind in a maiden's place ; a virgin in reality has become a soldier. I have been told—though I did not believe it—that Christ changed water into wine ; now He has begun to change the sexes. Let us be going, while we are still what we were. Am I, too, changed, who see things different from what I thought ? I came to a brothel and see a bailee. And yet indeed I am changed, for I came here to wanton and am walking chastely away."

When the matter became known, the soldier, who had been seized in the virgin's dress, was now condemned to death in the virgin's place. To such a conqueror the crown was plainly due, and from the brothel not only the virgin but a pair of martyrs came forth. We are told that the maiden ran to the place of execution and that they both contended for the privilege of dying. The soldier said : " I am condemned to death, but the sentence passed on me lets you go free." But the maiden cried out : " I chose you as a guarantor of chastity, not as a surety against death. If they seek my virtue, my sex is still the same ; if they want my blood, I need no one to go bail for me ; I have the means to pay them. The sentence passed on you in my stead was passed upon me. Certainly if I had given your name as security for a debt and in my absence the judge had assigned your property to my creditor, his verdict would have put you and me on the same footing and I should have paid off your obligations from my estate. If I refused, who would not think me worthy of a shameful death ? How much greater is my debt when you have lent me life ? Let me die innocent, that I may not die guilty. There is no middle course here ; to-day I shall either be guilty of your blood or bear a martyr's witness with my own. If I came back quickly, who dares to shut me out ? If I delayed, who dares acquit me ? I owe a double debt to the law, for I am guilty not only of my own escape but of another's execution. My limbs are strong enough to bear death, though they were not strong enough to bear dishonour. A virgin can accept a wound who could not accept insult. I shrank from shame, not from martyrdom. I gave you my virgin's dress, but I did not break my virgin's vow. If you deprive me of death, you will have rather tricked than rescued me. I pray you not to argue with me or venture to contend. Take not away the kindness you have conferred upon me. If you refuse me the execution of this sentence, you set up again the former one. This sentence merely takes the place of the first, and that one is binding on me even if this one is not. We can each satisfy judgement, if you will allow me to be slain first. From you they have but one penalty to exact ; but a virgin has also her chastity to consider. To make a martyr out of a wanton will be a greater glory for you in men's eyes than to make a wanton out of a martyr."

What more would you have ? The two contended and both gained the victory. The crown was not divided, but became double. The holy martyrs, conferring mutual benefits in turns, gave the one the impulse to martyrdom, the other the final achievement.

SELECTIONS FROM *CLERGYMEN'S DUTIES*

(*a*) MODESTY (i, 18–20)

Lovely is the virtue of modesty and sweet is its grace. It is seen not only in our deeds, but in our talk. It prevents us from overstepping the bounds in speech, it ensures that there shall be nothing indecorous in what we say. Words are often a mirror reflecting the mind. The very sound of our voice is fixed for us by modesty, so that too loud an utterance may not offend any one's ears. Nay, in singing and in every kind of speech, the first rule is modesty. A man must advance gradually when he is learning to play or to sing or to speak ; and progress is always enhanced by a modest beginning.

Even silence, where the other virtues find nothing to do, is one of modesty's great achievements. Of course, if men suppose it due to childishness or pride it is held a reproach ; but if it is a sign of modesty it is reckoned as praiseworthy. Susanna was silent in danger, and thought the loss of modesty worse than the loss of life. She did not think it right to risk her chastity in guarding her safety. To God alone she spoke, for to Him she could speak out in chaste modesty. She avoided looking men in the face. For there is a modesty of the eye, which makes a woman unwilling to look at men or to be looked at by them.

Let no one suppose that our praise should be given to chastity alone. Modesty goes hand in hand with purity, and chastity herself is safer when she stands close by their side. Shame, too, is a good companion in guiding chastity aright, for by offering itself at once as a shield against danger it saves purity from violation. This feeling, at the very outset of her recognition, commends the Mother of the Lord to readers of the Scriptures and like a trusty witness declares her worthy of her high office. When she is sitting in her chamber alone and is saluted by the angel, she is silent and troubled at his entrance, and the Virgin's look is disturbed by the strange appearance of a man's form. Great as was her humility, it was not on that account but on account of her modesty that she did not return his salutation nor make any reply. She merely asked, when she had learnt that she should conceive the Lord, how this should be ; but she did not enter into a conversation.

In our very prayers modesty is a pleasing thing and wins us grace from our God. Was it not this virtue that set the publican first and commended him, when he himself did not dare to lift even his eyes to heaven ? Therefore in the Lord's judgement he was justified rather than the Pharisee whom presumption marred. " *Let us pray then in the incorruptibility of a meek and quiet spirit, which is in the sight of God of great price*," as St. Peter says. Great, therefore, is modesty ; it gives up its rights, takes nothing for itself, claims nothing, never expands to its full strength ; and yet it is rich in the sight of God, in whose sight no man is rich. Rich is modesty ; it is God's portion. Paul also tells us to offer up prayer with modesty and sobriety. It is his wish that the first prayer, which leads the way for the others, should not be boastful of our sins but rather veiled with the blush of shame. The more modesty it shows in remembering its fault, the more abundant grace will it earn.

Even in our movements and gestures and gait, we must observe the rules of modesty. The body's attitude reveals the mind's condition. By our gestures our inner man is judged : " He is a frivolous, loud, and boastful fellow " ; men say, or else : " He is steady, firm, upright, and dependable." Thus the movement of the body is the voice of the soul. You remember, my sons, a certain friend of ours, who seemed to be anxious to recommend himself by his assiduity, but was not admitted by me into the clerical order because of the extreme unseemliness of his gestures. You remember too that I told another cleric, whom I found already here, that he was never to walk in front of me ; the arrogance of his gait was like a whip lash across my eyes. I told him that, when he returned to his duties after some offence, and that was the one criticism I made. But my judgement did not deceive me. Both those men have now left the Church. What their gait betrayed them to be, such were they proved to be by the faithlessness of their hearts. The one forsook the faith at the time of the Arian troubles ; the other through love of money denied that he was one of us, so that he might not have to appear before a Bishop's Court. Their worthlessness was reflected in their walk ; for they really looked like a pair of strolling buffoons.

Some people walk slowly with an actor's gestures. They pace like bearers in a procession and sway their bodies as though they were statues, and seem to be keeping time even as they put one foot in front of the other. Still, I think that a hurried walk is unbecoming, except when a case of some danger demands it, or a real necessity. If people hurry, they come up to us panting, and with distorted features : and if there is no reason which renders haste necessary we have just cause of offence. I am not talking of those who have to hurry occasionally for a particular reason, but of those who by constant use have made hurry a second nature. I disapprove of your slow walker, for he looks like a moving image : I disapprove of your hustler, for he reminds me of a shell that is just about to burst. A proper gait is one in which there is an appearance of authority and weight and dignity and tranquility. It should be perfectly simple and plain, without any affectation or conceit ; for nothing artificial is really pleasing. Let nature fashion our movements and if there is any fault in nature let care amend it. We do not need artifice, but we may need correction.

But if such points as these deserve investigation, how much more careful should we be to let nothing shameful proceed out of our mouth ; for that is man's gravest defilement. It is not food that defiles, but unjust criticism and foul talk. Even among laymen that is shameful, but in our office not a word must be let fall that is unseemly or might offend modesty. Not only must we ourselves say nothing indecorous, we must not lend ear to anything of the kind. So it was that Joseph left his garment behind and fled, that he might not hear words inconsistent with his modesty. For he who takes pleasure in listening challenges the other to go on talking.

Knowledge of foulness is a thing to be ashamed of. As for seeing it, if perchance it should come our way, how dreadful it would be ! Can a thing then be pleasing in ourselves which displeases in others ? Is not nature herself our teacher, who has formed to perfection every part of our body, taking due thought for necessities and also bestowing beauty and grace ? The parts that are comely to look upon, the head, for example, which holds the body's citadel, the pleasant lines of the figure, the appearance of the face ; these she has left open to sight and ready for use. But the parts that must obey nature's needs she has either put away and hidden within the body, to spare us their unsightliness, or else has taught and persuaded us to conceal them with coverings.

Does not nature herself, then, teach us modesty ? Following her example, men's modesty—so called, I imagine, from the mode of knowing what is seemly—has covered and veiled that part of our body's fabric which it found already hidden away. Even as the door which Noah was bidden to make in the side of the ark is a figure both of the church and of our body ; for through that door the remnants of food were cast out. Therefore the Maker of our substance so studied modesty and so guarded what was seemly and honourable in our body that those passages and channel exits were placed in its rear out of view of our eyes, lest the process of voiding should offend the sight. Of this the apostle well says : " *Those members of*

*the body which seem to be more feeble are necessary, and
those members of the body which we think to be less honourable
upon these we bestow more abundant honour, and our
uncomely parts have more abundant comeliness."*   Truly,
by following nature's guidance care has added to the body's
grace. In another place I have explained this matter more
fully, and have said that not only do we hide those parts
that have been given us to hide but also that we think it
unseemly to name these organs or to describe their
appearance and use.

If these parts are exposed by accident, modesty is
violated ; if by design, it is reckoned as utter shamelessness. Therefore Ham, the son of Noah, brought disgrace
upon himself ; for he laughed when he saw his father
naked. But those sons who covered their father's nakedness
received the gift of his blessing. So it was an old custom
in Rome and in many other states that grown-up sons
should not bathe with their parents, or sons-in-law with
their fathers-in-law, in order that the authority and
reverence due to a father should not be diminished. Not
but what many men cover themselves as far as possible
even in the bath, and where the whole body is naked try
at least to hide that part of it. The priests also, under the
old law, as we read in Exodus, wore breeches, as it was
told Moses by the Lord : " *And thou shalt make them
linen breeches to cover their shame ; from their loins even
to their thighs they shall reach, and Aaron and his sons shall
wear them when they enter into the tabernacle of witness and
when they come unto the altar of the holy place to offer
sacrifice, that they lay not sin upon themselves and die."*
Some of us are said still to observe this custom, but most
think that the command has a spiritual interpretation and
was designed to guard modesty and preserve chastity.

It has given me pleasure to dwell at some length on
the various functions of modesty ; for I was addressing
you who are aware of its virtue in your own persons, or,
at least, know nothing of its loss. Fitted as it is for all

ages, persons, times, and places, it is especially becoming in the period of youth and early manhood. At every age, however, we must take care that all our acts be seemly and decorous, so that the order of our life may form one harmonious whole. Therefore Cicero thinks that even in what is seemly a certain order must be observed. He says that it depends on beauty, order, and appointments fitted for action ; which, though difficult to explain in words, can be quite clearly understood.

Why Cicero should have introduced beauty, I do not altogether comprehend ; although he certainly praises bodily strength as well. We do not assign any place to virtue in bodily beauty, even if we recognize a certain grace, as when modesty is wont to cover the face with a blush of shame and make it more pleasing. For as the excellence of a craftsman's work is conditioned by the quality of his materials, so modesty is more noticeable in a comely person. Only the comeliness of the body should not be artificial : it should be frank and natural, careless rather than studied, not heightened by costly and glistening dresses, but clad in ordinary garb. Nothing should be lacking that one's position or necessity demands, but nothing should be added for the sake of effect.

The voice should not be languid nor feeble nor effeminate—although many people, thinking to be important, affect that sort of tone—but should keep the form and rule and vigour suitable to a man. To attain to beauty of life one must act in harmony with one's sex and character. Then we get the best order in all we do, and appointments suited to every form of action. As regards voice and gesture I neither approve of effeminate weakness nor of boorish asperity. Let us follow nature. Her mirror gives us a sure rule of training and a plain pattern of propriety.

It must be allowed that modesty has its rocks—not those that she brings but those which often she encounters, when we fall in company with the intemperate who under

a pretence of good fellowship pour out poison for honest
men. If we come frequently to their banquets and take
part in their merry-making and jests, our manly gravity
is destroyed. Let us beware lest any desire for relaxation
should mar the harmony of our life, which is the blended
concord, as it were, of good works. For habit quickly
bends nature. Therefore, I think that you do wisely to
shun outside entertainments, as being unsuitable to the
clerical, and especially to the priestly, office ; provided that
you offer hospitality to travellers and that your refusal
gives no cause for complaints. Outside entertainments are
distracting in themselves, and soon induce a love of feasting.
Tales of the world and its pleasures frequently creep in ;
you cannot close your ears against them, and to cut them
short is reckoned overbearing. Your glass, too, is filled
without your knowing or wishing it. It is better to excuse
yourself once for all in your own house than to have to do
so again and again in another's. You may be sober enough
yourself when you get up from table, but you should not
by your presence lay yourself open to the condemnation
that the intemperance of others deserves.

There is no need for the younger clergy to go to the
houses of widows or virgins, unless thay are making an
official call ; and even then they should be accompanied
by some of the elder clergy, by the bishop for example,
or if it is an important matter, by the presbyters. Why
should we give the worldly an opportunity for scandal ?
What need is there that can authorize those frequent
visits ? What if one of these women perchance should
make a false step ? Why should you incur the odium of
another's fall ? How many firm hearts have been led
astray by passion ! How many are there who, while not
yielding to sin, have still given room for suspicion ! Why
should you not spend those hours, which your church
duties leave free, in reading ? Why not visit Christ again,
address Him and hear His voice ? We address Him when
we pray, we hear Him when we read the oracles of God.

What have we to do with other people's houses? There is one house that holds all. Let those who want us come to us. What have we to do with gossip? The office of minister at Christ's altar is what we have received; we are under no obligation to make ourselves agreeable to men.

(b) KINDNESS (i, 30; ii, 15)

Let us now consider kindness, under its two headings of benevolence and liberality. Kindness to be perfect must embrace both these virtues. It is not enough to wish well; we must also do well. Nor are good deeds enough; unless they spring from a good source, that is from good will. "*For God loveth a cheerful giver.*" If you act unwillingly, what reward do you deserve? Therefore the apostle, speaking generally, says: "*If I do this thing willingly I have a reward, but if unwillingly a dispensation is given unto me.*" In the Gospel also many rules of just liberality are given to us.

Good will is a comely thing, and so is liberality when it is inspired by the idea of doing good, not doing harm. If you were to think it right to give an extravagant man the means to live extravagantly or an adulterer the money to pay for his adultery, yours would not be a good act of kindness, for there would be no good will behind it. You would be doing harm, not good, if you gave a man money to help him in plotting against his country or in trying to get rogues together at your expense to attack the Church. Nor is it proper liberality to assist a man who abuses widows and orphans or attempts to seize their property by force.

It is no proof of generosity to give to one man the money you have extorted from another. You cannot make

unrighteous gains and then think to spend them
righteously ; unless indeed you do as Zacchaeus did and
repay the man you have cheated fourfold, making up for
the faults of your heathen life by a zealous faith and true
Christian labour. Your generosity should have a firm
foundation. The first requisite is to contribute honestly :
do not say that you are giving a large amount and then
give a small one. What is the use of such pretences? Yours
is a fraudulent promise, for it rests entirely with you to
give what you please. A fraud undermines the foundation,
and your work collapses. Was Peter so hot with anger
that he desired the death of Ananias and his wife ? Nay,
indeed : but he wished that from their example others
might escape death.

Again, it is not true liberality if you give not out of
compassion but for the sake of boasting. Your inward
feelings give your deeds their name. An act is valued by
its primary motive. See what a judge of character you have
to face. He consults you as to how he is to regard your
work, and questions your thoughts first : " *Let not,*"
he says, " *thy left hand know what thy right hand doeth.*"
He is not speaking of our actual body ; the meaning is :
Let not your closest friend or your brother know what
you do, lest, seeking in this world your wages in boastfulness, you lose in the next world the enjoyment of your true
reward. It is true liberality when a man hides what he
does in silence and secretly assists individuals in their
need. His praises come, not from his own lips, but from
the mouths of the poor.

Case, time, place, and faith ; by all these true liberality
is enhanced. Let your first care be for the household of
faith. It is a grave fault if a believer is in need and you
know it and are aware that he has no money and that he is
hungry and distressed, especially if he is ashamed of his
poverty. It is a fault if a believer is falsely accused or if
any of his family are taken prisoners, and you do not help
him. If a just man be in prison suffering pain and punish-

ment for some debt—and though we ought to show mercy to all, we ought especially to show it to the just—if in the time of his trouble he obtains nothing from you, and if in the hour of danger when he is carried off to die your money seems more to you than the life of a dying man, how great is your sin.   Therefore. Job says beautifully : " *Let the blessing of him that was ready to perish come upon me.*"

God indeed is no respecter of persons, for He knows all things ; and we ought to show mercy to all men. But as many seek help on false pretences and make out imaginary losses, the stream of pity should flow with especial generosity when the case is plain, the person known, and the occasion urgent. The Lord is not exacting to demand the utmost. Blessed, indeed, is the man who forsakes all and follows Him, but blessed also is he who does the best he can with what he has. The Lord preferred the widow's two mites to all the offerings of the rich ; she gave all she had, they only gave a small part of their abundance. It is the intention that gives things their value and makes a gift seem handsome or poor. The Lord does not wish us to throw away all our money at once, but rather to parcel it out ; unless perchance our case is like that of Elisha who killed his oxen and fed the people with what he got, so that no household cares might detain him, and that he might give up everything and devote himself to training as a prophet.

But this liberality can only be approved provided that you do not neglect your own near kinsmen if you know they are in need. It is better for you to assist your own people, since they would feel ashamed to ask money from others or to beg from strangers assistance in their distress. Not that they should try and enrich themselves with what you could give to the poor. We must consider the facts of each case and leave out personal feeling. You did not dedicate yourself to the Lord in order to make your family rich, but rather to win eternal life by the fruit of good works and to redeem yourself from the guilt of your own sins by showing mercy to others. Your people think that they are asking little, but they are really seeking what is your ransom. They think that they are acting rightly, but they are really striving to rob you of your life's best fruit. They blame you for not making them rich, but they wish to cheat you of the reward of eternal life.

There are, indeed, many kinds of liberality. Not only can we distribute and give away food day by day to the needy so that they may sustain life, but we can also give advice and assistance to those who are ashamed to confess their poverty, so long as the common poor-box is not exhausted. I am now speaking of an official of the church, a priest or an almoner. Such cases he should report to his bishop, and not keep back the name of anyone whom he knows to be in straits, or to be reduced from wealth to poverty; especially if they have fallen into this distress, not owing to youthful extravagance, but because of another's theft or loss of their estate, so that they cannot earn their daily bread.

The highest form of liberality is to ransom prisoners, to snatch them from the hands of the enemy, to save men from death, and women above all from shame, to restore children to parents and parents to children, and to give back citizens to their native land. Only too familiar to us was this when Illyria and Thrace were laid waste. How many prisoners were then on sale all over the world! If you left them in captivity not one single province would have its proper total of citizens. And yet there were some people who wished to send back into slavery those whom the Church had ransomed, men more cruel than captivity itself, for they grudged the mercy that was shown by others. If they themselves had been taken captive, they said, they, though free-born, would have been made slaves; if they had been sold, they would not have refused to perform a slave's tasks. And yet they now wish to undo the freedom of others, although then they would not have been able to undo their own slavery, unless perchance their buyer had consented to accept a ransom. And by that method slavery is not undone but redeemed.

It is therefore a special form of liberality to redeem captives, especially from barbarian enemies who are not influenced by any feelings of humanity to show mercy but only by a greedy desire to secure ransom. And so it is also to take up another's debt, if the debtor is insolvent and is pressed to pay, while the money is justly due and has been left unpaid through want. So, again, is it to bring up little children and to look after orphans. Another thing is to arrange a marriage for girls who have lost their parents and so preserve their virtue, helping them both with good wishes and with money. A further kind of liberality is that which the apostle teaches : " *If any that believeth hath widows let him relieve them, that the Church be not burdened by supplying them, that it may have enough for those that are widows indeed.*"

Liberality of this sort is useful but it is not possible in all cases. Many good men have but slender means and while satisfied with a little for their own use, they are not able to be of help in relieving the poverty of others. But there is another sort of kindness ready to their hand, whereby they can help their weaker neighbours. Liberality is twofold ; one sort gives material assistance in money ; the other takes the form of helpful deeds, and is often the finer and nobler of the two. How much grander, for example, was it for Abraham to recover his captured son-in-law by force of his victorious arms than to ransom him ! What a much more useful help was the counsel of foresight given by holy Joseph to King Pharaoh than any contribution in money ! Money could not have bought back fertility even in the case of one city ; but foresight kept off famine from all Egypt for five years.

Money is easily spent ; advice never runs dry. Advice grows by use : money is diminished and quickly fails. It even leaves kindness itself stranded, so that the more you wish to be generous to, the fewer you can actually help, and often you find yourself wanting that which you thought it your duty to give to others. But as regards offers of advice and assistance in work, that is a stream that runs back ever to its source and the more widely it spreads the more copiously it flows. The richness of prudence returns upon itself, and the further its water reaches the more active is that which remains.

It is plain, then, that there must be a limit to liberality, or else generosity will become useless. Moderation must be observed, especially by priests, who should dispense their charities, not in ostentatious fashion, but with due regard to justice. Never was the greed of beggars greater than it is to-day. Strong men come to you and their one plea is " I am on the road." And yet they would clear out your poor box and leave it without a penny. They are not satisfied with a little, they always ask for more. Their candidature for assistance is backed up by a grand display of rags and with invented tales of coming birthdays they bid for an increase in their dole. If anyone trusts them too readily he will soon exhaust the funds that are meant for the support of the poor. Let there be method in our generosity, so that while these vagrants do not go away quite empty, the subsistence of the poor may not be wasted and made a prize for cheats. Let us make such an apportionment as will neither forget the claims of humanity nor leave necessity stranded.

Many people pretend they have debts. Look into the real facts. Many complain that they have been stripped by robbers. Help them generously ; but only when their distress is manifest and you are acquainted with them personally. To those who have been banished from church communion supplies must be granted if they are in actual want of food. The man who works by method is harsh to none and generous to all. We ought to lend our ears to hear the cries of our petitioners, but we also ought to use our eyes to look into their needs. To the good almoner weakness appeals more loudly than the pauper's clamour.

The importunity of the vociferous must inevitably get more than it should, but we should not always allow shamelessness its opportunity. You must see those who do not come to see you : you must seek those out who blush to be discovered. You must remember those who are in prison ; and the sick whose voices cannot reach your ears must reach your thoughts instead.

The more zealous people see you in good works, the more they will love you. With many priests I know the more they give away the more abundant are their means. Anyone who sees a good almoner will give him something to distribute on his behalf, being sure that his act of mercy will reach some poor man ; for no one wishes to benefit any save the poor by charity. But if an almoner appears to be too lavish or too stingy, he will in either case be looked at askance ; on the one hand because he is wasting the fruit of other men's labours by unnecessary payments, on the other because he is hoarding it in his money bags. And so while a limit must be set to liberality, it seems that occasionally the spur should be applied. A limit, so that your kindness may be shown day by day and you may not have to refuse to necessity what you have wasted on indulgence. A spur, because money does better work in buying food for the poor than in filling the rich man's purse. Beware lest you shut up within your coffers the welfare of the needy and bury in that sepulchre the very life of the poor.

JEROME

JEROME—or to give him his real and highly significant name Eusebius Sophronius Hieronymus, " The pious puritan, the man of the Holy Word "—was born 345 A.D. at Stridon in Dalmatia, a small town near Aquileia, which was partly destroyed by the Goths during their invasion in 377. Like most young provincials of talent he was attracted to Rome and there studied rhetoric under Donatus, the commentator on Virgil, returning to Aquileia in 370. In that town he established his first society of ascetics, which lasted for just three years. Then some event—referred to by him variously as " a sudden storm " and " a monstrous rending asunder "—broke up the fellowship, and Jerome with a few of his closer associates went eastwards to Antioch. The adjacent desert of Chalcis was already full of hermits and Jerome soon joined their company, living in a bare cell, submitting himself to vigorous penances, and giving all his days to study and devotional exercise. This went on for five years, when he returned to Antioch, was ordained presbyter by Bishop Paulinus, and with him came to Rome for the Church Council held there in 382.

For the next three years Jerome lived in the great city. He became the friend and trusted adviser of Pope Damasus, who constantly consulted him on points of biblical scholarship and commissioned him to write a revised version in Latin of the Psalms and the New Testament. He also found amid the wealth and luxury of Rome a few ardent souls, most of them women, who were ready to embrace and follow his ascetic teaching. One of his pupils was Paula the heiress of the great Aemilian family, who brought over her two daughters Blesilla and Eustochium. Another was the wealthy Marcella, at whose palace on the Aventine

211

the little company used to meet for the study of Hebrew, to pray together, and to sing psalms. During this interval Jerome was perhaps as happy as he ever thought it right to be ; but the death of his protector Damasus unchained against him all the enmities that his rigorous virtues had challenged and his bitter sarcasms provoked. The new pope, Siricius, regarded him as a dangerous rival ; the mob were enraged by the sudden death of Blesilla, which was believed to have been caused by her prolonged fastings and penances ; the cry was raised " The monks to the Tiber " : and Jerome left Rome and Europe for ever.

Thus the second period of Jerome's life begins. He resolved that he would no longer sing the Lord's song in a strange land, and taking Paula and Eustochium with him he went once more to the East, the true home of ascetic belief, and after some little delay settled down in Judaea at Bethlehem, where he remained for the last thirty-four years of his existence. At Bethlehem he built a monastery, of which he was head, a convent over which first Paula and then Eustochium presided, a church where both communities assembled for worship, and a hospice to lodge the pilgrims who came from all parts of the world to that holy ground. The administration of these various activities must have occupied a portion of his time, but the greater part of his energy was given at Bethlehem, as everywhere, to writing and study, and in the history of his later years the chief events are the innumerable books that flowed from his pen. Not that his life was peaceful, or that he passed his days in quietude. His own character always ensured a certain amount of friction ; he quarrelled bitterly with the Bishop of Jerusalem ; his health was never of the best ; and the calm of his monastery was continually being broken by rumours of wars and by the actual shock of barbarian invasion.

The sack of Rome in 410, for example, spread terror even in Palestine, and it is from Jerome perhaps that we get the clearest idea of the consternation caused throughout the world by the fall of the imperial city. In the preface to his Ezekiel he writes : " I was so stupefied and dismayed that day and night I could think of nothing but the welfare of the Roman community. It seemed to me that I was sharing the captivity of the saints and I could not open my lips until I received some more definite news. All the while, full of anxiety, I wavered between hope and despair, torturing myself with the misfortunes of others. But when I heard that the bright light of all the world was quenched, or rather that the Roman Empire had lost its head and that the whole universe had perished in one city : then, indeed, " *I became dumb and humbled myself and kept silence from good words*." And even two years later we see that the impression of horror had scarcely abated. Writing to Principia in 412 he says : " A dreadful rumour came from the West. Rome was besieged and its citizens forced to buy their lives with gold. Then thus despoiled they were attacked a second time, so as to lose their lives as well as their substance. My voice sticks in my throat and even as I dictate this letter sobs choke my utterance. The city which had taken the whole world was itself taken ; nay, more, famine anticipated the sword, and but few citizens were left to be made prisoners. In their frenzy the starving people had recourse to hideous food and tore each other limb from limb that they might have flesh to eat. Even the mother did not spare the babe at her breast."

Still, however troubled at heart Jerome might be, neither public calamity nor private sorrow could stop his labours for long. Paula passed away, her great fortune spent to the last penny in good works ; Marcella only survived the barbarities of the sack of Rome by a few days ; even Eustochium, although she was of a younger generation, succumbed to the rigours of the ascetic life. But the old man, nearly blind, and over seventy, was still working at his commentary on Jeremiah when his last illness came. He died 20th September, 420, and his body was buried beside Paula near the grotto of the Nativity

at Bethlehem, in later days to be transferred and to be the
cause of many a miracle at the Church of Santa Maria
Maggiore in Rome.

As Ambrose before him is the type of the clerical
administrator and man of affairs ; as Augustine after him
is the type of the clerical psychologist and director of
consciences ; so Jerome is the type of the third class of
great divines, the ascetic scholar. Ambrose, as Bishop of
Milan, played a great part in politics and was one of the
most striking figures of his age. Augustine, although less
immersed in worldly affairs, held a high position in the
church hierarchy and was only saved from the deadening
influence of routine administration by the extraordinary
force of his genius. But Jerome steadfastly refused all
through his life to surrender his independence ; he never
held any higher office than that of presbyter, and he was
able to give all of himself to literary work. His early years
he spent in making himself familiar with Latin and Greek
literature, and while he was living in the desert he began
that profound study of the Hebrew scriptures which lasted
till his death. The result of his labours is to be seen in the
ten closely printed volumes in Migne, and in what is
perhaps the most permanent memorial that any man has
left behind him, the Vulgate.

That great version has exercised an influence on Catholic
Christianity, equal to that of the Authorized Version on
our own literature. But quotations from it in this volume
would be unnecessary. Nor need we do more than mention
Jerome's twenty-four books of biblical commentary,
ranging from the *Epistle to Philemon* written in 386 to
the *Jeremiah* left unfinished in 420. Putting aside then the
translations and commentaries there remain the controversial treatises such as *Against Helridius*, *Against
Rufinus*, and *Against Jovinianus*, in which the acrimonious
spirit so often seen in great scholars finds full vent ; the
two histories, the *Chronicle* and the *Illustrious Men*,
books which with all their faults are the basis of much of our

historical knowledge : and the curious and delightful hermit biographies *The Life of Paul*, *The Life of Hilarion*, and *The Story of Malchus*, this last written at Bethlehem in Jerome's old age and given here.

Jerome's literary powers are clearly displayed in all his writings ; but perhaps they have their most attractive expression in his *Letters*. Of these we have 154 written between the years 370 and 419, a collection that can well hold its own in Latin with the letters of Cicero and Pliny and Seneca. The topics with which Jerome and his correspondents deal are so various that it would be easy to make a volume of selections from the letters alone. But when space is limited the long epistle to Eustochium on the nun's vocation chooses itself; for in it we see at their best Jerome's gift of picturesque narrative, his power of satirical description, and, above all, his immense fertility of scriptural quotation.

Those who are going to fight a sea-battle prepare for it beforehand in a harbour on calm water. They turn the tiller, ply the oars, make ready the hooks and grappling irons. They draw up the soldiers on the deck and train them to stand steady on a slippery surface with one foot in the air. And then they feel no fear in the real encounter, since they have gained experience in their sham fights. So I, who have long held my peace—for silence was laid upon me by one who found my words a punishment— now desire some previous practice on a small work, so that I may wipe the rust from my tongue before I approach the wider field of history. For, if God grants me life and if my critics will allow me peace now that I have fled to the seclusion of a monastery, I propose to write a history of the church of Christ from the coming of our Saviour down to our own days, that is, from the apostles to the dregs of this present age. I shall describe by what means and by whose agency the church came into existence, and how, as it gained strength, it grew by persecution and was crowned with martyrdom, and then, coming to the Christian emperors, increased in power and wealth but decreased in virtue. But of this elsewhere. Now to the matter in hand.

Maronia is a little village about thirty miles from Antioch the capital of Syria. When as a young man I was living in that country, after having had several owners and patrons the hamlet had passed into the hands of my friend the Bishop Evagrius, whose name I now give to show the source of my information. Well, at that time an old man was living there called Malchus, a name which in Syriac means " king ", a Syrian by birth and speech, in fact a genuine son of the soil. His house companion was

an old woman very decrepit who seemed to be at death's
door. The pair were devotedly pious and so haunted the
church door that you might have thought them the
Zacharias and Elizabeth of the gospel except for the fact
that they had no John. I made careful inquiries of the
villagers as to what was the bond between them; was it
marriage, kinship, or a spiritual union? All with one
accord replied that they were righteous folk well pleasing
to God, and added further some strange details about them.
Attracted by their story I approached the man and
inquiring eagerly about the truth of what I heard, learnt
the following facts.

My son, the old man said, I was my parents' only child
and used to farm a piece of ground at Nisibis. As I was
the sole representative of our line and the family heir,
my people tried to force me into marriage but I told them
that I would rather be a monk. The mere fact that at last
I ran away from home and parents will prove to you what
threats were used by my father and what persuasions by
my mother to make me betray my chastity. I could not
go eastwards, since Persia was close by and the Roman
soldiers were on guard; and so I turned my steps to the
west, taking with me a little store of provisions just
sufficient to ward off destitution. To cut a long tale short,
I came at last to the desert of Chalcis between Immae
and Beroa to the south. There I found some monks
under whose direction I placed myself, earning a livelihood
by manual labour and curbing the wantonness of the flesh
by fasting; but after some years a longing came over me
to return to my native place. I had heard that my father
was dead, and I thought that I would comfort my widowed
mother as long as she lived, and then sell my little property
and give one-third to the poor, one-third to the monastery,
and—why blush to confess my lack of faith?—keep one-
third to supply myself with comforts.

My abbot cried out that it was a temptation of the devil,
and that under pretext of a good deed some snare of the

old enemy lay concealed. This is a case, he said, of the
dog returning to his vomit; many monks had been
deceived in this fashion, for the devil never showed himself
openly. He set before me many examples from the
scriptures; among others how at the beginning he over-
threw Adam and Eve by giving them the hope of becoming
gods. Finally, when arguments proved useless, he fell
upon his knees and begged me not to forsake him to my
own destruction, nor look back after putting my hand to
the plough. Alas, alas! I won a fatal victory and disregarded his advice; for I thought that he was seeking,
not my salvation, but his own comfort. He followed me
from the monastery as though he were walking at my
funeral, and when at last he bade me farewell he said:
" I see that you are branded as a son of Satan. I ask not
your reasons. I do not accept your excuses. The sheep
that leaves the fold is at once exposed to the jaws of the
wolf."

As you go from Beroa to Edessa there is a piece of lonely
country near the high road, across which the Saracens
who have no fixed abode are continually roaming in all
directions. Through fear of them travellers in that district
usually assemble in a party so that by mutual assistance
they may escape impending danger. In my company
there were about seventy persons, men, women, and
children, old and young. Suddenly the Ishmaelites
attacked us, riding on horses and camels. Their long hair
was bound with fillets, their bodies were half naked, their
cloaks trailed behind them and they wore loose boots.
They had slung their quivers over their shoulders and
carrying their bows unstrung they brandished long spears;
for they had come not to fight, but to plunder. We were
seized, divided, and carried off in different directions.
I, meanwhile, repenting too late of my plans and very far
now from entering into possession of my inheritance, was
assigned as slave to a master together with one other
woman captive. We were led off, or, rather, carried high

on camels' backs, through a desert waste, expecting every
moment to fall and hanging rather than sitting in our
place. Our only food was half-raw meat, our drink camel's
milk.

At length we crossed a wide river and came to the
interior of the desert, where we were bidden to make
obeisance to our master's wife and children and bow our
heads humbly to them, as is the custom with that people.
There like a prison captive I changed my dress ; that is,
I learned to go about naked. For the excessive heat
rendered any covering but a loin cloth unbearable. Some
sheep were given me to feed ; and when I came to compare
troubles I found that I had at least one advantage ; I
seldom saw my masters or my fellow-slaves. I thought that
I was in somewhat the same case as that holy man Jacob,
and I remembered the life of Moses ; for both of these
had once been shepherds in the desert. My food was
fresh cheese and milk ; I prayed continually and sung
the psalms I had learned in the monastery. My captivity
was a pleasure to me, and I rendered grateful thanks to
God's judgement, inasmuch as I had found in the desert
that monk whom I was on the point of losing in my own
country.

But how true is it that with the devil safety is impossible !
How manifold and ineffable are his snares ! Hid
though I was his malice found me out. My master, seeing
that his flock was growing and finding no dishonesty in
me—for I knew that the apostle bade us serve our masters
as faithfully as we serve God—wished to reward me and
thus secure my fidelity. Accordingly, he gave me the slave
woman who had previously been taken captive with me.
I refused to take her and said I was a Christian and that
it was not lawful for me to have a woman for wife whose
husband was still alive ; for her husband had been taken
prisoner with us and carried off by another owner. At this
my master went mad with anger, and drawing his sword
came furiously at me. Indeed, if I had not at once stretched

out my hand and taken possession of the woman he would have killed me on the spot.

Soon night came on, for me all too early, a night darker than its wont. I led my new bride into a tumbledown cave, with grief as bridesmaid, both of us shrinking from one another, although we did not confess it. Then truly I realized that I was a slave, and flinging myself upon the ground began to lament the monk that I had ceased to be. " Was it for this misery that my life was spared ? " I cried. " Have my sins brought me to this, that I who have lived a virgin should in my old age take a wife ? What avails it me to have scorned parents, country, and estate for the Lord's sake, if now I do the thing which I scorned them to avoid. Unless indeed it is because I regretted my native land that I now have these troubles to bear ! What are we to do, my soul ? Die, or conquer ? Wait for the hand of God, or stab ourselves with our own sword ? Do thou turn the blade upon thyself : the soul's death is more to be feared than the body's. Chastity even if preserved has its own martyrdom. Let the witness to Christ lie unburied in the desert : I will be both persecutor and martyr."

So speaking, I drew my sword, which gleamed still in the darkness, and turning its point towards me said : " Farewell, unhappy woman ; take me as a martyr rather than as a husband." At that she threw herself at my feet and cried : " I pray you by Jesus Christ and by the dread compulsion of this hour, do not shed your blood and make me a criminal. If you are resolved on death, turn your sword against me first. Let that be our union. Even if my husband came back to me I should cling to the chastity which I have learned in captivity. I would die rather than lose it now. Why kill yourself to prevent a union with me ? I should kill myself if you insisted on our mating. Take me, therefore, as your partner in chastity, and love the bond of the spirit more than you could ever love the bond of the flesh. Let our masters fancy that you are my husband, but let Christ know you for my brother. We shall easily convince people of our marriage when they see us so loving." I confess, I was astonished : I had admired the woman's virtue before, but I loved her as a wife still more. Yet I never looked upon her naked body ; I never touched her flesh ; I feared to lose in peace that which I had kept in battle. In this strange wedlock many days passed. Our marriage had increased our master's liking for us, and he had no fear that we should run away. Indeed, I was sometimes absent for a whole month, a faithful shepherd in the wilderness.

A long time passed, and as I sat alone one day in the desert with nothing in sight save earth and sky, I began quietly to turn things over in my mind. Among other things I called back to memory the monks with whom I had lived, and especially the look of the father who had taught me, detained me, and lost me. While busied with these thoughts I suddenly noticed a crowd of ants swarming over a narrow pathway. You could see that the loads they carried were larger than themselves. Some with their mandibles were dragging grass seed along ; others were throwing the earth out of pits they had made and banking it up to prevent an overflow of water. One party, mindful of the winter's approach, were cutting off the tips of the grain they had brought in, so that the damp might not turn their store into grass. Another company with mournful ceremonies were carrying out the bodies of their dead comrades. And, what is especially strange in such a host, those who were coming out did not hinder those who were going in ; nay, rather, if they saw anyone sink beneath the weight of his load, they would put their shoulders to it and assist him. To be brief, that day gave me a delightful entertainment.

The result of it was that I remembered how Solomon sends us to the shrewdness of the ant and by its example rouses our sluggish wits. I began to be weary of captivity and to regret the monastery cells, and long to take pattern by these ants who work for the community, and, since nothing belongs to anyone all things belong to all. When I returned to my lodging my wife met me, and my looks could not disguise the sadness that I felt. She asked why I was so depressed. I told her the reasons and urged her to escape. She made no objection. I begged her to say nothing. She gave me her word. We spoke all the time in whispers, wavering between hope and fear. I had in my flock two particularly large he-goats : these I killed, made their skins into leather bottles and prepared their flesh as food on our way. In the early evening, when our masters thought we had retired to rest, we set off, taking with us the skins and portions of the meat. When we reached the river, which was ten miles off, we inflated the skins and getting astride them trusted ourselves to the water, rowing slowly with our feet for oars, so that the stream should carry us down to a point on the further bank much below that at which we had embarked, and so our pursuers would lose track of us. In the crossing, however, part of our meat became sodden with water, and part was carried away, so that we had scarcely three days' food to depend on. We drank till we could drink no more, in preparation for the thirst that we knew would come upon us, and then hurried away, looking continually behind us, and moving more by night than by day for fear of an ambush of the roaming Saracens and also because of the sun's excessive heat. Even now I shudder when I recall our misery ; and though my mind is at ease every part of my body is trembling.

On the fourth day of our flight we saw in the dim distance two men on camels riding quickly towards us. I foreboded trouble at once, the sun turned dark before my eyes, and I thought that my master would certainly put us to death. We realized that our footsteps in the sand had betrayed us ; but at the height of our fear we suddenly saw on our right a cavern extending far underground. We entered it in deadly fear of venomous beasts—for

vipers, basilisks, scorpions, and such like are wont to
frequent these dark places out of the heat of the sun—
and stopping just inside its mouth took refuge in a pit
on the left, not going any further in lest we should come
upon destruction while flying from it. We thought to
ourselves : " If the Lord helps us in our trouble, we are
saved. If he heeds us not because of our sins, we have a
grave here." Suddenly we saw our master and one of his
slaves standing in front of the cave quite close to us. Our
footsteps had again betrayed us, and they had discovered
our hiding-place. What do you imagine were our feelings,
what our terror ?   Ah, how much more cruel is the
expectation of death than death itself ! Even now my
tongue stammers with the terror and distress which then
I knew. I fancy that I hear my master calling and am
afraid to mutter.

Well, he sent the slave to drag us from the cavern,
while he himself holding the camels waited for us to come
out with his sword ready. The man came in for about
five or six feet, and we in our hiding place saw his back
though he did not see us, for the nature of the eye is such
that people coming into the dark from sunlight find
themselves quite blinded. His voice echoed through the
cave : " Come out, you rogues ; come out and die ;
why are you standing there ? Why do you delay ? Come
out ; your master calls and patiently awaits you." He was
still speaking when lo ! in the dark we saw a lioness spring
upon the fellow, grip him by the throat, and drag him all
bloody into the inner cave. Good Jesus ! How great
then was our terror and our joy ! We beheld our enemy
perish while our owner stood in ignorance of his fate.

Soon, however, the master himself, impatient of delay
and suspecting that one man was no match for two, rushed
furiously angry into the cave. Sword in hand he fiercely
upbraided his slave's slowness ; but before he could reach
our hiding place he, too, was seized by the wild beast.
Who would ever have thought that before our very eyes

a brute would fight for us ? Our first fears were thus dis-
pelled, but we had still facing us the prospect of a death
like theirs, although we preferred the rage of the lioness
to the anger of the man. We trembled in our retreat,
and not daring to move awaited the issue, only protected
by our consciousness of chastity as by a wall. Early in
the morning the lioness, afraid of a trap and aware that she
had been seen, took up her cub in her teeth and carried
it away, leaving us in possession. We did not have enough
confidence to come out at once ; and even after a long wait
whenever we thought of leaving we pictured to ourselves
the horror of meeting her again.

Well, we got rid of our fright at last, and at the end of the
day, towards evening we sallied forth and saw the camels—
called dromedaries because of their excessive speed—
quietly chewing the cud. We got on their backs and after
recruiting our strength with the fresh provisions started
to cross the desert. On the tenth day we arrived at a Roman
camp, and being presented to the tribune told him the
whole story. He sent us on to Sabianus, general in
command of Mesopotamia, and we there sold the camels.
My dear old abbot by this time was sleeping in the Lord ;
I therefore came back here and joined the monks for a
time, handing over my companion to the care of the virgins ;
for though I loved her as a sister, I could not trust myself
with her as a sister.

I was quite a young man and Malchus was old when
he related all this to me. I in my old age have now repeated
it to you, a story of chastity for the chaste. I exhort you,
virgins, to guard your chastity. Tell this tale to those that
come after, so that they may know that even in the midst
of swords and deserts and wild beasts virtue is never made
a captive, and that he who has surrendered himself to
Christ may be slain but cannot be conquered.

" *Hear, O daughter, and consider, and incline thine ear ;
forget also thine own people and thy father's house, and the
king shall desire thy beauty.*" So in the forty-fourth psalm
God speaks to the human soul, that, following Abraham's
example, it should go out from its own land and from its
kinsmen, and leave the Chaldæans, that is the demons,
and dwell in the country of the living, for which elsewhere
the prophet sighs, saying : " *I trust to see the good things
of the Lord in the land of the living.*" But for you it is not
enough to go out from your own land unless you forget
your people and your father's house, so that despising the
flesh you may be joined to your bridegroom's embrace.
" *Look not behind thee,*" he says, " *neither stay thou in all
the plain ; escape to the mountain lest thou be consumed.*"
It is not right for one who has grasped the plough to look
behind him or return home from the field, or after putting
on Christ's garment to descend from the roof for other
raiment. A wondrous thing indeed is it that a father should
charge his daughter not to remember her father. " *Ye are
of your father the devil, and the lusts of our father it is
your will to do.*" So it was said to the Jews. And in another
place, " *He that committeth sin is of the devil.*" Born of
such a parent first we are black by nature, and even after
repentance until we have climbed to virtue's height we
may say, " *I am black but comely, O ye daughters of
Jerusalem.*"

You may say : " I have gone out from my childhood's
home, I have forgotten my father, I am born again in
Christ. What reward do I receive for this ? " The context
tells you : " *And the king shall desire thy beauty.*" This,
then, is the great sacrament. " *For this cause shall a man
leave his father and his mother and shall be joined unto his*

wife, and they two shall be "—not as is there said, " *of one flesh,*" but of one spirit. Your bridegroom is not arrogant or haughty; He has married a women of Ethiopia. As soon as you resolve to hear the wisdom of the true Solomon, and come to Him, He will avow to you all His knowledge; He will lead you as a king to His chamber; your colour will be miraculously changed, and to you the words will be fitting : " *Who is this that goeth up and hath been made white ?* "

I am writing this to you, Lady Eustochium (I am bound to call my Lord's bride " lady ") that from the very beginning of my discourse you may realize that I do not to-day intend to sing the praises of the virginity which you have adopted and proved to be so good. Nor shall I now reckon up the disadvantages of marriage, such as pregnancy, a crying baby, the tortures of jealousy, the cares of household management, and the cutting short by death of all its fancied blessings. Married women have their due allotted place, if they live in honourable marriage and keep their bed undefiled. My purpose in this letter is to show you that you are fleeing from Sodom and that you should take warning by Lot's wife. There is no flattery in these pages. A flatterer is a bland enemy. Nor will there be any pomp of rhetoric in expounding the beatitude of virginity, setting you among the angels and putting the world beneath your feet.

I would have you draw from your vows not pride but fear. When you walk laden with gold you must beware of robbers. For mortals this life is a race : we run it on earth that we may receive our crown elsewhere. No man can walk secure amid serpents and scorpions. The Lord says : " *My sword hath drunk its fill in heaven* "; and do you expect peace on the earth, which yields only thorns and thistles and is itself the serpent's food ? " *Our wrestling is not against flesh and blood, but against the principalities, against the powers, against the world rulers of this darkness, against the spiritual hosts of wickedness in the heavenly places.*" We are surrounded by the thronging hosts of our foes, our enemies are on every side. The flesh is weak and soon it will be ashes, but to-day it fights alone against a multitude.

But when the flesh has been melted away and the Prince of this world has come and found in it no sin, then in safety you shall listen to the prophet's words : " *Thou shalt not be afraid for the terror by night nor for the arrow that flieth by day ; nor for the trouble which haunteth thee in the darkness ; nor for the demon and his attacks at noonday ; A thousand shall fall at thy side and ten thousand at thy right hand ; but it shall not come nigh thee.*" If the hosts of the enemy beset you, if the allurements of sin begin to burn within your breast, if in your troubled thoughts you ask : " What shall I do ? " Elisha's words will give you an answer. " *Fear not, for they that be with us are more than they that be with them.*" He will pray for you and will say : " Lord, open the eyes of thy handmaid that she may see." And when your eyes have been opened you will see a chariot of fire which will carry you, as it carried Elijah, up to the stars ; and then you will joyfully sing : " *Our soul is escaped as a bird out of the snare of the fowlers : the snare is broken and we are escaped.*"

As long as we are held down by this frail body ; as long as we keep our treasure in earthen vessels and the flesh lusteth against the spirit, the spirit against the flesh ; so long can there be no sure victory. Our adversary the devil goeth about as a roaring lion seeking whom he may devour. David says : " *Thou maketh darkness and it is night ; wherein all the beasts of the forest do creep forth. The young lions roar after their prey and seek their meat from God.*" The devil does not look for unbelievers or for those who are without, whose flesh the Assyrian king roasted in a pot ; it is the church of Christ that he hastens to ravish. According to Habakkuk—" *His dainty morsels are of the choicest.*" He desires Job's ruin, and after devouring Judas he seeks power to put all the apostles through his sieve. The Saviour came not to send peace upon the earth but a sword. Lucifer fell, Lucifer who used to rise with the dawn ; and he who was nurtured in a paradise of delight heard the well-earned sentence : " *Though thou exalt thyself as the eagle, and though thou set thy nest among the stars, thence will I bring thee down, saith the Lord.*" For he had said in his heart, " I will exalt my throne above God's stars, and I will be like the Most High." Wherefore God every day says to the angels as they go down the stairway which Jacob saw in his dream : " *I have said ye are God's and all of you are children of the Most High. But ye shall die like men and fall like one of the princes.*" The devil fell first, and since God stands in the congregation of the Gods and judges them in the midst, the apostle writes to those who are ceasing to be Gods—" *Whereas there is among you envying and strife, are ye not carnal and walk as men ?* "

The apostle, who was a chosen vessel set apart for the gospel of Christ, because of the spur of the flesh and the allurements of sin keeps his body down and subjects it to slavery, lest in preaching to others he himself be found a reprobate. But still he sees that there is another law in his members fighting against the law of his will, and that he is still led captive to the law of sin. After nakedness, fasting, hunger, prison, scourging and torture, he turns back upon himself and cries : " *Oh wretched man that I am, who shall deliver me from the body of this death ?* " If that is so with him, do you think that you ought to lay aside all fear ? Beware, pray, lest God some day should say of you : " *The virgin of Israel is fallen, and there is none to raise her up.*" I will say it boldly, though God can do all things he cannot raise a virgin up after she has fallen. He is able to free one who has been corrupted from the penalty of her sin, but he refuses her the crown. Let us be fearful lest in our case also the prophecy be fulilled : " *Good virgins shall faint.*" Note that it is of good virgins he speaks, for there are bad ones as well. The Scripture says : " *Whosoever looketh on a woman to lust after her hath committed adultery with her already in his heart.*" Virginity therefore can be lost even by a thought. Those are the evil virgins, virgins in the flesh, but not in the spirit : foolish virgins, who having no oil in the lamps, are shut out by the Bridegroom.

But if even true virgins are not saved by their bodily virginity if they have other faults, what shall be done to those who have prostituted the members of Christ and changed the temple of the Holy Spirit into a brothel ? Straightway they shall hear the words : " *Come down and sit in the dust, O virgin daughter of Babylon ; sit in the dust, for there is no throne for the daughter of the Chaldæans ; no more shalt thou be called tender and delicate . Take the millstone and grind meal ; uncover thy locks, make bare thy legs, pass over the rivers ; thy nakedness shall be uncovered, yea, thy shame shall be seen.*" And this, after the bride-chamber of God the Son, after the kisses of her kinsman and her bridegroom, she of whom once the word of the prophet sang : " *Upon thy right hand stood the queen in a vestment of gold wrought about with divers colours.*" But now she shall be made naked and her skirts shall be discovered upon her face : she shall sit by the waters of loneliness, her pitcher laid aside ; and shall open her feet to every one that passeth by and shall be polluted to the crown of her head. Better had it been for her to have submitted to marriage with a man and to have walked on the plain rather than to strain for the heights and fall into the depths of hell.

Let not the faithful city of Sion become a harlot, I pray you ; let not demons dance and sirens nest in the place that once sheltered the Trinity. Loose not the belt that confines the bosom. As soon as lust begins to tickle the senses, and the soft fires of pleasure envelope us with their delightful warmth, let us break forth and cry : " *The Lord is on my side ; I will not fear what the flesh can do unto me.*" When for a moment the inner man shows signs of wavering between vice and virtue, say : " *Why are thou cast down, O my soul, and why art thou disquieted within me?　Hope thou in God, for I shall yet praise Him who is the health of my countenance and my God.*" I would not have you allow any such thoughts to rise. Let nothing disorderly, nothing that is of Babylon find shelter in your breast. Slay the enemy while he is small : nip evil in the bud, and then you will not have a crop of tares. Harken to the words of the Psalmist : " *Hapless daughter of Babylon, happy shall he be that rewardeth thee as thou hast served us.　Happy shall he be that taketh and dasheth thy little ones against the stones.*" It is impossible that the body's natural heat should not sometimes assail a man and kindle sensual desire ; but he is praised and accounted blessed, who, when foul thoughts begin to rise, gives them no quarter, but dashes them straightway against the rock. " *And the Rock is Christ.*"

Oh, how often, when I was living in the desert, in that lonely waste, scorched by the burning sun, which affords to hermits a savage dwelling place, how often did I fancy myself surrounded by the pleasures of Rome. I used to sit alone ; for I was filled with bitterness. My unkempt limbs were covered in shapeless sackcloth ; my skin through long neglect had become as rough and black as an Ethiopian's. Tears and groans were everyday my portion ; and if sleep ever overcame my resistance and fell upon my eyes I bruised my restless bones against the naked earth. Of food and drink I will not speak. Hermits have nothing but cold water even when they are sick, and for them it is sinful luxury to partake of cooked dishes. But though in my fear of hell I had condemned myself to this prison house, where my only companions were scorpions and wild beasts, I often found myself surrounded by bands of dancing girls. My face was pale with fasting ; but though my limbs were cold as ice, my mind was burning with desire, and the fires of lust kept bubbling up before me when my flesh was as good as dead.

And so, when all other help failed me, I used to fling

myself at Jesus' feet, I watered them with my tears, I
wiped them with my hair ; and if my flesh still rebelled
I subdued it by weeks of fasting. I do not blush to confess
my misery ; nay, rather I lament that I am not now what once
I was. I remember that often I joined night to day with
my wailings and ceased not from beating my breast till
tranquillity returned to me at the Lord's behest. I used
to dread my poor cell as though it knew my secret thoughts.
Filled with stiff anger against myself, I would make my
way alone into the desert ; and when I came upon some
hollow valley or rough mountain or precipitous cliff, there
I would set up my oratory, and make that spot a place of
torture for my unhappy flesh. There sometimes also—
the Lord Himself is my witness—after many a tear and
straining of my eyes to heaven, I felt myself in the presence
of the angelic hosts and in joy and gladness would sing :
" *Because of the savour of thy good ointments we will run
after thee.*"

If such are the temptations of men whose bodies are
emaciated with fasting, so that they have only evil thoughts
to withstand, how must it fare with a girl who clings to
the enjoyment of luxuries ? Surely, as the apostle says :
" *She is dead while yet she liveth.*" Therefore, if I may
advise you and if experience gives my advice weight, I
would begin with urgent exhortation : as Christ's spouse
avoid wine as you would avoid poison. Wine is the first
weapon that devils use in attacking the young. The restless-
ness of greed, the windiness of pride, the delights of
ostentation, are nothing to this. Other vices we easily
forego : this is an enemy within our walls, and wherever
we go we carry our foe with us. Wine and Youth—behold
a double source for pleasure's fire. Why throw oil on the
flame : why give fresh fuel to a wretched body that is
already ablaze ?

Paul says to Timothy : " *Drink no longer water, but use
a little wine for thy stomach's sake, and for thine often
infirmities.*" Notice the reasons why wine is allowed :

it is to cure pain in the stomach and to relieve a frequent infirmity. And lest perchance we should indulge ourselves on the ground of illness, Paul recommends that but a little wine should be taken, advising rather as a physician than as an apostle—although indeed an apostle is a spiritual physician. He was afraid that Timothy might be overcome by weakness and might not be able to complete the many journeys that the preaching of the Gospel rendered necessary. In any case, he remembered that he had said elsewhere : " *Wine, wherein is wantonness* " and " *It is good for a man neither to drink wine nor to eat flesh* ". Noah took wine and became drunken. But living in the rude age after the Flood when the vine first was planted he was unaware perhaps of its inebriating qualities. And that you may see the mystery of the Scripture in all its fulness— for the word of God is a pearl and may be pierced right through—note that after his drunkenness there followed the uncovering of his thighs : lust was near neighbour to wantonness. First the belly is swollen : then the other members are roused. " *The people sat down to eat and drink and rose up to play.*" Lot, the friend of God, after he had been saved upon the mountain as the one man found righteous among all those thousands, was intoxicated by his daughters. They may have thought that the human race had ended and have acted rather from a desire for offspring than from love of sinful pleasure ; but they knew full well that the righteous man would not abet them unless he were drunken. In fact, he did not know what he was doing : but although there be no wilfulness in his sin the error of his fault remains. As the result he became the father of Moab and Ammon, Israel's enemies, who " *even to the fourteenth generation shall not enter into the congregation of the Lord for ever.*"

When Elijah in his flight from Jezabel was lying weary and alone beneath the oak-tree, an angel came and raised him up and said : " Arise and eat." And he looked, and behold there was a cake and a cruse of water at his head.

Could not God have sent him spiced wine and dainty condiments and tenderly basted meats, if He had willed ? Elisha invited the sons of the prophets to dinner, and when he gave them field herbs to eat he heard his guests cry out with one accord " There is death in the pot ". The man of God, however, was not angry with the cooks—for he was not used to very sumptuous fare—but threw some meal upon the herbs, and thus sweetened their bitterness by the same spiritual virtue as Moses once sweetened the waters of Mara. Again, when the men sent to seize the prophet had been blinded alike in eyes and understanding, that he might bring them unawares to Samaria, notice the food with which Elisha ordered them to be refreshed. " Set bread and water before them," he said, " let them eat and drink and go back to their master." Daniel too might have had rich dishes served him from the king's table ; but he preferred the mower's breakfast that Habakkuk brought, which must, methinks, have been but country fare. Therefore he was called " the man of desires ", because he refused to eat the bread of desire or drink the wine of lustfulness.

From the Scriptures we may get countless divine answers condemning gluttony and approving simple food. But as it is not my present purpose to discuss the question of fasting and an exhaustive inquiry would need a volume to itself, these few remarks from the many I could make must suffice. In any case, the examples I have given will enable you to understand why the first man, obeying his belly rather than God, was cast down from Paradise into this vale of tears. You will see also why Satan tempted Our Lord himself with hunger in the wilderness, and why the apostle cries : " *Meats for the belly and the belly for meats, but God shall destroy both it and them*," and why he says of the wanton : " *Whose God is their belly.*" Every man worships what he loves. Wherefore we must take all care that abstinence may bring back to Paradise those whom repletion once drove out.

You may choose perhaps to answer that a girl of good family like yourself, accustomed to luxury and down pillows, cannot do without wine and tasty food and would find a stricter rule of life impossible. To that I can only say : " Live then by your own rule, since you cannot live by God's." Not that God, the Lord and Creator of the universe, takes any delight in the rumbling of our intestines or the emptiness of our stomach or the inflammation of our lungs ; but because this is the only way of preserving chastity. Job was dear to God, his purity and frankness witnessed by God's own testimony ; yet hear what he thinks of the devil : " *His strength is in the loins and his force is in the navel.*" The words are used for decency's sake, but the male and female generative organs are meant. So the descendant of David, destined according to the promise, to sit upon his throne is said to come from his loins. The seventy-five souls who entered into Egypt are said in the same way to have come from Jacob's thigh. And when after wrestling with the Lord the stoutness of his thigh shrank away Jacob begat no more children. Those who celebrate the Passover also are bidden to do so with their loins girded and mortified. God says to Job : " *Gird up thy loins like a man.*" John wears a leather girdle ; and the Apostles are bidden to gird their loins before they take the lamps of the Gospel. Ezekiel tells us how Jerusalem is found in the plain of wandering, all bespattered with blood, and he says : " *Thy navel has not been cut.*" In his assaults on men therefore all the devil's strength is in the loins : against women his force is in the navel.

Would you like to be sure that it is as I say ? Here are some examples. Samson was stronger than a lion and harder than rock ; alone and unprotected he chased a thousand armed men ; but in Dalilah's soft arms his vigour melted away. David was chosen as a man after God's heart and his lips had often sung of the future coming of Christ the Holy One : but as he walked upon his housetop he was fascinated by Bathsheba's nakedness and added murder to adultery. Notice for a moment that even in one's own house the eyes are never safe from danger. Therefore in repentance he says to the Lord : " *Against Thee, Thee only, have I sinned, and done this evil in Thy sight.*" He was a king and feared no one else but God. Solomon, too, by whose lips wisdom herself used to speak, who knew of all plants from the cedar of Lebanon to the hyssop that grows out of the wall, went back from God because he became a lover of women. And that no one may trust in kinship by blood, remember that Ammon was fired by an illicit passion for his sister Thamar.

I am ashamed to speak of the many virgins who every day are falling and being lost to the bosom of our Mother Church : stars over which the proud enemy sets his throne and hollow rocks in whose crevices the serpent makes his habitation. You may see many women who have been left widows before they were ever wed, trying to conceal their consciousness of guilt by means of a lying garb. Unless they are betrayed by a swelling womb or by the crying of their little ones they walk abroad with tripping feet and lifted head. Some even insure barrenness by the help of potions, murdering human beings before they are fully conceived. Others when they find that they are with child as the result of their sin, practice abortion with drugs, and so frequently bring about their own death, taking with them to the lower world the guilt of three crimes : suicide, adultery against Christ, and child murder. Yet these are the women who will say : " To the pure all things are pure. My conscience is enough for me. A pure heart is what God craves. Why should I refrain from the food which God made for enjoyment ? " When they wish to appear bright and merry, they drench themselves with wine, and then joining profanity to drunkenness they cry : " Heaven forbid that I should abstain from the blood of Christ." When they see a woman with a pale sad face, they call her " a miserable Manichæan " ; and quite logically, too, for on their principles fasting is heresy. As they walk the streets they try to attract attention, and with stealthy nods and winks draw after them troops of young men. Of them the prophet's words are true : " *Thou hast a whore's forehead : thou refusest to be ashamed.*" Their dress is only a piece of transparent purple with the lilac cape which they call a " Maforte " fluttering from their shoulders : on their head they wear a loose bandeau. so as to leave their hair free : their feet are shod in cheap slippers and their arms confined in tight sleeves. Add to all this a very loose-kneed walk, and you have all their marks of virginity. Such women may have their admirers, and it may cost more to ruin them because they are called virgins. But to such virgins as these I prefer to be displeasing.

There is another scandal of which I blush to speak ; yet, though sad, it is true. From what source has this plague of " dearly beloved sisters " found its way into the Church ? Whence come these unwedded wives, these new types of concubine, nay, I will go further, these one-man harlots ? They live in the same house with their male friend ; they occupy the same room and often even the same bed ; and yet they call us suspicious if we think that anything is wrong. A brother leaves his virgin sister ; a virgin, scorning her unmarried brother, seeks a stranger to take his place. Both alike pretend to have but one object : they are seeking spiritual consolation among strangers : but their real aim is to indulge privately in sexual intercourse. About such folk as these Solomon in Proverbs speaks the scornful words : " *Can a man take fire in his bosom and his clothes not be burned ? Can one go upon hot coals and not burn his feet ?* "

Let us therefore drive off and expel from our company such women as only wish to seem and not to be virgins. Now I would direct all my words to you who, inasmuch as you have been at the beginning the first virgin of high rank at Rome, will now have to labour the more diligently so as not to lose your present and your future happiness. As for the troubles of wedded life and the uncertainties of marriage, you know of them by an example in your own family. Your sister Blaesilla, superior to you in age but inferior in firmness of will, has become a widow seven months after taking a husband. How luckless is our mortal state, how ignorant of the future ! She has lost both the crown of virginity and the pleasures of wedlock. Although the widowed state ranks as the second degree of chastity, can you not imagine the crosses which every moment she must bear, seeing in her sister daily that which she herself has lost ? It is harder for her than for you to forego the delights that she once knew, and yet she receives a less reward for her present continence. Still, she, too, may rejoice and be not afraid. The fruit that is an hundredfold and that which is sixtyfold both spring from one seed, the seed of chastity.

I would not have you consort over much with married women or frequent the houses of the great. I would not have you look too often on what you spurned when you became a virgin. Women of the world, you know, plume themselves if their husband is a judge or holds some high position. Even if an eager crowd of visitors flocks to greet the Emperor's wife, why should you insult your husband ? Why should you, who are God's bride, hasten to visit the wife of a mortal man ? In this regard you must learn a holy pride ; know that you are better than they. And not only do I desire you to avoid the company of those who are puffed up by their husband's honours, who surround themselves with troops of eunuchs, and wear robes inwrought with fine threads of gold : you must also shun such women as are widows from compulsion not choice. Not that they ought to have desired their husband's death ; but they have been unwilling to accept their opportunity for chastity. As it is, they only change their dress : their old love of show remains unchanged.

Look at them as they ride in their roomy litters with a

row of eunuchs walking in front : see their red lips and
their plump sleek skins ; you would not think they had
lost a husband, you would fancy they were looking for one.
Their houses are filled with flatterers and guests. The very
clergy, whose teaching and authority ought to inspire
respect, kiss these ladies on the forehead, and then stretch
out their hand—you would think, if you did not know,
that they were giving a benediction—to receive the fee
for their visit. The women meanwhile, seeing that priests
need their help, are lifted up with pride. They know by
experience what a husband's rule is like and they prefer
their liberty as widows. They call themselves chaste nuns,
and after an immoderate supper they dream of the apostles.

Let your companions be those who are pale of face and
thin with fasting, approved by their years and their conduct,
who daily within their hearts sing the words : " *Tell me
where thou feedest thy flock, where thou makest it to rest at
noon*," and lovingly say : " *I have a desire to depart and
to be with Christ*." Follow your husband's example, and
like him be subject to your parents. Walk not often abroad,
and if you wish the help of the martyrs seek it in your own
chamber. You will never lack a reason for going out if
you always go out when there is need. Take food in
moderation, and never overload your stomach. Many
women are temperate over wine, but intemperate as to
the amount of food they take. When you rise at night to
pray let any uneasiness of breath be caused not by
indigestion but by an empty stomach. Read often and
learn all you can. Let sleep steal upon you with a book
in your hand and let the sacred page catch your drooping
head. Let your fasts be of daily occurrence and let
refreshment ever avoid satiety. It is of no avail to carry
an empty stomach for two or three days if that fast is
to be made up for by a clogging repletion. The mind when
cloyed straightway grows sluggish and the watered ground
puts forth the thorns of lust. If ever you feel that your
outward being is sighing for the bloom of youth, and if,

as you lie on your couch after a meal, you are shaken by the vision of lust's alluring train ; then snatch up the shield of faith and it will quench the devil's fiery darts. " *They are all adulterers,*" says the prophet, " *they have made their hearts like an oven.*"

But do you keep close to Christ's footsteps and intent upon his words. Say to yourself " *Did not our heart burn within us by the way while Jesus opened to us the Scriptures ?* " And again : " *Thy word is tried to the uttermost, and thy servant loveth it.*" It is hard for the human soul not to love something, and our mind of necessity must be drawn to some sort of affection. Carnal love is overcome by spiritual love : desire is quenched by desire ; what is taken from the one is added to the other. Nay, rather, as you lie upon your couch say these words, and repeat them continually : " *By night have I sought Him whom my soul loveth.*" " *Mortify your members on earth,*" says the apostle ; and because he did so himself he could afterwards boldly say : " *I live, yet not I but Christ liveth in me.*" He who mortifies his members, and as he walks through this world knows it to be vanity, is not afraid to say : " *I am become like a leather bottle in the frost. Whatever there was in me of the moisture of lust has dried away.*" And again : " *My knees are weak with fasting. I forget to eat my bread. By reason of the voice of my groaning my bones cleave to my skin.*"

Be like the grasshopper and make night musical. Wash your bed and water your couch nightly with tears. Keep vigil and be like the sparrow alone upon the housetop. Let your spirit be your harp, and let all your senses join in the psalm : " *Bless the Lord, O my soul, and forget not all his benefits ; who forgiveth all thine iniquities ; who healeth all thy diseases ; who redeemeth thy life from destruction.*" Who of us can say from our heart ? " *I have eaten ashes like bread and mingled my drink with weeping.*" And yet ought I not to weep and groan when the serpent again invites me to take forbidden fruit, and when, after driving us from the paradise of virginity, he tries to clothe us in tunics of skin such as Elijah on his return to paradise left behind him on earth ? What have I to do with the short-lived pleasures of sense ? What have I to do with the sirens' sweet and deadly songs ? You must not be subject to the sentence whereby condemnation was passed upon mankind : " *In pain and in sorrow shalt thou bring forth children.*" Say to yourself, " That is a law for a married woman, but not for me." " *And thy desire shall be to thy husband.*" Say to yourself : " Let her desire be to her husband, who has not a husband in Christ." " *Thou shalt surely die.*" Say once more, " Death is the end of marriage. But my vows are independent of sex. Let married women keep to their own place and title. For me virginity is consecrated in the persons of Mary and of Christ."

Some one may say, " Do you dare to disparage wedlock, a state which God has blessed ? " It is not to disparage wedlock, to prefer virginity to it. No one can make a comparison between two things, if one is good and the other evil. Let married women take pride in coming next after virgins. " *Be fruitful,*" God said, " *and multiply and replenish the earth.*" Let him then be fruitful and multiply who intends to replenish the earth. But your company is in heaven. The command to increase and multiply is fulfilled after the expulsion from Paradise, after the realization of nakedness, after the putting on of the fig-leaves which augured the approach of marital desire. Let them marry and be given in marriage who eat their bread in the sweat of their brow, whose land brings forth thorns and thistles, and whose crops are choked with brambles. My seed produces fruit a hundredfold.

" *All men cannot receive God's saying, but only those to whom it is given.*" Some men may be eunuchs of necessity : I am one by choice. " *There is a time to embrace, and a time to refrain from embracing. There is a time to cast away stones, and a time to gather stones together.*" Now that out of the hardness of the Gentiles sons have been born to Abraham, they begin to be "*holy stones rolling upon the earth*." So they pass through the storms of this world and roll on with rapid wheels in God's chariot. Let those stitch themselves coats who have lost that raiment which was woven from the top in one piece, and delight in the cries of infants lamenting that they are born as soon as they see the light of day. Eve in Paradise was a virgin : it was only after she put on a garment of skins that her married life began. Paradise is your home. Keep therefore as you were born, and say : "*Return unto thy rest, O my soul.*"

That you may realize that virginity is natural and that marriage came after the Fall, remember that what is born of wedlock is virgin flesh and that by its fruit it renders what in its parent root it had lost. "*There shall come forth a rod out of the stem of Jesse, and a flower shall grow out of his roots.*" That virgin rod is the mother of Our Lord, simple, pure, unsullied ; drawing no germ of life from without, but like God Himself fruitful in singleness. The flower of the rod is Christ, who says : "*I am the rose of Sharon and the lily of the valleys.*" In another passage He is foretold to be "*a stone cut out of the mountain without hands.*" The prophet signifying thereby that He will be born a virgin of a virgin. The word "hands" is to be taken as meaning the marital act as in the passage : "*His left hand is under my head and his right hand doth embrace me.*" It agrees also with this interpretation that the unclean animals are led into Noah's ark in pairs, while of the clean an uneven number is taken. In the same way Moses and Joshua were bidden to take off their shoes before they walked on holy ground. When the disciples were appointed to preach the new Gospel they were told not to burden themselves with shoes or shoe-latchets. And when the soldiers cast lots for Jesus' garments they found no shoes that they could take away. For the Lord could not Himself possess what he had forbidden to his servants.

R

I praise wedlock, I praise marriage ; but it is because they produce me virgins. I gather the rose from the thorn, the gold from the earth, the pearl from the oyster. Shall the ploughman plough all day ? Shall he not also enjoy the fruit of his labour ? Wedlock is the more honoured when the fruit of wedlock is the more loved. Why, mother, grudge your daughter her virginity ? She has been reared on your milk, she has come from your body, she has grown strong in your arms. Your watchful love has kept her a virgin. Are you vexed with her because she chooses to wed not a soldier but a king. She has rendered you a high service ; from to-day you are the mother by marriage of God.

The Apostle says : " *Concerning virgins I have no commandment of the Lord.*" Why so ? Because he himself was a virgin, not by order but of his own free will. Those people must not be listened to who pretend that he had a wife. When he is discussing continence and recommending perpetual chastity, he says : " *I wish that all men were even as I myself.*" And later : " *I say therefore to the unmarried and widows, it is good for them if they abide even as I.*" And in another place : " *Have we not power to circumvent women even as the other apostles.*" Why, then, has he no commandment from the Lord concerning virginity ? Because that which is freely offered is worth more than what is extorted by force, and to command virginity would have been to abrogate wedlock. It would have been a stern task to force men against their nature and to extort from them the life that angels enjoy. Moreover, it would have meant condemning in a way that which is a divine ordinance.

The old law had a different ideal of felicity. There it is said : " *Blessed is he who hath seed in Zion and a family in Jerusalem ; and cursed is the barren woman who beareth not children.*" And again : " *Thy children shall be as olive plants around thy table.*" To such riches are promised, and we are told that there was not one feeble man among the tribes. But to-day even eunuchs are told : " *Say not that I am a dry tree ; for instead of sons and daughters you have a place for ever in heaven.*" Now the poor are blessed and Lazarus is set before Dives in his purple. Now he who is weak has thereby the greater strength. But in the old days the world was empty of people, and, omitting those whose childlessness was but a type for the future, the only benediction possible was the gift of children. It was for this reason that Abraham in his old age married Keturah ; that Jacob was hired with mandrakes ; and that fair Rachel—a type of the Church—complained of the closing of her womb.

But gradually the crop grew high and the reaper was sent in. Elijah was a virgin, and so was Elisha, and so were many of the sons of the prophets. Jeremiah was told that he must not take a wife. He had been sanctified in his mother's womb, and now that the captivity was drawing near he was forbidden to marry. The apostle gives the same injunction in different words : " *I think therefore that this is good by reason of the present distress, namely that it is good for a man to be as he is.*" What is this distress, which abrogates the joys of wedlock ? The apostle tells us : " *The time is short : it remaineth that those who have wives be as though they had none.*"

Now is Nebuchadnezzar again drawing nigh. Now has the lion come out from his den. What to me is a wife, if she shall fall as a slave to some proud king ? What good will little ones do, if their lot must be that which the prophet deplores ? " *The tongue of the sucking child cleaveth to the roof of his mouth for thirst ; the young children ask for bread and no man breaketh it unto them.*" In the old days, as I have said, the virtue of continence was confined to men, and Eve continually bore children in travail. But now that a virgin has conceived in the womb a child, upon whose shoulders is government, a mighty God, Father of the age to come, the fetters of the old curse are broken. Death came through Eve : life has come through Mary.

For this reason the gift of virginity has been poured most abundantly upon women, seeing that it was from a woman it began. As soon as the Son of God set foot on earth, He formed for Himself a new household, that as He was adored by angels in heaven He might have angels also on earth. Then chaste Judith once more cut off the head of Holofernes. Then Haman—whose name means iniquity—was once more burned in his own fire. Then James and John forsook father and net and ship and followed the Saviour : they put behind them the love of their kin, the ties of this world, and the care of their home. Then first the words were heard : " *Whosoever will come after me, let him deny himself and take up his cross and follow me.*"

No soldier takes a wife with him when he is marching into battle. Even when a disciple was fain to go and bury his father, the Lord forbade him and said : " *Foxes have holes and the birds of the air have nests ; but the Son of Man hath not where to lay His head.*" So you must not complain if you are scantily lodged. " *He that is unmarried careth for the things that belong to the Lord, how he may please the Lord : but he that is married careth for the things of the world how he may please his wife.*" There is a difference also between a wife and a virgin. The unmarried woman cares for the things of the Lord that she may be holy both in body and spirit. But she that is married cares for the things of the world how she may please her husband.

How great are the inconveniences involved in wedlock and how many anxieties encompass it I think I have briefly described in my treatise against Helvidius on the perpetual virginity of the blessed Mary. It would be tedious to go over the same ground again, and anyone who wishes to can draw from my little spring. But lest I should be thought to have passed over this subject completely, I will say now that the apostle bids us pray without ceasing and that the man who in the married state renders his wife her due

cannot so pray. Either we pray always and are virgins ;
or we cease to pray that we may perform our marital
service. The apostle says also : " *If a virgin marry she
hath not sinned. Nevertheless, such shall have trouble in
the flesh.*" At the outset I promised that I should say
little or nothing of the troubles of wedlock, and now I
give you the same warning again. If you wish to know
from how many vexations a virgin is free and by how many
a wife is fettered you should read Tertullian's " *To a
philosophic friend,*" and his other treatises on virginity ;
the blessed Cyprian's notable book ; the writings of
Pope Damasus in prose and verse ; and the essays recently
written by our own Ambrose for his sister. In these he has
poured forth his soul with such eloquence that he has
sought out, set forth, and arranged all that bears on the
praise of virgins.

I must proceed by a different path. Far from trumpeting
the praises of virginity, I only wish to keep it safe. To
know what is good is not enough ; when you have chosen
it you must guard it with jealous care. The first is a matter
of judgement and we share it with many ; the second calls
for labour and for that few care. The Lord says : " *He
that shall endure unto the end, the same shall be saved.*"
and " *Many are called but few are chosen.*" Therefore,
before God and Jesus Christ and his chosen angels I
adjure you to guard what you have and not lightly to expose
to the public gaze the vessels of the Lord's temple which
priests alone are allowed to see. No man that is profane
may look upon God's sanctuary. When Uzzah laid hands
upon the ark which it was not lawful to touch, he was
struck down by sudden death. And no vessel of gold
or silver was ever so dear to God as the temple of a virgin's
body. What was shadowed in the past presaged the reality
of to-day. You, indeed, may speak frankly to strangers
and look at them with kindly eyes ; but the unchaste see
differently. They cannot appreciate the beauty of the soul,
they only regard the beauty of the body. Hezekiah showed

God's treasure to the Assyrians, who ought never to have seen what they were sure to covet. And so it was that Judaea was rent asunder by continual wars, and that the first things taken and carried away were the Lord's vessels. From them as drinking cups Belshazzar quaffed his wine— for the crown of vice is to pollute what is noble— surrounded by his concubines at the feast.

Never incline your ear to words of mischief. Men often make an improper remark that they may test a virgin's real purpose and see if she hears it with pleasure, and is ready to unbend at a joke. Such people approve of all you say, and anything you refuse they refuse also. They call you both merry and good, one in whom there is no guile. " Behold," they cry, " a true handmaid of Christ : behold complete frankness. She is not like that rough ugly country fright who probably never married because she could never find a husband." A natural weakness easily beguiles us. We willingly smile on such flatterers and although we may blush and say we are unworthy of their praise, the soul within us rejoices to hear their words.

Like the ark of the Covenant, Christ's bride should be overlaid with gold within and without ; she should guard the law of the Lord. As in the ark there was nothing but the tablets of the covenant, so in you let there be no thought of anything outside. On that mercy seat it is God's pleasure to sit as once he sat upon the cherubim. He sends his disciples, that as He rode upon the foal of an ass so He may ride upon you, setting you free from the cares of this world so that you may leave the bricks and straw of Egypt and follow Him, the true Moses, through the wilderness and enter the land of promise. Let no one prevent you, neither mother nor sister nor kinswoman nor brother : " *The Lord hath need of thee.*" If they seek to hinder let them fear the scourges that fell on Pharoah, who, because he would not let God's people go to worship Him suffered what is written in the Scriptures. Jesus entered into the temple and cast out those things which were not of the temple. For God is jealous, and He does not allow His Father's house to be made a den of robbers. Where money is counted, where there are pens of doves for sale, where simplicity is slain, where a virgin's breast is disturbed by thoughts of worldly business ; there at once the veil of the temple is rent and the bridegroom rising in anger says : " *Your house is left unto you desolate.*"

Read the Gospel and see how Mary sitting at the feet of the Lord is preferred to the busy Martha. Martha in her anxious and hospitable zeal was preparing a meal for the Lord and His disciples ; but Jesus said to her : " *Martha, Martha, thou art careful and troubled about many things. But few things are needful or one. And Mary hath chosen that good part which shall not be taken away from her.*" Be thou too Mary, and prefer the Lord's teaching to food. Let your sisters run to and fro and seek how they may entertain Christ as a guest. Do you once for all cast away the burden of this world, and sit at the Lord's feet, and say : " *I have found him whom my soul loveth ; I will hold him, I will not let him go.*" And He will answer : " *My dove, my undefiled is but one ; she is the only one of her mother, she is the choice one of her that bare her.*" And that mother is the Jerusalem that is in heaven.

Let the seclusion of your own chamber ever guard you ; ever let the Bridegroom sport with you within. If you pray, you are speaking to your spouse : if you read He is speaking to you. When sleep falls on you, He will come behind the wall and will put His hand through the hole in the door and will touch your flesh. And you will awake and rise up and cry : " *I am sick with love.*" And you will hear Him answer : " *A garden enclosed is my sister, my spouse ; a spring shut up, a fountain sealed.*" Go not from home nor visit the daughters of a strange land, though you have patriarchs for brothers and rejoice in Israel as your father. Dinah went out and was seduced. I would not have you seek the Bridegroom in the public squares ; I would not have you go about the corners of the city. You may say : " *I will rise now and go about the city : in the streets and in the broad ways I will seek Him whom my soul loveth.*" But though you ask the watchmen " *Saw ye Him whom my soul loveth ?* " no one will deign to answer you. The Bridegroom cannot be found in the city squares. " *Straight and narrow is the way that leadeth unto life.*" And the song goes on : " *I sought him but I could not find him : I called him but he gave me no answer.*"

Would that failure to find Him were all. You will be wounded and stripped, you will lament and say : " *The watchmen who go about the city found me : they smote me, they wounded me, they took away my veil from me.*" If this was the punishment that going forth brought to her who said : " *I sleep but my heart waketh,*" and " *A bundle of myrrh is my well-beloved unto me ; he shall lie all night between my breasts.*" If she, I say, suffered so much because she went abroad, what shall be done to us who are but young girls, to us who, when the bride goes in with the Bridegroom, still remain without ? Jesus is jealous : He does not wish others to see your face. You may excuse yourself and say : " I have drawn my veil, I have covered my face, I have sought Thee there, and I have said : ' *Tell me, O Thou whom my soul loveth, where Thou feedest Thy flock, where Thou makest it to rest at noon. For why should I be as one that is veiled beside the flocks of Thy companions ?* ' " But He will be wroth and angry, and He will say : " *If thou know not thyself, O thou fairest among women, go thy way forth by the footsteps of the flock and feed thy goats beside the shepherd's tents.*" Though you be fair, and though of all faces yours be dearest to the Bridegroom, yet unless you know yourself and keep your heart with all diligence and avoid the eyes of lovers, you will be turned from My bridal-chamber to feed the goats which shall be set on the left hand.

Therefore, my Eustochium, daughter, lady, fellow-servant, sister—for the first name suits your age, the second your rank, the third our religion, and the last our affection—hear the words of Isaiah : "*Come, my people, enter thou into thy chambers, and shut thy doors about thee : hide thyself as it were for a little moment, until the indignation of the Lord be overpast.*" Let foolish virgins roam abroad ; do you for your part stay within with the Bridegroom. If you shut your door and according to the Gospel precept pray to your Father in secret, He will come and knock, and He will say : "*Behold I stand at the door and knock : if any man open, I will come in to him and will sup with him, and he with me.*" And you forthwith will eagerly make reply : "*It is the voice of my beloved that knocketh, saying ' Open to me, my sister, my love, my dove, my undefiled.'*" You must not say : "*I have put off my coat ; how shall I put it on? I have washed my feet, how shall I defile them?*" Arise straightway and open ; lest, if you linger, he pass on and leave you mournfully to cry : "*I opened to my beloved, but my beloved was gone.*" Why need the door of your heart be closed to the Bridegroom. Let it be open to Christ, but closed to the devil, according to the saying : "*If the spirit of him who hath power to rise up against thee, leave not thy place.*" Daniel when he could no longer remain below withdrew to an upper room, but he kept its windows open towards Jerusalem. Do you, too, keep your windows open on the side where light may enter and you may see the eye of the Lord. Open not those other windows of which it is said : "*By our windows death came in.*"

You must also avoid with especial care the traps that are set for you by a desire for vain glory. Jesus says : "*How can ye believe, which receive glory one from another?*" Consider then how evil that thing must be whose presence forbids belief. Let us rather say : "*Thou art my glorying,*" and "*He that glorieth, let him glory in the Lord,*" and "*If I yet pleased men, I should not be the servant of Christ,*" and "*Far be it from me to glory save in the cross of our Lord Jesus Christ, through whom the world hath been crucified unto me and I unto the world,*" and again "*In God we*

*boast all the day long ; my soul shall make her boast in
the Lord.*"

When you are giving alms, let God alone see you. When
you are fasting, keep a cheerful face. Let your dress be
neither elegant nor slovenly, and let it not be noticeable
by any strangeness that might attract the notice of passers-
by and make people point their fingers at you. If a brother
dies or the body of a beloved sister has to be carried to
burial, take care that you do not attend such funerals too
often, or you may die yourself. Do not try and seem
very devout, nor more humble than is necessary. It is
possible to seek glory by avoiding it. Many men who screen
from view their poverty, charity, and fasting, reveal their
desire for admiration by the very fact that they spurn it,
and, strangely enough, seek the praise which they avoid.
From the other perturbations of the mind, from exultation,
despondency, hope, and fear, I find many free ; but desire
for praise is a fault which few escape and that man is best
whose character, like a fair skin, is disfigured by the fewest
blemishes.

I am not going to warn you against boasting of your
wealth or priding yourself on your birth or setting yourself
up as superior to others. I know your humility. I know
that you can say from your heart : " *Lord, my heart is
not haughty nor my eyes lofty.*" I know that with you, as
with your mother, the pride through which the devil
fell finds no lodging. Therefore it would be superfluous
to write to you on this subject : it is the height of folly
to teach a pupil what he already knows. But beware lest
your contempt for the world's boastfulness breed in you
a boastfulness of another kind. Harbour not the secret
thought that as you have ceased to please in cloth of gold
you may now try to please in homespun.

When you come into a gathering of the brethren and
sisters do not sit in too lowly a place, or pretend that you
are unworthy of a footstool. Do not lower your voice on
purpose, as though you were exhausted by fasting ; nor

yet lean upon a friend's shoulder imitating the gait of one
who is about to faint. Some women indeed actually dis-
figure themselves, so as to make it obvious that they have
been fasting ; as soon as they catch sight of anyone they
drop their eyes and begin sobbing, covering up their
face all but one eye, which they keep free to watch the
effect they make. They wear a black dress and a girdle
of sackcloth ; their feet and hands are unwashed : but
their stomach—which cannot be seen—is busy churning
food. Of these the psalm is sung every day : " *The Lord
will scatter the bones of them that please themselves.*" Other
women change their garb and put on men's dress ; they
cut their hair short and lift up their chins in shameless
fashion ; they blush to be what they were born to be—
women ; and prefer to look like eunuchs. Others again
dress themselves in goat's hair, and returning to their
childhood's fashions put on a baby's hood and make themselves look like so many owls.

Women are not the only persons of whom I must warn
you. Avoid those men also whom you see loaded with
chains and wearing their hair long like a woman's in contravention of the apostle's precept ; and with all this, a
pointed goat's beard, a black cloak, and bare feet braving
the cold. Antimus some time ago was the sort of man I
mean, and just lately Sophronius has been another for
Rome to groan over. Such men as these make their way
into noble houses and deceive " *silly women laden with sins,
ever learning and never able to come to the knowledge of the
truth.*" They put on a mournful face and pretend to make
long fasts, which for them are rendered easy by secret
nocturnal banquets. I am ashamed to say more, lest I
should seem to be using the language of invective rather
than of admonition.

There are other men—I speak of those of my own
order—who only seek the office of presbyter and deacon
that they may be able to visit women freely. These fellows
think of nothing but dress ; they must be nicely

scented and their shoes must fit without a crease. Their hair is curled and still shows traces of the tongs ; their fingers glisten with rings ; and if there is wet on the road they walk across on tiptoe so as not to splash their feet. When you see these gentry think of them rather as potential bridegrooms than as clergymen, Indeed, some of them devote their whole life and all their energies to finding out about the names, the households, and the characters of married ladies.

I will give you a brief and summary portrait of the chief practitioner in this line, that from the master's likeness you may recognize his disciples. He rises with the sun in haste ; the order of his morning calls is duly arranged ; he takes short cuts, and importunately thrusts his old head almost into the bedchambers of ladies still asleep. If he sees a cushion, or an elegant table cover, or, indeed, any article of furniture that he fancies, he starts praising and admiring it and takes it in his hand, and so, lamenting that he has nothing like this, he begs or rather extorts it from the owner, as all the women are afraid to offend the town gossip. He hates chastity, and he hates fasting : what he likes is a savoury lunch—say a plump young crane such as is commonly called a cheeper. He has a rough and saucy tongue always well equipped with abusive words. Wherever you betake yourself, he is the first man you see. What-ever news is noised abroad, he either originates the story or else exaggerates it. He changes horses every hour ; and his nags are so sleek and spirited that you might take him to be own brother to Diomede of Thrace.

Our cunning enemy fights against us with many varied stratagems. " *The serpent was more subtile than any beast of the field which the Lord God had made.*" So the apostle says : " *We are not ignorant of his devices.*" Neither an affected shabbiness nor an elaborate elegance of attire becomes a Christian. If you feel ignorant or have any doubt about some passage in Scripture, ask advice from some man whose life commends him, whose age puts him above suspicion, and whose reputation stands high with all ; one who can say : " *I have espoused you to one husband, a chaste virgin to present to Christ.*" If there is no one at hand able to resolve your difficulty, remember that peaceful ignorance is better than dangerous instruction. You walk in the midst of snares, and many veteran virgins, whose chastity never was doubted, on the very threshhold of death have let the crown slip from their hands.

If any of your handmaids have taken the vow with you, do not lift yourself up against them, or pride yourself as being the mistress. From now you all have one Bride-groom ; you sing psalms together ; together you receive the body of Christ. Why, then, should you not think alike ? You must challenge other mistresses : let the respect paid to your virgins be an invitation for the rest to do the same. If you find one of your girls weak in faith, take her aside, comfort and caress her, make her chastity your treasure. But if one merely pretends to have a vocation in order to escape from service, read aloud to her the apostle's words : " *It is better to marry than to burn.*"

Cast from you like the plague those idle and inquisitive virgins and widows who go about to married women's houses and surpass the very parasites in a play by their unblushing effrontery. " *Evil communications corrupt good manners,*" and these women care for nothing but their belly and its adjacent members. Creatures of this sort will give you wheedling advice : " My pretty pet, make the best of what you have and live your own life. What is the use of saving for your children ? " Flown with wine and wantonness, they instill all sorts of mischief into a girl's mind and tempt even the firmest soul with the soft delights of pleasure. " *And when they have begun to wax wanton against Christ, they will marry, having condemnation because they have rejected their first faith.*"

Do not seek to appear over-eloquent or compose trifling songs in verse. Do not in false refinement follow the sickly taste of those married ladies who habitually speak with a lisp and clip all their words, now pressing their teeth together, and now opening their lips wide. They fancy that a natural utterance is the sign of country breeding, and find pleasure in making even their tongue commit adultery. " *What communion hath light with darkness? What concord hath Christ with Belial?* " What has Horace to do with the Psalter, Virgil with the gospels, and Cicero with Paul ? Is not a brother made to stumble if he sees you sitting at table in an idol's temple ? Although unto the pure all things are pure and nothing is to be refused if it be received with thanksgiving, still we ought not to drink the cup of Christ and the cup of devils at the same time. I will tell you the story of my own unhappy experience.

Many years ago for the sake of the kingdom of heaven I cut myself from home, parents, sister, relations, and, what was harder, from the dainty food to which I had been used. But even when I was on my way to Jerusalem to fight the good fight there, I could not bring myself to forego the library which with great care and labour I had got together at Rome. And so, miserable man that I was, I would fast, only to read Cicero afterwards. I would spend long nights in vigil, I would shed bitter tears called from my inmost heart by the remembrance of my past sins ; and then I would take up Plautus again. Whenever I returned to my right senses and began to read the prophets, their language seemed harsh and barbarous. With my blind eyes I could not see the light ; but I attributed the fault not to my eyes but to the sun. While the old serpent was thus mocking me, about the middle of Lent a fever attacked my weakened body and spread through my inmost veins. It may sound incredible, but the ravages it wrought on my unhappy frame were so persistent that at last my bones scarcely held together.

Meantime, preparations were made for my funeral ; my whole body grew gradually cold, and life's vital warmth only lingered faintly in my poor throbbing breast.

Suddenly, I was caught up in the spirit and dragged before the Judge's judgement seat ; and here the light was so dazzling and the brightness shining from those who stood around so radiant that I flung myself upon the ground and did not dare to look up. I was asked to state my condition and replied that I was a Christian. But He who presided said : " Thou liest : thou art a Ciceronian, not a Christian ' *For where thy treasure is there will thy heart be also.*' " Straightway I became dumb, and amid the strokes of the whip—for he had ordered me to be scourged—I was even more bitterly tortured by the fire of conscience, considering with myself the verse : " *In the grave who shall give thee thanks ?* " Yet for all that I began to cry out and to bewail myself saying : " Have mercy upon me, O Lord, have mercy upon me " ; and even amid the noise of the lash my voice made itself heard. At last the bystanders fell at the knees of Him who presided and prayed him to pardon my youth and give me opportunity to repent of my error, on the understanding that the extreme of torture should be inflicted on me if ever I read again the works of Gentile authors. In the stress of that dread hour I should have been willing to make even larger promises and taking oath I called upon His name : " O Lord, if ever again I possess worldly books or read them, I have denied Thee."

After swearing this oath I was dismissed and returned to the upper world. There, to the surprise of all, I opened my eyes again and they were so drenched with tears that my distress convinced even the incredulous. That this experience was no sleep nor idle dream, such as often mocks us, I call to witness the judgement seat before which I fell and the terrible verdict which I feared. May it never be my lot again to come before such a court as that ! I profess that my shoulders were black and blue, and that I felt the bruises long after I awoke from my sleep. And I acknowledge that henceforth I read the books of God with a greater zeal than I had ever given before to the books of men.

You must also avoid the sin of attaching any importance to money. Not merely must you refuse to claim what belongs to another, for that is an offence punished by the laws of the state ; you must also give up clinging to your own property, which has now become no longer yours. The Lord says : " *If ye have not been faithful in that which is another man's, who shall give you that which is your own ?* " " That which is another man's " is a mass of gold and silver ; " that which is your own " is the spiritual heritage of which it is said elsewhere " *The ransom of a man's life is his riches* ", " *No man can serve two masters, for either he will hate the one and love the other ; or else he will hold to the one and despise the other. Ye cannot serve God and Mammon.*" By Mammon understand riches : for in the heathen tongue of the Syrians riches are so called. The thorns that choke our faith are the taking thought for our subsistence. Care for the things of the Gentiles is the root of avarice.

But you say : " I am a delicate girl and I cannot work with my hands. If I reach old age and fall sick who will take pity on me ? " Hear Jesus speaking to the apostles : " *Take no thought of what ye shall eat ; nor yet for your body what ye shall put on. Is not the life more than meat and the body more than raiment ? Behold the fowls of the air ; for they sow not neither do they gather into barns : yet your heavenly Father feedeth them.*" If clothing fail you, regard the lilies . If you are hungry, hear how blessed are the poor and hungry among men. If any pain afflict you, read the words : " *Therefore I take pleasure in my infirmities* " and " *There was given to me a thorn in the flesh, the messenger of Satan to buffet me, lest I should be exalted above measure.*" Rejoice in all God's judgements ; for does not the psalmist say : " *The daughters of Judah rejoiced because of thy judgements, O Lord ?* " Let the words be ever on your lips : " *Naked came I out of my mother's womb and naked shall I return thither,*" and " *We brought nothing into this world and it is certain we can carry nothing out.*"

To-day you see many women packing their wardrobes with dresses, putting on a fresh frock every day, and even so unable to get the better of the moth. The more scrupulous sort wear one dress till it is threadbare, but though they go about in rags their boxes are full of clothes. Parchments are dyed purple, gold is melted for lettering, manuscripts are decked with jewels : and Christ lies at their door naked and dying. When they hold a hand out to the needy they sound the trumpet. When they invite to a love-feast they hire a crier. Just lately I saw the greatest lady in Rome—I will not give her name, for this is not a satire—standing in the church of the blessed Peter with her band of eunuchs in front. She was giving money to the poor with her own hand to increase her reputation for sanctity ; and she gave them each a penny ! At that moment an old woman full of years and rags ran in front of the line to get a second coin ; but when her turn came she got, not a penny, but the lady's fist in her face, and for her dreadful offence she had to pay with her blood.

" *The love of money is the root of all evil*," and therefore the apostle calls it slavery to idols. " *Seek ye first the kingdom of God and all these things shall be added unto you.*" The Lord will never let a righteous soul die of hunger. The psalmist says : " *I have been young and now am old, yet have I not seen the righteous forsaken nor his seed begging bread.*" Elijah was fed by ministering ravens. The widow of Zarephath, herself and her sons within an ace of death that night, went hungry that she might feed the prophet : by a miracle the flour barrel was filled, and he who had come to be fed supplied food. The apostle Peter says : " *Silver and gold have I none, but such as I have give I thee. In the name of Jesus Christ, rise up and walk.*"

To-day many people, though they do not say it in words, by their deeds declare : " Faith and pity have I none ; but such as I have, gold and silver, these give I thee not." Having food and raiment let us be content. Hear the words

s

of Jacob in his prayer : " *If God will be with me and will keep me in this way that I go, and will give me bread to eat and raiment to put on, then shall the Lord be my God.*" He prayed only for necessities ; yet twenty years afterwards he returned to the land of Canaan rich in goods and richer still in children. Endless are the examples that Scripture supplies, teaching us to beware of love of money.

As I have touched on this subject—if Christ allows I keep it for a special book—I will relate an incident that occurred not many years ago at Nitria. A brother, rather thrifty than avaricious, forgetting that the Lord was sold for thirty pieces of silver, left behind him at his death a hundred ducats, which he had earned by weaving linen. The monks held a council as to what was to be done with it, for there were about five thousand of them in the neighbourhood living in separate cells. Some said that the money should be distributed among the poor ; others that it should be given to the Church ; others that it should be sent back to the dead man's parents. But Macarius, Pambo, Isidore, and the other Fathers, the Holy Spirit speaking by them, decreed that the coins should be buried with their owner, saying : " *Thy money perish with thee.*" Let no one think their decision too harsh ; for so great a fear has fallen upon all in Egypt that it is now a crime to leave a single ducat.

Since I have mentioned the monks, and know that you like to hear about holy things, lend me your ear awhile. There are in Egypt three classes of monks. First, there are the cenobites, called in their Gentile tongue Sauses, or as we should say, men living in a community. Secondly, there are the anchorites, who live in the desert as solitaries, so called because they have withdrawn from the society of men. Thirdly, there is the class called Remoboth, a very inferior and despised kind, though in my own province they are the chief if not the only sort of monks. These men live together in twos and threes, seldom in larger numbers, and live according to their own will and ruling.

A portion of what they make they contribute to a common fund which provides food for all. In most cases they live in cities or in fortified places, and anything they sell is very dear, the idea being that their workmanship is sanctified, not their life. Quarrels are frequent among them ; for while they supply their own food they will not brook subordination. It is true that they compete with one another in fasting, making what should be a private matter an occasion for a triumph. Everything with them is done for effect : loose sleeves, big boots, clumsy dress. They are always sighing, or visiting virgins, or disparaging the clergy ; and when a feast day comes they eat so much that they make themselves ill.

Avoiding these, then, as though they were the plague, let us come to the more numerous class who live together and are called, as we have said, cenobites. Among them the first principle of their association is to obey superiors and do whatever they command. They are divided into sections of ten and a hundred ; each tenth man is over nine others, while the hundredth has ten such officers under him. They live apart from each other, in separate cells. According to their rule, no monk may visit another before three o'clock in the afternoon, except only the deans or leaders of ten, whose business it is to comfort with soothing words anyone disturbed by restless thoughts. After three o'clock they meet together to sing psalms and duly read the Scriptures. When the prayers have ended and all have sat down, one of the so-called Fathers stands up in their midst and discourses, a silence so complete being observed while he is speaking that no one dares to look at his neighbour or to clear his throat. The highest praise that can be given to the preacher is the weeping of his audience. But the tears that run down their cheeks are silent and not even a sob reveals their emotion. When he begins to announce the kingdom of Christ, the future happiness, and the coming glory, you may see everyone with a gentle sigh and lifted gaze saying to himself :

" *Oh, that I had the wings of a dove. For then would I fly away and be at rest.*"

After the discourse the meeting breaks up, and each set of ten goes with its Father to its own table ; taking in turns to serve each man for a week at a time. No noise is made over the food ; no one talks while eating. The fare consists of bread, pulse and greens, and salt is their only condiment. The old men alone receive wine, they often having a special meal prepared in company with the children so that the weariness of age is refreshed and the weakness of childhood is strengthened. They then rise from table together, and after singing a hymn return to their quarters. There each one talks till evening, with his friends, thus : " Have you noticed so-and-so ? What grace he has, and what powers of silence ! How soberly he walks ! " If they see that anyone is weak, they comfort him ; if he is fervent in love for God, they encourage his zeal. At night, besides the common prayers, each man keeps vigil in his own cell ; and so they go round to each room and putting their ears to the doors carefully ascertain what the inmates are doing. If they catch a monk in sloth-fulness, they do not upbraid him : but, hiding what they know, they visit him more frequently, and by beginning themselves to pray exhort rather than drive him to his devotions. Every day has its allotted task ; the work done is handed to a dean and by him brought to the bursar who once a month with fear and trembling gives an account to the Community Father. The bursar also tastes the dishes when they are cooked, and as no one is allowed to say : " I am without a tunic or a cloak or a rush mattress," he so arranges their entire store, that none need ask and none go without. If anyone is taken ill, he is moved to a larger room and is there so sedulously tended by the older monks that he misses neither the luxuries of cities nor a mother's loving care. Every Lord's day they give their whole time to prayer and reading : which, indeed, are their usual occupations on ordinary days when work is over. Every day they learn by heart a passage of Scripture. Fasting is regular throughout the year, but in Lent an increase of strictness is permitted. After Whitsuntide a midday meal takes the place of the evening repast, and thus the tradition of the Church is satisfied and they avoid overloading their stomachs with a double quantity of food. The Essenes also follow these rules, as we learn from Philo, Plato's imitator, and from Josephus, the Greek Livy, in the second book of his *Jewish Captivity*.

As I am writing now about virgins, all these details about monks may seem rather superfluous. I will proceed to the third class, who are called anchorites. They go out from a monastery and live in the desert, taking nothing with them but bread and salt. The founder of the system was Paul, and Anthony made it famous : going back, the first example was given by John the Baptist. The prophet Jeremiah describes such a solitary : " *It is good for a man that he bear the yoke in his youth. He sitteth alone and keepeth silence, because he hath borne it upon him. He giveth his cheek to him that smiteth him, he is filled full of reproach. For the Lord will not cast off for ever.*" The struggles of the anchorites and their life, in the flesh but not of the flesh, I will unfold to you one some other occasion, if you wish. Let me now return to my subject, for I was speaking of love of money, when I digressed to the monks. With them as examples before you, you will look down not only on gold and silver and worldly possessions, but even on earth itself and the sky. United to Christ, you will sing : " *The Lord is my portion.*"

Moreover, although the apostle bids us to pray without ceasing and although to the saints their very sleep is an oraison, yet we ought to have fixed hours for prayer, so that if perchance we are occupied with any business the time itself may remind us of our duty. Every one knows that the set times are the third, the sixth, and the ninth hours, at dawn and at evening. No food should be taken except after prayer, and before leaving the table thanks

should be rendered to our Creator. We should rise from
our bed two or three times in the night and go over those
passages of Scripture which we know by heart. Let prayer
arm us when we leave our lodging : when we return from
the streets let us pray before we sit down, nor give our
miserable body rest until our soul is fed. In everything
we do, in every step we take, let our hand trace the sign
of the Lord's cross. Speak against no one and slander not
your mother's son. " *Who art thou that judgest the servant
of another ? To his own lord he standeth or falleth ; yea,
he shall be made to stand, for the Lord hath power to make
him stand.*" If you have fasted for the space of two or
three days, do not think that you are better than those who
have not fasted. You fast and are angry ; another eats
and wears a smiling face. You work off your irritation
and hunger by quarrelling with others ; your neighbour
feeds in moderation and gives thanks to God. Therefore
Isaiah proclaims to us every day : " *Is it such a fast that
I have chosen, saith the Lord ?* " And again : " *In the day
of your fast ye find your own pleasure and oppress all your
labourers. Behold ye fast for strife and contention and to
smite with the fist of wickedness. How fast ye unto me ?* "
What sort of fast can that be whose wrath not only does
the night go down upon, but even the moon leaves
unchanged. Look to yourself and glory not in the fall of
others but only in your own works.

Do not take pattern by those women who take thought
for the flesh and are always reckoning up their income
and their daily household expenditure. The eleven
apostles were not crushed by Judas' treachery, and though
Phygellus and Alexander made shipwreck, the rest did not
falter in the race of faith. Say not—" So-and-so enjoys
her own property ; she is honoured by men ; the brethren
and the sisters assemble at her house. Has she ceased to
be a virgin for that ? " In the first place it is doubtful if
such an one is a virgin. " *For the Lord seeth not as man
seeth ; for man looketh upon the outward appearance, but*

the Lord looketh upon the heart." Furthermore, even if
she is a virgin in body, I am not sure that she is a virgin
in spirit. The apostle has defined a virgin thus : " *She
must be holy both in body and in spirit.*" In fine, let her keep
her own glory. Let her override Paul's judgement and live
in the enjoyment of her good things. But let us follow
better examples.

Set before your eyes the blessed Mary, whose purity
was such that she earned the reward of being the mother
of the Lord. When the angel Gabriel came down to her in
man's form and said : " Hail thou that art highly favoured ;
the Lord is with thee," she was filled with terror and
consternation and could not reply ; for she had never
been greeted by a man before. Soon, however, she learned
who the messenger was, and spoke to him : she who had
been afraid of a man conversed fearlessly with an angel.
You, too, may be perhaps the Lord's mother. " *Take thee
a great new roll and write in it with a man's pen 'Quickly
carry off the spoils'.*" And when you have gone to the
prophetess, and conceived in your womb, and brought
forth a son, say : " *Lord, we have been with child by thy
fear, we have been in pain, we have brought forth the spirit
of thy salvation which we have wrought upon the earth.*"
Then shall your Son reply : " *Behold my mother and my
brethren.*" And He whose name just before you had
inscribed upon the tablet of your heart, and had written
with a pen upon its new surface, after He has recovered
the spoils from the enemies and has stripped principalities
and powers nailing them to His cross, He having been
conceived grows to manhood, and as he becomes older
regards you not as His mother but as His bride. To be as
the martyrs or as the apostles or as Christ is a great struggle,
but for that struggle there is a great reward.

All such efforts are only of avail when they are made
within the Church ; when we celebrate the passover in one
house ; if we enter the ark with Noah ; if, while Jericho
is falling, we shelter beneath the roof of the justified harlot

Rahab. Such virgins as there are said to be among the different kinds of heretics or with the followers of the filthy Manes must be considered, not virgins, but prostitutes. If the devil is the author of their body, how can they honour a thing fashioned by their foe ? It is because they know that the name of virgin brings glory with it that they go about as wolves in sheep's clothing. Antichrist pretends to be Christ : and even so they falsely cloak their shameful lives under an honourable title. Rejoice, my sister ; rejoice my daughter ; rejoice my virgin ; you have begun to be in truth that which these others only feign to be.

All the things that I have set out in this letter will seem hard to her who loves not Christ. But one who regards all the pomp of this world as dross and holds everything under the sun as vain if only he may win Christ ; one who has died with his Lord and risen again and crucified the flesh with its weaknesses and lusts ; he will freely cry : *" Who shall separate us from the love of Christ ? Shall tribulation, or distress, or persecution, or famine, or nakedness, or peril, or sword ? "* And, again : *" I am persuaded that neither death, nor life, nor angels, nor principalities, nor powers, nor things present, nor things to come, nor height, nor depth nor any other creature shall be able to separate us from the love of God which is in Jesus Christ, our Lord."*

For our salvation the Son of God became the Son of Man. Nine months He awaits birth in the womb, He endures distress, He comes forth covered with blood, He is swathed in napkins, He is comforted with caresses. Though He holds the world in His closed hand, He is contained by the narrow space of a manger. I say nothing of the thirty years He lives in obscurity, content with His parents' poverty. He is scourged and says not a word. He is crucified and prays for His crucifiers. *" What, then, shall I render unto the Lord for all his benefits towards me ? I will take the cup of salvation and call upon the name of the Lord. Precious in the sight of the Lord is the death of His saints."* The only fitting return we can make Him is to pay for blood with blood ; and as we are redeemed by the blood of Christ to die willingly for our Redeemer. What saint was ever crowned without a contest ? Righteous Abel is murdered. Abraham runs the risk of losing his wife. And, not to enlarge my screed beyond all measure, look for yourself and you will find that all the saints have suffered adversity. Solomon alone lived in luxury, and that is perhaps the reason why he fell. " *Whom the Lord loveth He chasteneth, and scourgeth every son whom He receiveth.*" Is it not better to fight for a short space, to carry timber, to put on arms, to faint beneath a breast-plate, and then to know the joy of victory, rather than to become slaves for ever because we could not hold out for a single hour ?

Love finds nothing hard : no task is difficult if you wish to do it. Consider all that Jacob bore to win Rachel, his promised bride. The Scripture tells us : " *Jacob served seven years for Rachel. And they seemed to him but a few days for the love he had to her.*" So he himself afterwards says : " *In the day the drought consumed me and the frost by night.*" Let us also love Christ and ever seek His embraces. Then everything difficult will seem easy ; all things long we shall think to be short ; and smitten with His javelin we shall say as each hour passes : " *Woe is me that I have prolonged my pilgrimage. For the sufferings of this present time are not worthy to be compared with the glory that shall be revealed in us. Tribulation worketh patience, and patience experience, and experience hope ; and hope maketh not ashamed.*" Whenever your lot seems hard, read Paul's second epistle to the Corinthians : " *In labours more abundant ; in stripes above measure ; in prisons more frequent ; in deaths oft. Of the Jews five times received I forty stripes save one ; thrice was I beaten with rods ; once was I stoned ; thrice I suffered shipwreck ; a night and a day have I been in the deep ; in journeyings often, in perils of robbers, in perils by mine own countrymen, in perils by the heathen, in perils in the city, in perils in the wilderness,*

*in perils in the sea, in perils among false brethren, in weariness
and painfulness, in watchings often, in hunger and thirst,
in fastings often, in cold and nakedness.*" Who of us at least
can claim for himself the smallest part of this catalogue of
virtues ? But became of these things he could afterwards
boldly say : "*I have finished my course, I have kept the
faith. Henceforth there is laid up for me a crown of righteousness which the Lord, the righteous Judge shall give me at that
day.*"

And yet we frown if our food seems to lack savour, and
fancy that we are doing God a favour when we drink water
with our wine. If that water is a trifle too warm, the servant
must pay for it with his blood : we smash the cup, knock
the table over, and the whip whistles in the air. "*The
kingdom of heaven suffereth violence and the violent take
it by force.*" But unless you use violence you will never
seize the kingdom of heaven. Unless you knock
importunately you will never receive the sacramental
bread. Does it not seem to you to be truly violence when
the flesh desires to be as God and ascends to the place
whence angels fell to judge angels ?

Come out, I pray you, awhile from your prison-house,
and picture before your eyes the reward of your present
labours, a reward "*which eye hath not seen nor ear heard,
neither hath it entered into the heart of man.*" What will
be the splendour of that day when Mary, the mother of
the Lord, shall come to meet you, attended by her bands
of virgins ; when, the Red Sea past and Pharaoh with his
hosts drowned beneath its waves, Miriam, sister of Aaron,
with timbrel in her hand, shall chant to her responsive
choir : "*Let us sing unto the Lord, for he hath triumphed
gloriously ; the horse and his rider he hath thrown into the
sea.*" Then shall Thecla fly rejoicing to your arms. Then
shall your spouse himself come to meet you and say :
"*Rise up, my love, my fair one, and come away, for lo,
the winter is past, the rain is over and gone.*" Then shall
the angels gaze in wonder and cry : "*Who is she that*

looketh forth as the morning, fair as the moon, clear as the sun? The daughters shall see you and bless you ; yea, the queens shall proclaim and the concubines shall praise you."

And then another chaste band will be there to greet you. Sarah will come with the wedded ; Anna, the daughter of Phanuel, with the widows. In the one company you will see your natural and in the other your spiritual mother. The one will rejoice in having borne you, the other will exult in having taught you. Then truly will the Lord ride upon His ass and enter the heavenly Jerusalem. Then the little ones—of whom in Isaiah the Saviour says : *" Behold I and the children whom the Lord hath given me "*— shall lift up palms of victory and with one accord shall sing : *" Hosanna in the highest, blessed is he that cometh in the name of the Lord, hosanna in the highest."* Then shall the hundred and forty-four thousand hold their harps before the throne and before the elders and sing the new song. And no man shall be able to sing that song save the appointed company. *" These are they which were not defiled with women ; for they are virgins. These are they which follow the Lamb whithersoever he goeth."* As often as this world's vain display delights you ; as often as you see in life some empty glory, transport yourself in thought to Paradise and begin to be now what you will be hereafter. Then will you hear your Spouse say : *" Set me as a sun-shade in thine heart, and as a seal upon thine arm."* And then, fortified alike in mind and body, you will cry : *" Many waters cannot quench love, neither can the floods drown it."*

AUGUSTINE

AURELIUS AUGUSTINUS was born 13th November, 354, at Thagaste, a small town in Numidia, his mother, Monica, being a very fervent Christian, his father, Patricius, a pagan. He learnt Greek at Madaurus, and when he was seventeen proceeded to Carthage to finish his education. His university course there, consisting chiefly of the study of Virgil and Cicero, strengthened his natural taste for literature, and when he was twenty he returned to his native town as a professor of rhetoric. But while living at Carthage he had, to his mother's great grief, been attracted to the Manichæans, and for some years he was inclined to support at least two of their heresies ; one, the existence of two co-eternal Principles, the Principle of good and the Principle of evil ; the other, the corporeal existence of God as a form of highly subtilized matter. He had also formed a connection with a woman, by whom he had a son, Adeodatus, and was living in sin with her, so that at this time of his life neither his faith nor his morals were beyond reproach.

In 383 he left Africa for Italy, and taught first at Rome and then in Milan, where Ambrose was then bishop. In that town in 386 the crisis of his life came, and in the garden where he had taken refuge from temptation a child's cry— " *tolle, lege*," " take and read," caused him to open his Bible and then and there renounce all the errors of the past. In 387 he was baptized together with his son and his devoted friend Alypius, and at the end of the year, after a short stay at Ostia, where Monica died, he returned to Africa. Giving his small inheritance to the poor, he lived quietly for three years with an association of friends at Thagaste, and then became assistant-priest to Valerius, the aged bishop of Hippo. On Valerius' decease, in 395, he was elected bishop in his stead, and remained in that office till his own death at the age of seventy-six, 28th August, 430.

It will be seen that the outward incidents of this career are simple enough, and they have been clearly narrated for us in the biography of Augustine, written by his friend Possidius, Bishop of Calama. But Augustine's character is by no means a simple one, and his inner life was never illumined by a clear light, but was rather one long struggle, firstly against himself and those human instincts which he came to regard as man's deadliest temptation, and secondly against all the various forms of heresy that in the forth and fifth centuries distracted the church. There were the Manichæans, with their recruits from the old Gnostic sects, who sought to establish some connection between Christianity and rationalism. There were the Donatists, stiff-backed puritans who maintained that the Sacraments had no efficacy unless the minister was duly ordained and in a proper state of grace. And, most dangerous of all in Augustine's view, there were the followers of the British monk, Pelagius, who maintained that Adam's sin was purely personal, that men were born into this world good, and that they had a free choice in the direction of their lives.

Against these ideas Augustus fought with all the strength he possessed, and it is probable that a weaker man would have succumbed to the stress of thought and emotion that these fierce controversies involved. But Augustine is perhaps the greatest mind revealed to us in Latin literature, and not only did he emerge triumphant from all his difficulties, but he succeeded in imprinting his mark more deeply than any other writer upon the life of the Middle Ages. He is the only Roman who can for a moment be compared with Plato ; and for the medieval man he took Plato's place and stood side by side with Aristotle as the guiding beacon of truth. " From his distant Africa," says Duchesne, " Augustine shed his light over the whole of Christendom. To the men of his own time he uttered profitable words. He knew how to explain their own souls to them, to console them for the calamities of the world, and to guide their understanding through mysteries. Even now, after the inevitable attrition of so many centuries, he is still the great authority in theology. It is through him in a special manner that we have intercourse with Christian antiquity. In certain aspects he is for every age."

Augustine's writings are very numerous, for in the assiduity of his pen he equalled even Tertullian and Jerome, and there are no less than one hundred and eighteen separate titles in the list of his works. A rough classification will divide them as follows. *First*, the controversial books, directed against Manichæans, Donatists, Pelagians, and Arians, and establishing his own stern doctrine of predestination. *Secondly*, the doctrinal treatises, concerned with church teaching and administration, the two most important being the *De Doctrina Christiana*, and the *De Catechizandis Rudibus*, "*On the Art of Catechizing novices*." *Thirdly*, the philosophical and rhetorical essays, a comparatively unimportant section, and mostly early works. *Fourthly*, volumes of biblical exegesis, such as the commentaries on the Book of Job, the Psalms, and the Epistle to the Romans. *Fifthly*, the sermons and letters, each class containing a large number of examples of very varying length and interest. *Sixthly*, the "*Retractations*", the work of Augustine's old age, in which he reviews and frankly criticises most of his previous writings and amends such statements in them as seem to his mature judgement incorrect.

Into one of these sections nearly all Augustine's writings will fall. But from the mass of his work there stands out a pair of great books, *The Confessions* and *The City of God*, the one an epitome of fifth century feeling, the other an encyclopaedia of fifth century knowledge. *The Confessions* is, or should be, familiar to all ; and the selections from

Augustine in this volume have therefore been taken only from " *The City of God* ". That amazing book occupied thirteen years of Augustine's life, and he himself in the Retractations gives his own summary of its contents. " The great work on the City of God was at last completed in twenty-two books. Of these the first five were occupied with the refutation of such persons as believe that human prosperity depends upon the worship of the pagan gods, and that the prohibition of their worship is the cause of our present misfortunes. The next five are directed against those who admit that troubles have always been the attributes of humanity, but argue that the worship of many gods possesses a value in relation to the life after death. In these ten books those two futile opinions, which are antagonistic to Christianity, are refuted. But as I did not wish to be accused of having merely controverted the doctrines of other people, without enunciating my own, this is the object of the second part of this work. The first four of its twelve books contain the origin of the two cities, The City of God and the city of this world ; the second four contain their process or progress ; the third four, the final books, their appointed ends. So, while the twenty-two books are all occupied with the description of both cities, yet they derived their title from the better city, and were called by preference " The City of God ".

The actual occasion of the book was, of course, the sack of Rome by Alaric in 410, a disaster which made not only the pagans but many Christians also believe that the end of the world was rapidly approaching. Every one was filled with uneasy apprehension, and Augustine realized that it was absolutely necessary to restore men's confidence. How far he succeeded is now a matter of history, and the *City of God* was one of the strongest bulwarks of faith all through medieval times, and one of the chief sources from which the temporal organization of the Catholic Church drew its inspiration. As Dean Weldon says in his excellent edition of the Latin text (S.P.C.K.,

1924) : " The *De Civitate Dei* has been one of the great books in human history, greater even in its effect or influence than in itself. For it is a book which breathed hope into a despondent, and faith into a sceptical, society, and which turned men's eyes away from the grave of a dead or dying world to the resurrection of a living and conquering Christ. The *De Civitate Dei* made its appeal at its publication, and may make the same appeal now, to an age crying aloud for reconstruction."

The book perhaps is best known to English readers in the very inadequate translation by J. Healey originally published in 1610 and re-issued in a somewhat mangled form in the Temple Classics. There is a much more workmanlike version by Dr. Marcus Dods, but this is not available in an altogether satisfactory form. To many, however, it will be new ground, which it is to be hoped the following extracts will tempt some to explore further.

SELECTIONS FROM *THE CITY OF GOD*

(I) THE PAGAN'S IDEAL STATE

(D.C.D., ii, 20)

The worshippers and admirers of these pagan gods, whose crimes and vices they delight to imitate, are not concerned at all to cure the villainous depravity of their state. Only let it stand firm, they say ; only let it flourish and abound in resources ; only let it be glorious in victory, or, better still, secure in peace. What else matters to us ? Our business is to see that every man has the opportunity to make money, so as to supply his daily extravagance and enable the powerful to keep the weak under their control.

Let the poor cringe to the rich for the sake of a full stomach, that under their patronage they may enjoy a sluggish tranquility. Let the rich misuse the help of the poor, to make them their dependants and to minister to their pride. Let the people applaud, not those who consult their true interests, but those who provide them lavishly with pleasures. Let no stern duty be commanded, no filthiness forbidden. Let it be a ruler's object to secure, not the loyalty, but the servility of his subjects. Let the provinces render obedience to their rulers, not as being their moral guides, but as being their worldly masters and the purveyors of their pleasures ; and let them feel not an honest respect but a slavish fear.

Let the laws take cognizance of any damage that you do to your neighbour's vines, but not of the damage that is done to yourself by your own vices. Let no man be brought before a judge unless he has shown himself a nuisance or a danger to his neighbour's life and person, his property and his household : in his own home let everyone do what he pleases in company with his own family, and anyone

who willingly joins him. Let there be a plentiful supply of
public prostitutes for all who wish to use them, and
especially for those who are too poor to keep one for themselves. Let houses be built in the grandest and most elegant
style and in them let sumptuous banquets be provided
where everyone who wishes by day or night may gamble,
drink, vomit, and waste his strength. Let the rattle of
dance music everywhere be heard and let the theatres
overflow with shouts of immodest laughter and with every
kind of cruel and shameful delights.

If such happiness as this is distasteful to any man, let
him be regarded as a public enemy : if any man attempt
to modify or make an end of it, let the people unhindered
drive him out of earshot, harry him from his home, make
an end of him as a living man. Let those be reckoned the
true gods, who procure this happiness for the people and
assure them its enjoyment. Let them be worshipped as
they wish : let them demand whatever games they wish,
to be observed in the company or at the expense of their
worshippers : only let them see to it that this happiness
has nothing to fear from enemies, pestilence, or disaster
of any kind.

What man in his senses would rank such a state as equal,
I will not say to the Roman Empire, but to the palace of
Sardanapalus, the ancient King who was so given over
to his pleasures that he had this inscription engraved upon
his tomb : " In death my sole possessions are those things
which in lifetime my fancy swallowed and consumed."
If these folk had such a king as this, indulgent to himself
in these vices and laying no stern restraint on anyone of
them, they would more gladly consecrate to him a temple
and a priest than did the ancient Romans to Romulus.

(II) Wonders of the Past

(XV, 9)

Therefore no one who carefully considers facts will hesitate to acknowledge that Cain not only was able to found a city but that his city was a great one, seeing that the life of men at that time extended to such length of days : unless, indeed, a sceptic takes exception to the very number of years for which our authorities vouch, and declares it to be incredible.

Such people, of course, refuse to believe that the size of men's bodies before the Flood was larger than it is now. And yet Virgil, the greatest of their poets, speaks of a huge stone, set in the fields as a boundary-mark, which a strong man of old snatched up, and ran, and hurled, and cast it as he fought ; and, says the poet :—

"Twelve men could scarcely bear that stone away,
  Such puny frames as earth brings forth to-day."

Thus declaring his belief that the earth then was wont to produce mightier men. And how much more so must it have been in the earlier days of the world before the famous and world-renowned Flood.

The huge size of early men's bodies has often been proved to the incredulous by the exposure of their burial places through lapse of time or the force of torrents or some other accidents, for in them dead men's bones have been found or started out of quite incredible dimensions. I myself and others with me, saw on the shore at Utica a man's molar tooth so huge that if it were cut piecemeal into teeth of our size, a hundred, I think, could have been made out of it. That tooth I should be inclined to believe belonged to a giant : for beside the fact that everyone then was bigger than we are, the giants also far surpassed their contemporaries. In other ages, too, as well as in our own there have not been wanting some cases of extraordinary bodily stature, though they may be rare.

The learned Pliny declares that the older the world grows the smaller are the men that nature produces ; and he mentions that Homer in his poems often lamented the same decline, not laughing at his complaint as being a poetical fiction, but as a recorder of natural marvels accepting it as historically true. As I have said, the bones that are frequently discovered reveal to much later ages the size of the bodies of men of old and will do so since they are slow to decay. But the length of life before the Flood cannot be proved by any such archæological evidence.

We should not, however, on that account refuse belief to the sacred history, whose narrative we are the less justified in discrediting, inasmuch as we see now how exactly its predictions are being fulfilled. Pliny tells us, too, that there is still one tribe whose men live for two hundred years. If, then, in places unknown to us men are believed to have a length of days which is altogether outside our own experience, why should we not believe that the same thing happened in times of which we know not ? Is it credible that something now exists in other places which does not exist here, but incredible that a thing existed in other days which to-day is not to be found ?

(III) The Eunuch Priests of Cybele

(VIII, 26)

As regards the eunuchs also, consecrated to the Great Mother in defiance of male and female modesty, Varro says nothing. Up till yesterday even these priests with their perfumed hair, whitened cheeks, soft bodies, and feminine gait used to go through the streets and squares of Carthage begging from our shopkeepers the means of maintaining their shameful existence. Of them Varro would not speak and I do not remember to have read about them in any author. Interpretation fails, argumentation blushes, demonstration is silent. The Great Mother has surpassed all her divine sons, not in the greatness of her deity, but in the greatness of her guilt. To this monster not even the monstrosity of Janus can be compared. His deformity was confined to his statues : hers was the cruel deformity of sacred rites. He had a superfluity of members in stone : she inflicted the loss of members on living men. Even Jove's countless deeds of vile lust cannot surpass this abomination. Amid all the seductions he practised on women he only disgraced heaven with one Ganymede : she has defiled the earth and insulted the skies with a host of eunuchs publicly confessed.

In this kind of shameful cruelty we might perhaps have been able to compare Saturn with her, or even to put him first ; for Saturn is said to have gelded his own Father. But in the rites of Saturn men were slain by the hands of others rather than mutilated by their own. Saturn devoured his sons, as the poets say, the physicists interpreting the story as they will : history tells us that he slew them. So it was that the Carthaginians sacrificed their sons to him, a custom that the Romans never adopted.

And yet this Great Mother of their gods brought eunuchs into Roman temples and kept alive the barbarous habit of castration, being believed to promote the virility of the Romans by this removal of the virile member. Compared with this crime, what are the thefts of Mercury, the wanton tricks of Venus, the vile debauchery of the other gods which I would bring forward from books were it not that every day they are represented by music and gesture in the theatres ? What are they, I repeat, compared with this crime, for whose greatness only the Great Mother was competent ?

Moreover, those stories are said to be the inventions of

the poets, the inference being that the poets also invented
their acceptability to the gods. Let us ascribe it then to
the poet's naughty audacity that such tales have been sung
in verse or put down in writing. But that they were made
part of the divine ritual at the urgent command of the gods
themselves, what else is that but a crime committed by
divinities ? Nay, more, a confession that the gods are
demons and a proof of the fraud they practise on unhappy
men. As for the fact, however, that the Mother of the
Gods has earned the right of being worshipped by the
consecration of eunuchs to her service, that is no invention
of the poets ; nay, they have preferred to shrink from it
in horror rather than sing of it in their verse.

(IV) THE MANICHÆAN HERESY

(XI, 22)

This cause, however, that is, the goodness of God
working for the creation of good ; this cause, I repeat, so
just and suitable, which, when weighed with pious care
and consideration puts an end to all the controversies of
those who inquire into the origin of the world, is not
recognized by some heretics. They see, forsooth, that there
are many things, such as fire, frost, wild beasts and so
forth, which do not suit the poor frail mortality of our
flesh, already sentenced to a just penalty, but rather work it
harm. But they do not consider how wonderful these things
are in their own place and nature and how beautifully
they are arranged, what grace they give, each in its due
proportion, to the commonwealth of the universe, what
services they render us, if only we use them suitably
and with knowledge. The poisons, for example, which
are deadly when they are injudiciously employed, become

salutary drugs if they are administered with discretion ; while, on the other hand, things that give us pleasure such as food, drink, and sunlight, are found to be hurtful when immoderately or unseasonably used.

Hence divine providence warns us not to depreciate things with foolish abuse but rather diligently to investigate their utility. If that utility be hidden from us, owing to our weakness and the failure of our discernment, we must remember those things in the past that we all but failed to discover, and still believe in its existence. The fact that a thing's utility can be thus concealed is for us an exercise in humility and a lesson against pride ; for nothing in nature is evil and the word " evil " itself does not mean anything save lack of good. From the earthly to the heavenly, from the visible to the invisible, all things are good but some are better than others, and the reason of their inequality is the possibility of the existence of them all. God, indeed, a great worker in great things is not less great in little things, and these little things are to be measured not by their own greatness, which is non-existent, but by the wisdom of their Maker. It is just like a man's visible aspect : if one eyebrow be shaved, how nearly nothing is taken from his body, but how much is taken from his comeliness, which depends not on bulk but on the correspondence and proportion of the limbs.

It is not, however, very surprising that people, who think that some evil nature has been produced and propagated by its own opposing principle, refuse to admit that the true cause of creation is that the good God created good things. They prefer to believe that He was forced into the great task of world-building by the urgent necessity of driving back the evil that rebelled against Him, and that with the idea of restraining and conquering that evil He mixed His good nature with it, which now, shamefully polluted and cruelly imprisoned and enchained, He now for all His labour can scarcely cleanse and deliver. Indeed, He does not seek to clean it all : that part of it which cannot be purified from defilement is to serve as a chain for the conquered enemy and to be the prison of his confinement. The Manichæans would not drivel, or rather, rave in this fashion, if they believed the nature of God to be, as it is, unchangeable and altogether incorruptible, so that nothing can injure it. Nor, again, would they do so, if with proper Christian orthodoxy they held that the soul, which by its own will can be changed for the worse and corrupted by sin and so deprived of the light of immutable truth, is not a part of God, nor of the same nature as God, but was created by Him, and is very different from its Creator.

(V) MIRACLES IN AUGUSTINE'S TIME

(XXII, 8)

There is a country house called Victoriana, less than thirty miles from Hippo Regius, where there is a monument to the two Milanese martyrs, Protasius and Gervasius. A young man was brought there who when he was watering his horse one summer day at noon in a river pool had become possessed by a devil. He was lying by the monument, near to death and, indeed, very like a dead person, when the lady of the manor with her maids and some pious women enter the shrine for the customary evening service of prayer and praise. Scarcely had they begun a hymn when the young man started up, as though the sound had pierced him through, and with a terrible scream seized hold of the altar; and then, either fearing or being unable to let go, clung to it as if he were fixed or tied. Meanwhile, the thing within him burst into loud lamentation and begging for mercy confessed where and when and how he had taken possession of the youth. At last, declaring that he meant to leave him, he named one by one the members of his body which he threatened to mutilate as he went out ; and with the words he departed from the man. At once the youth's eye fell out on his cheek, hanging by one slender vein as by a root, and the whole of the pupil which had been black became white. When the spectators saw this—for others had been brought to the place by his cries and were now on their knees praying for him—although they were rejoiced that he had recovered his sanity, they yet were grieved about his eye, and said that a doctor ought to be fetched. But his sister's husband, who had brought him there, said : " God, who has routed the devil, is able to restore the eye at the prayers of His saints." He then replaced the eye that had fallen and was hanging loose, and bound it in its place as well as he could with his handkerchief, recommending him not to take it off for a week. When the young man did so, he found his eye perfectly sound. Other people also have been cured at this shrine, but it would be tedious to give details of their cases.

I have a neighbour called Hesperius, a man of tribunician rank, who has an estate called Zubedi in the Fussalian district. Finding that his family, his cattle and his servants were suffering from the violent attacks of malicious demons, he asked our presbyters during my absence to send one of their number to banish the spirits by his prayers. One went, offered there the sacrifice of the body of Christ, and prayed with all his strength that this persecution might cease ; and by God's mercy it did cease immediately. Now Hesperius had received from a friend some holy earth brought from Jerusalem, where Christ was buried and rose again on the third day. This earth he had hung up in his bedroom to preserve him from harm. But when his house was cleansed from the visitation of demons, he began to think what should be done with the earth ; for out of reverence he did not wish to keep it any longer in his bedroom. It happened that I and a colleague of mine, Bishop Maximinus of Sinita, were in the neighbourhood.

He asked us to visit him, and we did so. He told us the whole story, and asked that the earth might be buried somewhere, and the place made a place of prayer where Christians might assemble for the worship of God. We made no objection, and his wishes were carried out. In the vicinity lived a young countryman, a paralytic, who, hearing of this begged his parents to take him to that holy place without delay. He was brought there and prayed and immediately went away on his own feet perfectly cured.

In the city of Carthage there lived a lady called Innocentia, a most devout Christian and a member of one of our principal families. She was suffering from cancer of the breast, a disease which, according to the doctors, is incurable. The usual method therefore is either to amputate the limb in which the cancer has appeared and so sever it from the body, or else give up all attempts at treatment ; this latter, they say, being in accordance with Hippocrates' views and securing for the patient some prolongation of life, though death, even if delayed, is inevitable. Such was the advice which Innocentia had received from a skilful physician, an intimate friend of the family ; and she had betaken herself in prayer to God alone. As Easter drew near she was admonished in a dream to keep watch in the place reserved for women, at the baptistery, and whoever might be the first woman to come out after baptism, to ask her to make the sign of Christ upon the spot where her cancer was. She did so ; and was immediately cured.

I am acquainted with a doctor in the same city of Carthage who suffers from gout. He had given in his name for baptism, but the day before the ceremony as he lay asleep, black woolly-haired boys, whom he realized to be demons, appeared to him in a dream and prohibited his appearance. On his refusing to obey them they trod on his feet and inflicted the acutest pain he had ever experienced, but he overcame them and refused to defer immersion in the laver of new birth. He was accordingly baptised and in the very act of baptism was relieved, not only of the extraordinary pain that then tortured him, but also of the gout itself, so that, though he lived a long time afterwards he never suffered with his feet again.

Florentius was a fellow townsman of mine at Hippo, a poor old man devoted to the faith, who supported himself as a tailor. Having lost his coat, and being without money to buy another, he prayed to the Twenty Martyrs, who have a famous shrine in our town, asking them loudly to clothe him. Some young men who were standing by heard him, and as he went away followed him with scoffing laughter, as though he had asked the martyrs for fifty pence to buy a coat. But he, walking along in silence, saw a great fish on the shore, gasping as if it had been just cast up by the waves. With the youths' kindly assistance he secured the fish and sold it for curing to a cook of the name of Catosus, a good Christian man, telling him how he had come by it. Catosus paid him three hundred pence, which he laid out in wool, so that his wife might make him a coat as best she could. On cutting up the fish, however, the cook found a gold ring in its belly ; and moved by compassion and influenced also by religious fear gave it up to the man, saying " Behold how the Twenty Martyrs have clothed you."

Audurus is the name of an estate where there is a church containing a shrine dedicated to the memory of the martyr Stephen. It happened that as a little boy was playing in the courtyard some oxen drawing a wagon went out of the track and crushed the child beneath the wheel, so that he seemed to be at his last gasp. His mother snatched him up and laid him at the shrine, and not only did he revive but also appeared to be unhurt.

A religious female who lived at Caspalium, an estate near Audurus, being so ill that her life was despaired of, had her dress taken to this shrine ; but before it was brought back she was defunct. However, her parents wrapped her corpse in the dress and her breath returned and she became quite well again.

There was a young women of Hippo, with whom I am acquainted, who was immediately healed of a devil by annointing herself with oil mixed with the tears of a presbyter who had been praying for her. I know also that a bishop once prayed for a demoniac whom he had never seen and that the young man was cured on the spot.

(VI) CAN MEN CHANGE THEIR SHAPE ?

(XVIII, 16–18)

The Romans say that Diomede's return home from Troy was prevented by a divinely imposed punishment, and they assert that his companions were turned into birds, relying for that not on fabulous and poetic falsehoods but on the evidence of history. As for Diomede, though he was, as they think, made a god he was neither himself able to restore his men to their human shape nor yet obtain that boon from Jupiter his overlord as a favour granted to a newcomer in heaven.

They tell us furthermore that his temple is in the island of Diomedea not far from Mount Garganus in Apulia, and that these birds fly round the shrine, and are so wonderfully tame that they fill their beaks with water and sprinkle it in ritual fashion. If any Greeks approach the altar, or people of Greek descent, the birds are quiet and even welcome them with soft twittering : but if they are men of an alien race, they fly at their heads and wound them with severe and even deadly blows. For with their huge hard beaks they are said to be well armed for such combats.

In support of this story Varro relates other tales no less incredible about that most notorious witch Circe, who changed the companions of Ulysses into swine, and also about the Arcadians, who used to draw lots and swim across a certain pool and in the water were changed into wolves and lived in the waste places of the country with wild beasts like themselves. But if they did not feed once on human flesh, after nine years they got back their human shape by swimming back across the same pool. Finally, Varro expressly names a certain Demaenetus who, on tasting the flesh of a boy offered as a ritual sacrifice by the Arcadians to their god Lycaeus, was turned into a wolf, and getting back his proper shape after ten years trained himself as a boxer and won a prize at the Olympic games.

Perhaps my readers may expect me to say something about these demoniacal tricks. Well, what can we say, save that it is best for men to fly from the midst of Babylon. That prophetic warning is to be understood now in a spiritual sense : we must fly from the city of this world, which is an association of wicked angels and wicked men, and by the path of faith working through love achieve to the living God. The greater we see the power of the demons to be in these depths, the more firmly must we cling to the Mediator through whom we rise from these lowest to those highest places.

If we should say that these things are incredible, there are not wanting people even now who declare that they have heard of similar things on the best authority or can even testify to them by their own experience. I myself, when I was in Italy, was told of a certain district in that country where landladies of inns, skilled in these mischievous arts, were said to be in the habit of giving to such travellers as they chose, or could manage, something in a piece of cheese by which they were changed immediately into beasts of burden, and carried whatever was necessary, being restored to their proper shape when the work was done. Their mind, however, did not become animal but remained rational and human, just as Apuleius in the book he wrote called *The Golden Ass* has told or pretended that it happened to himself that on taking poison he became an ass, while still retaining a human mind.

These things are either false or so unusual as rightly to be disbelieved. But we should most firmly believe that Almighty God can do whatever he pleases either to punish or to help, and that the demons can accomplish nothing by their own natural power (for their created being is in itself angelic although it has been made mischievous by their own fault) except in so far as He allows, whose judgements are often hidden but never unjust. Certainly the demons, if they really do the things into which we are now inquiring, do not create real substances but only change the appearance of things created by the true God so that they seem to be that which they are not.

I cannot therefore in any way believe that even the body, much less the mind, can really be changed into animal shapes and lineaments by any demoniacal art or power. I think that the phantasm of a man, which even in thought or in dreams goes through innumerable changes and though it is not the body assumes with wonderful rapidity shapes that are like the body, may possibly, when the man's corporeal senses are asleep or overpowered, in some undescribable way be presented to another's vision in his corporeal form. Men's bodies themselves will then lie somewhere, living, indeed, but with their senses enchained much more firmly than by sleep, while the phantasm embodied in the shape of some animal will appear to the senses of others. Even the man himself may think that he is changed as in dreams he fancies that he is changed, and that he is carrying burdens ; these burdens, if they are real substances being actually carried by demons in order that men may be deceived by beholding at the same time the real substance of the burdens and the simulated bodies of the beasts of burden.

A certain man named Praestantius used to tell the following tale of what once happened to his father. After taking the cheese poison I have mentioned in his own house he went to bed and lay there as though asleep but could not possibly be awakened. After some days, however, he woke up and told his family the things that had happened to him as though they had been dreams. He said that he had been changed into a horse and among the other beasts of burden had carried for the soldiers the corn that is called Rhaetian since it is taken to that province. All the details of his story were found to be exactly true, although it seemed to him that it was only a dream.

Another man declared that in his own house one night, before he went to sleep, he saw a certain philosopher, with whom he was very well acquainted, come in and explain to him some points of Platonic doctrine which he had previously refused to expound when requested to do so. The philosopher was asked afterwards why he had done in the other man's house what he had refused to do in his own home : " I did not do it," he replied, " I dreamed that I had done it." So what the one man saw in his sleep was shown to the other man when awake by means of a phantasmal image.

These tales have come to me not from persons who might be thought unworthy of belief but from men whom I cannot think to have been telling lies. Therefore what men say and have recorded about the Arcadians being often changed into wolves by the Arcadian gods, or rather by the Arcadian demons, and the other story also of how " By Circe's charms Ulysses' men were changed " seem to me, if they really happened, possibly to have happened in the way I have described. As for Diomede's birds, since their race is alleged to have been perpetuated by constant propagation, I believe that they are not changed men but that the men disappeared and these birds were substituted for them, just as a hind was substituted for Iphigenia the daughter of King Agamemnon. Tricks of this kind would not be difficult for demons if they had God's permission ; and as Iphigenia was afterwards found alive it is easy to see that a hind was sacrificed in her stead.

Diomede's men for their part suddenly disappeared and could not be found anywhere, being destroyed by bad avenging angels, and so it is believed that they were changed into birds, although as a matter of fact the birds were merely brought from the places where they breed and suddenly substituted for them. Finally, that these birds now bring water in their beaks and sprinkle it in Diomede's shrine, and that they flatter men of Greek stock and attack those of other races, is not very surprising, since it is due to the prompting of demons whose interest it is to persuade people that Diomede was made a god. Thus they beguile men into worshipping many false gods to the true God's injury, and into serving dead mortals, who even in their lifetime did not truly live, with temples, altars, sacrifices, and priests, all things which, when they are of the right kind, are due only to the one true and living God.

(VII) Lessons for Christians from Roman History
(V, 18)

Is it then so great a thing for the sake of that eternal city in the skies to despise all the allurements of this world, however pleasant they be, seeing that Brutus for the sake of this temporal city on earth was able even to put his own sons to death, a sacrifice which our heavenly fatherland forces no one to make? Surely it is a harder thing to kill one's sons than to do what we must do for her, that is, either give to the poor the goods which once we thought to amass and lay up for our children, or else throw them away altogether if we be faced with a temptation which renders that the way of faith and righteousness.

It is not earthly riches that make us or our sons happy: either we lose them in our lifetime or when we are dead they are taken by whom we know not or perhaps by whom we would not. It is God, the mind's true wealth, that gives us happiness. As for Brutus, even the poet who sings his praises testifies that he was an unhappy man, in that he slew his sons; for he says:—

> " Upon his reckless sons, who seek to make,
>   A second war of strife, for freedom's sake
> The father shall take vengeance, hapless man."

Although in the next lines he consoles him in his unhappiness:—

> " Howe'er the doubtful deed is understood,
>   'Twas love of honour and his country's good."

These two things, liberty, and the desire for men's praise, spurred the Romans on to wondrous deeds. If, then, for the freedom of men doomed to death and for the desire of mortal glory a father was able to kill his own sons, is it so great a thing if we for the true freedom, which liberates us from the dominion of sin and death and the devil, do not indeed kill our sons, but rather reckon Christ's poor children as our sons, moved not by a desire for human praise but by a loving wish to set men free, not from King Tarquin, but from demons and the prince of demons?

Again, if another Roman chief, surnamed Torquatus, slew his son, not because he fought against his country—he was fighting for his country—but because he fought against his orders, that is against the orders which the father had issued as commander-in-chief—and that too although the lad had accepted an enemy's challenge in youthful impetuosity and won the day—fearing lest the precedent of disobedience would do more harm than the glory of victory would do good: if, I say, Torquatus did this, why should those men vaunt themselves who for the laws of an eternal city despise the good things of earth, which are loved far less than sons?

Again, if Furius Camillus, who was condemned by his envious countrymen, although he had cast off from their necks the yoke of their bitter enemies of Veii, delivered his ungrateful city a second time from the Gauls, because there was no other place where he could live with a better chance of fame; if he could act thus, why should that man be extolled, as though he had done some great thing, who, though perchance in the church he has suffered serious and slighting wrongs from carnal enemies, has not betaken himself to the camp of our heretical foes or himself raised some heresy against her, but rather has defended her with all his strength from the mischievous perversity of schismatics, there being no other church in which I will not say one can live a life of mortal glory, but in which eternal life can be obtained?

If Mucius to secure peace with King Porsenna, who was pressing the Romans very hard in war, failed to kill the king himself and in error slew another man in his stead, and then before Porsenna's eyes stretched out his right hand and laid it on a blazing altar, saying that there were many others left of a like resolution who had solemnly sworn his death, so that the king terrified by his fortitude and the thought of such a conspiracy without further hesitation stopped the war, and made peace; if Mucius, I say, did this, who is going to reckon his merits as claims upon the kingdom of heaven, if for its sake he has given to the flames not one hand but even his whole body, and even so not by his own voluntary act but as the result of persecution?

If Curtius in full armour spurring on his horse flung himself headlong into a sheer gulf, obeying the oracles of his gods who had ordered the Romans to throw into it the best thing they had, and excelling as they did in arms and men they could only understand thereby that they should cast an armed man headlong down to destruction; if he did this, can any man say that he has done a great thing for the eternal city, when he suffers this death at the hands of some enemy of the faith, not throwing himself down of his own accord but being another man's victim, especially when he has received from his Lord who is King of his city, a more certain oracle : " Fear not them who kill the body but cannot kill the soul " ?

If the Decii devoted themselves to death and consecrated themselves as victims by a definite vow, in order that the anger of the gods might be appeased by their blood and the Roman army freed by their destruction : if they did this, the holy martyrs should not walk too proudly, as though they had done something that entitles them to a share in the city where true happiness reigns for ever, even if to the shedding of their blood they have vied with one another in faith of love and love of faith, cherishing, not only their brethren for whom their blood was shed, but also their enemies by whom it was shed, according to the command that has been given us.

If Marcus Pulvillus when dedicating a temple to Jupiter, Juno and Minerva received with indifference the news of his son's death falsely brought to him by envious rivals in the hope that he would go away in grief and leave the glory of dedication to his colleague ; if he, I say, treated the news so lightly that he even bade them cast out his son unburied, the love of glory in his heart overcoming the grief of bereavement, what great service for the preaching of the holy gospel, whereby the citizens of the heavenly city are freed and brought together from diverse wanderings, can that man say he has done, to whom the Lord said, when he was troubled about his father's burial : " *Follow me, and let the dead bury their dead* " ?

If Marcus Regulus, according to the story, returned from Rome to his cruel enemies rather than break his oath ; since, as he told his countrymen when they wished to keep him, he could not live as an honourable man in Rome after having been a slave in Africa ; if we know that he went back and was put to death with the most painful torments because he had spoken in the senate against

Carthage, ought we not to despise every kind of torture compared with the faith required of us by that city to whose beatitude faith itself leads us ? How, indeed, can anyone render back to the Lord all that He has rendered to us, even if to pay his debt of honour he suffers the death that Regulus endured to pay his debt to his ruthless enemies ?

How shall a Christian dare to boast of the voluntary poverty, which he has chosen so that while he sojourns in this life he may walk unencumbered along the road which leads to his fatherland, where true riches are, even God Himself ? How shall he boast when he hears or reads that Lucius Valerius, who died in the year that he was consul, was so poor that a public collection had to be made to pay for his funeral ? Or, again, when he hears or reads that Quintius Cincinnatus possessed only four acres of land which he tilled with his own hands when he was taken from the plough to become dictator, an office greater even than that of consul, and that after having won great glory by conquering the enemy he still preferred to continue in his poverty.

Will any man declare that he has done a great thing in that he has not been tempted by any of this world's prizes to give up his partnership in the eternal city, when he learns that Fabricius could not be induced to forsake the city of Rome by the great gifts, even to the fourth part of his kingdom, which Pyrrhus King of Epirus offered, but preferred to stay there in his poverty as a private citizen ?

For if, when their republic—that is the interests of the people, the country, the community—was most prosperous and wealthy, the Romans in private life were so poor that one of them, who had already twice been consul, was expelled ignominiously by the censor from the senate because he was discovered to possess ten pounds weight of silver plate ; if these men, whose triumphs enriched the treasury of the state, were themselves so poor, ought not all Christians, who make common purse for a nobler end, that they may distribute to each one according to his needs, as it is written in the Acts of the Apostles, and none may say that anything is his own but that all things are held in common—ought not they to understand that they have no cause for windy boasting because they accept poverty in order to stay partners with the angels, seeing that the ancient Romans did almost the same thing in order to preserve the glory of Rome ?

How could these examples, and others of the same kind found in Roman history, have become so well known and have been proclaimed so loudly by fame, had not the Roman empire, extending far and wide, grown to greatness by a succession of magnificent victories ?   Therefore, by the fact that their empire was made so wide lasting, so famous and illustrious by the virtues of such great men, the reward they sought was granted to their endeavours and an example is set before us by them containing a necessary admonition. If for the sake of God's glorious city we do not hold fast to the virtues which those other virtues in some degree resemble to which the Romans held for the sake of an earthly city's fame, then indeed we may be stung to the soul with shame.   But if we do hold to them, we must not be lifted up with pride, since, as the apostle says, " *The sufferings of the present time are not worthy to be compared to the glory that shall be revealed in us.*"

So far as regards human and temporal glory, the lives of these ancient Romans must be regarded as sufficiently worthy ;   and hence we see that the Jews were most righteously given over to Rome to swell her renown. The New Testament reveals to us the truth which is veiled in the Old, that it is not for the sake of terrestrial and temporal benefits which divine providence distributes promiscuously to good men and to bad, but for the sake of eternal life, perpetual blessings, and a share in the heavenly city itself that the one true God is to be worshipped.   So it was that the Romans who used such virtues as they had to seek after and acquire earthly glory

overcame the Jews who in signal depravity slew and
rejected Him who gives both true glory and the eternal
city.

(VIII) THE HORRORS OF THE SACK OF ROME

(I, 16–19)

The pagans certainly think that they are bringing a
conclusive charge against the Christians, when they add
to their tales of prisoners taken by saying that not only
matrons and unmarried maidens, but even nuns were
raped. As regards this, it is not a question of faith nor
piety nor the virtue of chastity : our difficulty is to keep
the discussion within the bounds of modesty and reason.
Our chief concern will be not so much to reply to strangers
as to comfort our own folk.

Let this, then, first be laid down and affirmed : the
virtue of right living is enthroned in the soul, and thence
rules the members of the body which becomes holy by
use of holy wishes. As long as the will remains firm and
unshaken, nothing that another person does with the body
or upon the body is any fault of the person who suffers it,
so long as he cannot escape it without himself committing
a sin. But as it is possible by certain acts not only to inflict
pain upon the body of another, but also to gratify lust,
whenever anything of this kind takes place, even though
it does not destroy the modesty which a firm virtue never
loses, it yet creates a feeling of shame, lest people should
think that an act which could not perhaps be done without
giving some pleasure to the flesh was also committed with
some assent of the will.

Consequently, who that has any human kindness can
refuse to forgive them if some of our nuns even killed

themselves to avoid suffering such treatment ? As for those of them who would not put an end to their lives for fear lest they should escape another's wickedness by themselves committing a sin, anyone who lays that to their charge will scarcely himself escape the charge of being a fool. In any case, if it is not permissible to take the law into our own hands and kill a man though he be guilty— and that is a permission which no code allows—obviously the man who kills himself is a murderer, and the more innocent he was in the matter which he thought a proper reason for his death, the more guilty he becomes.

Rightly do we execrate the deed of Judas, and truth declares that when he hanged himself he rather aggravated than expiated the guilt of that impious treachery, since by a penitence of death he left himself no opportunity for a penitence that might have brought salvation, and showed that he despaired of the mercy of God. How much more, then, should a man refrain from killing himself when he has done nothing to deserve such a punishment. Judas, when he killed himself, killed a criminal, and yet in thus passing from this life he made himself chargeable not only with Christ's death but with his own ; for though it was his own crime he punished he committed another crime by killing himself. Why, then, should a man who has done no wrong wrong himself, and by killing himself kill a guiltless person rather than submit to another's guilt ? Why should he commit upon himself a sin for which he is responsible in order that the sin of another may not be committed upon him ?

But you may say, the pollution of lust is to be feared even when another is responsible. There will be no pollution if another is responsible : if there is pollution, the responsibility is not his alone. Modesty is a virtue of the soul and has for its companion virtue the fortitude that resolves to endure all evils rather than consent to evil. But since no one, however courageous and modest, is always the master of his own body, but can only control the consent and refusal of his will, what man in his senses can suppose that his modesty is lost if perchance his body be forcibly seized for the exercise and satisfaction of another's lust? If modesty can be lost in this way, then obviously modesty is not a virtue of the soul nor will it be counted among the good things that make good living. It will rather rank with the good things of the body, with strength, beauty, health, and so forth : good things whose diminution does not diminish at all the goodness and righteousness of our lives.

If modesty is a thing of this kind, why should the body be endangered that modesty may be saved ? But if it is a thing of the soul, then it is not lost even when the body is violated. Nay, more, the virtue of holy continence, when it resists the uncleanness of fleshly desires, sanctifies even the body ; and therefore when continence with unshaken firmness refuses to yield, the holiness of the body is preserved, since the will to use it only in a holy fashion remains, and the power thus to use it also, in so far as lies with the body itself.

The sanctity of the body does not consist in the integrity of its members nor in their freedom from contact with others. They may receive wounds and endure violence of various kinds ; indeed, surgeons at times to save life perform operations on them which make the spectators shudder. Suppose that a midwife while testing a girl's virginity either maliciously or carelessly or accidentally destroys that for which she was looking : I do not imagine that anyone is such a wise fool as to think that the girl has lost anything of her body's sanctity even though one organ is no longer intact. Therefore, so long as the soul remains unshaken it secures the sanctity of the body, which cannot be destroyed by the violence of another's lust, but is preserved by a continence that never falters.

When an abandoned woman breaks the vows that she has made to God and goes to meet her seducer prepared already to yield, can we say that as she goes she is possessed even of bodily sanctity seeing that she has lost and destroyed that sanctity of the soul whereby the body is sanctified ? Let us beware of such an error, and remind ourselves rather that even if the body is violated, its sanctity is not destroyed so long as the sanctity of the soul remains ; and that similarly the sanctity of the body is lost when the soul's sanctity is violated, though the body itself be still intact. Accordingly, there is no reason why a woman should punish herself by a voluntary death because she has been taken without her own consent, and raped. That is another's sin, not hers. And much less has she cause to commit suicide before the rape takes place ; for then she is committing certain murder herself, while the other crime, which in any case is not hers, is still in the future and uncertain.

This is our way of reckoning. We assert that when a woman is raped her firm purpose of chastity not being changed by any consent to the iniquity, the sin is not hers who was taken by force and never consented to her assailant's embraces, the crime is done by the man who violated her. Will this plain statement be denied by those against whom we defend not only the minds but the sacred bodies also of those Christian women who were outraged in captivity ?

In the case of Lucretia, that noble matron of ancient Rome, we all know how loudly her modesty is praised. When King Tarquin's son by violence had taken her and lustfully got possession of her person, she revealed the wickedness of the profligate prince to her husband, Collatinus, and her kinsman, Brutus, both men of rank and spirit, and made them take an oath to avenge her. Then, suffering still from the foul wrong that had been done her and unable to bear the pain she killed herself. What is our verdict ? Is she to be judged an adulteress or a chaste wife ? Who will think there is any need to labour the question ? Not more happily than truly did a rhetorician say of the deed : " Here is a marvel : there were two

persons, and only one committed adultery." A striking
and a true saying. In those two bodies joined together
our author saw the foul lust of the one and the chaste
determination of the other, and paying heed not to the
contact of their limbs but to the diversity of their souls,
he says: "There were two persons, and only one
committed adultery."

But how is it that the woman who did not commit
adultery, receives the heavier punishment? The prince
was merely banished along with his father: Lucretia
paid the penalty of death. If it is not immodesty when a
woman is raped against her will, it is not justice when a
chaste wife is punished. To you I appeal, ye laws and
judges of Rome. Even when signal enormities have been
committed, you do not allow the criminal to be put to
death without a trial. If, then, one were to bring this
charge before your court and were to prove to you that a
chaste and innocent women had been put to death untried,
would you not visit the person responsible for her death
with all proper severity of punishment? Well, the famous
Lucretia was responsible: the famous heroine Lucretia
slew the chaste and innocent Lucretia after she had been
outraged. Pronounce sentence you cannot. There is no
one in the dock for you to punish. But why do you so
loudly praise the women who slew a chaste and innocent
wife? Certainly you cannot reasonably defend her before
the judges in the realm below, if they are such as your poets
love to represent them in their verse. Her place then will
be among those, of whom we read :—

> " The next in place and punishment are they
>   Who prodigally threw their lives away."

And if she should desire to return to the upper world :—

> " Stern Fate forbids, the Stygian floods oppose
>   And with nine circling streams the captive souls
>   enclose."

Perhaps, however, she is not there at all; because when

she killed herself she was conscious, not of innocence, but of guilt. She herself alone knows the truth, but what if beguiled by her own pleasure she gave some consent to Sextus when he violently fell upon her and then was so overcome with remorse that she thought death alone could expiate her sin? Although even so she ought not to have killed herself, if she could with her false gods have accomplished a fruitful repentance.

However, if this was the case and if the rhetorician was wrong when he said : " There were two persons and only one committed adultery " ; if in fact both persons committed adultery the one by open assault, the other by secret consent; then the woman she killed was not innocent ; and therefore her learned defenders may declare that in the nether world she is not in the class of those—

" Who prodigally threw their lives away."

The case, indeed, is reduced to a dilemma. Extenuate the murder and you confirm the adultery. Acquit her of adultery, and you aggravate the murder charge. There is no way out when the question is put thus : " If she was an adulteress, why is she praised? If she was a chaste wife, why was she killed ? "

Still, to refute those men who, unable to understand the nature of true holiness, insult the Christian women who were outraged in captivity it is enough for us that in the well-known case of this Roman matron it was said in her praise : " There were two persons, and only one committed adultery." Lucretia was confidently believed to be a woman of such virtue that she could not contaminate herself by consenting to adultery. That, then, she killed herself because she had submitted to an adulterer without herself being an adulteress, is a proof not that she held modesty dear, but that she was not strong enough to bear shame. She blushed to think that another had committed this foul deed upon her even without her consent, and being

a Roman matron, over greedy for praise, she feared that
men would think if she continued to live that she had
submitted willingly to the act of violence done to her while
she was alive. She could not exhibit her conscience to the
eyes of men, but she thought that her self-inflicted punishment would testify to her state of mind ; and she burned
with shame at the idea that her tame endurance of the foul
wrong done to her by another might make people suppose
that she was his accomplice.

Not such as hers was the conduct of our Christian women
who suffered as she did and are still alive. They did not
avenge upon themselves the guilt of others, lest they should
add crimes of their own to those that were not theirs.
And that is what they would have done, if their shame had
driven them to self-murder as the lust of the enemy had
driven him to rape. Within their hearts they enjoy the
glory of chastity, the witness of their own pure conscience.
In the sight of their God also they are esteemed pure and
they want nothing more. It suffices them to have the
opportunity of doing good, and they decline to evade the
distress of human suspicion, lest thereby they deviate
from the authority of the divine law.

(IX) THE TROUBLES AND THE BLESSINGS OF LIFE

(XII, 22, 24)

That the whole human race has been damned from its
first beginning is proved by life itself, beset on earth, as it
is, by a host of grievous ills. What else can we infer from
the dreadful depth of ignorance, cause of all the errors which
hold the sons of Adam in their dark embrace, wherefrom
no man can be delivered without labour, pain, and fear ?
What of men's endless desires for vain and harmful

things, and their gnawing cares ; their disquiet, grief, fear, mad joy, quarrels, lawsuits, wars, treachery, anger, enmity, deceit, flattery, fraud, theft, rapine, perfidy, pride, ambition, envy, murder, parricide, cruelty, barbarity, dishonesty, luxury, insolence, impudence, shamelessness, fornication, adultery, incest, and the countless acts of filthy and unnatural vice in which both sexes indulge and which it is shameful even to mention ? What of their sacrilege, heresy, blasphemy, perjury, oppression of the innocent, calumny, plots, tricks, false evidence, unrighteous judgements, deeds of violence and highway robbery, and all the other crimes which we can scarce conceive, although they are never far away from human life ?

It is true that these things are the sign of wickedness ; but they spring from that root of error and perverse desire with which every son of Adam is born. Who does not know with what ignorance of truth, manifest even in infancy, and with what abundance of vain desires, which begin to appear in boyhood, a man comes into this world, so that if he were let loose to live as he pleased and to do as he liked, he would come to all, or, at least, to many of the crimes and iniquities which I have mentioned or have been unable to mention ? But God's governance does not altogether desert those whom He has condemned nor does He in His anger completely close the door of compassion. Therefore it is that deep in the hearts of men two sentinels are ever keeping guard against the darkness in which we are born and opposing its attacks. Instruction and Prohibition are their names, and they are themselves full of labour and pain. What else is the meaning of those multifarious threats which are used to restrain the folly of children ? What else mean our pedagogues and teachers, the birch, the strap, the rod, and all the schooling which the holy scripture tells us we must give to the child we love, beating him on the sides, lest he wax stubborn and it be scarcely possible, or perhaps become impossible, to subdue him ?

What is the purpose of all these punishments except
to overcome ignorance and to check perverse desires,
evils that are in us when we first come into the world ?
Why else is it that we remember with difficulty and
without difficulty forget ; that we learn with difficulty and
without difficulty remain ignorant ; that we are diligent
with difficulty and without difficulty are idle ? Is it not
plain in what direction our faulty nature by its own
weight tends and inclines, and what assistance it needs if
it is to be delivered ? Love of ease, sloth, laziness,
negligence, are merely methods of escaping work, since
work, even if it be useful, is itself a penalty.

But, besides the punishments of childhood, without
which children would not learn what their parents wish—
and parents scarcely ever wish for anything really useful—
what words can describe the number and severity of the
punishments which afflict the human race, punishments
which have to do not with the crimes and wickedness
of godless men, but with the common lot of human misery ?
Who in thought even can conceive what fear and trouble
are caused by bereavement and mourning, by loss of money
and condemnation at law, by fraud and falsehood, by false
suspicions, and all the crimes and violent deeds of other
men ? At their hands we suffer robbery, captivity, chains,
imprisonment, exile, torture, mutilation, blinding,
violation to satisfy a debauchee's foul lust, and many
other horrible evils.

Moreover, what endless dangers from without threaten
our lives—extremes of heat and cold, tempests, rain, floods,
lightning, thunder, hail, earthquakes, pitfalls ; houses
tumbling down upon us ; horses stumbling, shying, or
turning vicious ; poisons lurking in fruit, in water, in
air, or in living creatures : painful or even deadly bites
from wild beasts ; the madness which a rabid dog com-
municates, so that even the animal which is most gentle
and friendly to its master becomes a thing more intensely
to be feared than a lion or a dragon, and the human being

whom it has by chance infected turns so frenzied under
the pestilential contagion that his parents, wife and children
dread him more than any wild beast.

Again, what troubles are endured by those who sail
the sea or travel by land ! Who can walk along the street
without being exposed to unforeseen accidents ? Returning
home from market sound in limb he slips, breaks his leg,
and never recovers. What seems safer than a man sitting
in a chair ? Eli the priest fell from his and died. How
many accidents do farmers, or, rather all men, fear the
fruits of the earth will suffer from the weather or the soil
or the ravages of insect pests ? Usually we feel secure
when the crops have been gathered in and stored away :
but, as I know well, a sudden flood even then sometimes
puts the farmer to flight and sweeps the finest harvest
clean out of his barns.

Against the thousandfold attacks of demons who can
think that his own guiltlessness will suffice ? That no
man might so believe, even baptized infants, than whom
nothing surely is more innocent, are sometimes so
tormented that God by allowing it plainly means to show
us in them how lamentable are the troubles of this life and
how desirable the felicity of the life to come. As for the
diseases of the body, they are so numerous that even in
medical books all of them are not included ; and in very
many or almost all of them the treatment used is itself a
torture, so that men are only rescued from the pain of
death by a cure equally painful. Have not the dreadful
pangs of thirst driven men to drink human urine or even
their own water ? Has not hunger forced them to devour
human flesh, and that not the flesh of men found dead,
but of men slain for that purpose ? Have not the pangs
of starvation driven women in madness to eat their own
children, incredibly savage as such an act must appear ?

Even sleep itself, which is properly called the time of
repose, who can describe how often its rest is disturbed
by the visions of dreams and how the wretched mind in

all its senses is harassed by false fears to which sleep gives
such a solid reality that we cannot distinguish them from
real alarms ?   How pitiably in certain diseases and cases
of poisoning are men distressed by delusive phantoms
even while they lie awake !   With what astonishing variety
of appearances are even healthy men deceived by malignant
demons who produce these delusions for the sake of
perplexing men's senses, even if they cannot win them over
to their side !   And from this hell upon earth there is
nothing that can save us except the grace of Christ the
Saviour, our God and Lord. . . .

God himself then gave to the human soul a mind, in
which during infancy reason and understanding lie asleep
and almost non-existent, but which is destined, as the years
roll on, to be awakened and exercised, so as to become
receptive of instruction and knowledge, fit to understand
what is true and to love what is good. By this capacity
the soul drinks in wisdom and is endowed with those
virtues whereby in prudence, fortitude, temperance, and
righteousness, it fights against error and the other inborn
faults and conquers them by craving nothing save the
supreme and unchangeable Good. And even when this
does not happen, who can adequately describe or conceive
the wonders of the Almighty's work and the blessings
conferred upon our rational nature by allowing it even
the capacity of such attainment ?

Beside the arts of goodly living that will lead us to
eternal   felicity,   the   arts   which   we   call   virtues
that are given to the children of the promise and the
kingdom by the grace of God alone in Christ, has
not the intellect of man invented and applied countless
other arts for necessity or pleasure, the vigour of his mind,
so active in the discovery not merely of superfluous but
even of dangerous and destructive things, testifying to the
blessings bestowed upon a nature that could invent, learn,
and employ them all ?

What marvellous and astonishing advances has human

industry made in the arts of weaving and building, of agriculture and navigation ! What various ingenuity it has expended on the production of pottery, statues, and paintings ! What wonderful spectacles it has devised for exhibition in the theatres, scarcely to be believed by those who only know of them by hearsay ! What cunning contrivances it has invented for catching, killing, and taming wild beasts !

For use against our fellow-creatures, too, how many kinds of poisons, weapons, and engines of destruction have been found, while for the preservation or restoration of health the appliances and remedies are infinite. How many sauces have cooks concocted to please the palate and provoke appetite ! What a multitude and variety of signs we have to invite and express thought, among which words and letters hold the first place ! What ornaments of rhetoric, what numerous kinds of verse are there to delight the mind ! How many musical instruments and strains of harmony to please the ear ! What skill has been attained in measures and numbers and with what sagacity have the movements and connections of the stars been traced ! In short, who could tell the thought that has been expended on nature, especially if he tried to give details and was not satisfied with a general view ?

Moreover, even in the body, though it shares mortality with the beasts and is weaker than many of them are, what goodness of God, what providence of the great Creator is evidenced ! Are not the organs of sense and the other members so placed, is not the appearance, shape, and stature of the whole body so fashioned, as to show that it was made for the service of a rational soul ? Man was not created with head drooping earthwards as we see is the case with animals devoid of reason : his bodily form, erect and looking heavenwards, admonishes him to mind the things that are above.

Again, the marvellous mobility that has been given to

the tongue and hands, fitting them conveniently to speak
and write and perform so many duties and practise so
many arts, does it not clearly show the quality of the soul
for which such bodily assistance was provided ?   Even if
we disregard the necessities of work, there is such a
symmetry in the various parts of the body and so beautiful
a proportion that you can scarcely say whether in its
construction greater regard was paid to utility or to grace.
It is certainly plain that no part of the body was created
merely for utility without having some beauty in it as well.

This truth would be all the more obvious to us if we
could count and measure how all its parts are connected
and adapted to one another. Perhaps, if we tried carefully,
human skill might trace out the exterior formation ; but
the intricate maze of veins and nerves and flesh tissue,
the secret of life hidden and withdrawn from our sight,
no one can possibly get at. For though the cruel zeal of
anatomists has dissected corpses, and even the bodies
of their patients, as they died beneath their knife, and has
barbarously pried into their recesses to learn the nature of
the disease, its exact seat, and the best method of treatment,
yet those relations of which I speak, which make a concord,
or, as the Greeks call it a harmony, for the whole body
within and without, as if it were an instrument of music,
no one has been able to discover because no one has had
the audacity to seek for them.

If they could be known, then even the inner tissues of
flesh, which seem to have no beauty, would so delight us
by the beauty of their adaptation that the mind's judgement,
to which the eyes are but servants, would prefer them
to any of those obvious beauties which give only a visual
satisfaction. There are some things also in the body
that are obviously set there for beauty, not for use ; the
teats on a man's breast, for example, and the beard on
his face ; for that the beard is for ornament and not for
protection is proved by the bare faces of women, who, as
being obviously of the weaker sex, ought, more properly,

to possess such a defence. If therefore everyone allows
that among all our visible members there is not one in
which beauty is sacrificed to utility, while there are some
that are beautiful only and have no practical use, I think
it can be easily understood that in arranging the human
body comeliness was preferred to necessity. Necessity,
indeed, is a transitory thing, and the day will come when
we shall enjoy one another's beauty without any thought
of lust, a joy that should redound to the praise of the
Creator, of whom the Psalmist says : " *Thou art clothed
with honour and majesty*."

How can I fully describe the beauty and utility of the
rest of creation, which God's goodness has given to man
to look upon and to use, condemned though he be to
trouble and plunged in misery ?   Shall I speak of the
manifold and various loveliness of heaven and earth and
sea, the abundant and marvellous glory of daylight, the
sun, the moon, and the stars, the shady recesses of the
forests, the hues and scents of the flowers, the multitude
of birds all differing in song and plumage, the variety of
living things among which the smallest are often the most
wonderful, the works of ants and bees being more amazing
to us than the huge bodies of whales ?   Shall I describe
the sea's majestic aspect when it clothes itself with a
diversity of colours as with a vestment, now running
through every shade of green and then becoming purple
or blue ?   What a glorious object it is even in a storm !
How the spectator's joy is intensified by the soothing
reflection that he is not on board ship to be tossed by it
and shaken ! What shall I say of the rich diversity of food
to alleviate hunger, or of the variety of seasonings to
stimulate appetite, and of all the abundance lavished by
nature's richness, not procured by any skill and toil of
cooks ? How many natural aids are there for preserving and
restoring health !   How grateful is the alternation of day
and night !   How pleasant the breezes that cool the air !
How abundant the supply of clothing furnished us by

trees and herds! Who can tell the whole story? If I
were to try to delineate one by one in detail these few
blessings which I have here indicated in the mass there
would be no end to my account.

(X) THE POSSIBILITY OF ETERNAL PUNISHMENT

(XXI, 1-5)

In this book to the best of my ability with God's help
I propose to consider what sort of punishment will be
assigned to the devil and all his followers when the two
cities, the city of God and the city of the devil, shall
through Jesus Christ our Lord, the Judge of quick and
dead, reach their due ends. I have chosen to adopt this
order and afterwards to speak of the felicity of the saints,
since the body will have a part both in felicity and punishment, and it seems harder to believe that bodies can endure
eternal torment than that they can continue in eternal
felicity free from all pain. Therefore the demonstration
that eternal punishment ought not to be held incredible
will be a material help to me in proving the credibility in
the case of the saints of a bodily immortality delivered
from all uneasiness.

This order is not in discordance with the divine oracles,
in which sometimes the blessedness of the good is placed
first, as in the words : " *They that have done good, into the
resurrection of life : and they who have done evil, into the
resurrection of damnation* " ; and sometimes also last, as :
" *The son of man shall send forth His angels, and they shall
gather out of His kingdom all things that offend, and shall
cast them into a furnace of fire : there shall be wailing and
gnashing of teeth. Then shall the righteous shine forth as
the sun in the kingdom of His Father* " ; and again : " *These*

shall go away into everlasting punishment, but the righteous into life eternal." It would be tedious to cite further examples ; any one who examines the prophets will find that they adopt now the one arrangement, now the other. My reason for choosing the present order I have now given.

What argument can I adduce to convince sceptics that human bodies, alive and breathing, can not only survive death, but also endure the torments of everlasting fires ? They will not have us refer this simply to the power of the Almighty ; they demand that we persuade them by a definite example. We could answer that there are animals which certainly are corruptible, since they are mortal, and yet maintain life in the midst of flames ; and also that in springs of boiling water so hot that no one can put his hand in it with impunity a kind of worm is found which not only lives there unharmed but cannot live elsewhere. But unless we can actually show them these creatures they refuse to believe us ; while if we are able to prove our statements by ocular demonstration or trustworthy evidence, they contend with persistent incredulity that these facts are not proper examples of what we are seeking to prove. They say that such animals do not live for ever, and also that the heat causes them no pain, the element of fire being congenial to their nature and making them thrive rather than suffer,—as though it were not more incredible that they should thrive in such surroundings than that they should suffer. It is miraculous that a thing should suffer in fire and yet live, but it is more miraculous that it should live in fire and not suffer. If you believe the second statement, why not also believe the first ?

There is no body, these sceptics say, which can feel pain and cannot also die. How do we know that ? Who can be certain that the demons do not feel pain in their bodies, seeing that they confess that they are grievously tormented ? If it is answered that there is no earthly body—that is, no solid and visible body, or, in a word, no flesh—which can feel pain and yet cannot die, does not such a statement depend solely on the evidence of the senses and bodily experience ?   Men have no acquaintance with any flesh save mortal flesh, and their reasoning merely comes to this—" Anything outside my experience cannot possibly exist." What sort of argument is it to make pain a presumption of death ? It is rather a plain indication of life. For though it be a question whether a thing that feels pain can live for ever, it is a certain fact that anything that feels pain is alive and that pain can only exist in a living subject.

It is necessary, then, that if a man is to feel pain he must be alive ; but it is not necessary that pain kill him ; for even with these mortal bodies of ours, doomed anyhow to die, every pain does not kill. That any pain can kill is caused by the fact that the soul is so closely connected with the body that it succumbs to extreme pains and departs : since, indeed, even the fabric of our limbs and vital members is so weak that it cannot hold out against the violence that causes great or extreme pain. But in the next world this connection of soul and body will be of such a kind that the bond will neither be dissolved by length of time nor broken by any agony. So even though to-day there is no flesh which can suffer pain and yet cannot die, in the next world there will be flesh such as does not exist here, even as there will be death such as we have not. Death will not be abolished but will be eternal, since the soul will neither be able to enjoy God and live, nor to escape from the pains of the body and die. The first death drives the soul from the body against her will : the second death holds the soul in the body against her will. The two have this in common that the soul against her will suffers from her own body.

Our opponents stress the fact that in this world there is no flesh that can feel pain and cannot die ; but they slur over the fact that there is something which is greater than the body. The spirit, whose presence animates and directs the body, can feel pain, and cannot die. Behold then something which though it can feel pain is immortal. And this faculty, which we recognize now in the spirit of all men, in the next world will exist also in the bodies of the damned. Moreover, if we look closely we shall see that what is called bodily pain has really more to do with the soul. It is the soul's function, not the body's, to feel pain even when the pain originates with the body, localized in the place where the body is hurt. As, then, we speak of bodies feeling and living, though feeling and life come to the body from the soul, so we speak of bodies suffering pain, though no pain can be suffered by the body apart from the soul. The soul then in conjunction with the body feels pain in that part of the body where something occurs to cause pain : and it feels pain by itself when it is distressed by some invisible cause while the body is unhurt. It feels pain even when it is not resident in the body : for assuredly that rich man was feeling pain in hell, when he cried : " I am tormented in this flame."

The body, however, suffers no pain when it is soulless, and even when it is animate it cannot suffer without the soul sharing in its pain. If, therefore, the argument, " pain implies death ", were correct, and we might infer that where pain can be felt death can occur, then death would rather be the property of the soul, for to the soul pain particularly belongs. But since that which especially feels pain cannot die, what sound reason have we to suppose that bodies destined to agony are for that reason destined to death ? The Platonists indeed have always said that our earthly bodies and dying members are the origin of the soul's fears and desires, griefs and joys. " Hence," says Virgil—that is, from the dying members of our earthly body—" come fear and desire, pain and joy ". But we have proved in the twelfth book of this work that according even to this theory souls which have been cleansed from all bodily stain are moved by an uncanny desire to return to bodies again. And where desire can exist, pain assuredly

can exist : for frustrated desire soon turns into pain, either
by missing what it aims at or losing all it has attained.

Therefore, if the soul, which is either the sole or at least
the chief sufferer, has a certain limited immortality of its
own, it is plain that the bodies of the damned will not be
able to die merely because they will be feeling pain. In
short, if the body makes the soul suffer, why is it that it
can cause pain but not cause death, unless that it does not
follow logically that what causes pain causes death as well ?
Why, too, is it incredible that the fires of hell may possibly
cause pain but not death to the bodies of the damned, just
as bodies themselves now cause pain to souls but do not
therefore force them to die ? Pain therefore is not a
necessary presumption of death.

If the salamander lives in fire, as close observers of
nature have recorded, and if certain famous mountains in
Sicily from immemorial ages up till the present time and
beyond it have been seething with flames and yet still
remain entire, we have before us convincing evidence that
everything which burns is not consumed. The soul shows
that not everything which can feel pain can also die ;
so why do sceptics require from us further examples ?
We can prove to them that the bodies of men condemned
to everlasting punishment may retain their soul in the fire,
and may continue to burn without being consumed, and
may feel pain without perishing. Such will be the quality
that the substance of their flesh will have.

And He will give that quality who has endowed the things
we see with qualities so marvellous and diverse that their
very multitude prevents our wonder. Who but God the
Creator of all things has given to peacock's flesh its freedom
from corruption ? I had heard of this and it seemed to
me incredible ; but it happened that at Carthage one of
these birds was cooked and served at my table, and taking
a suitable slice from its breast I ordered it to be kept, and
after it had been kept as long as would have made any other
cooked meat putrid, it was brought out and set before me,

and did not offend my nose at all. It was then put back again, and after more than a month it was still the same : indeed, a year passed and it remained unchanged except that it was a little drier in substance and rather shrivelled.

Who gave to straw such power to freeze that it preserves snow buried under it, and such power to heat that it ripens green fruit ? Who can explain the miracle of fire, which blackens everything it burns, though itself it is bright ; and which itself most beautiful in colour discolours everything it licks and surrounds, and turns gleaming fuel into grimy charcoal ? Although even here there is no definite uniformity ; for stones follow just the opposite rule, and if they are baked in glowing heat they glow also, and though the fire is red and they white, yet white is congruous with light and black with darkness. Thus, fire burns wood and bakes stones, producing opposite effects on them although the two substances are not opposites. Wood and stone are different, but they are not opposites like black and white, one of which colours is produced in stone and the other in wood by fire, which gives its own brightness to stone and begrimes wood, and which would fail to heat the stone unless it were kept alive by wood.

In charcoal, too, what wonderful properties are to be found It is so fragile that a light tap will break it, a gentle pressure crush it to dust ; and yet it is so strong that no moisture can rot it, no lapse of time cause it to decay. It has, indeed, such lasting qualities that it is usual in laying down boundary marks to put charcoal underneath them, so that if anyone, however long afterwards, brings an action and pleads that no boundary stone was fixed he may be refuted by the charcoal below. When it is buried in damp earth where its mother wood would rot away, what is it that enables charcoal to remain undestroyed except this same fire which destroys all things ?

Let us consider next the wonders of lime. Besides the fact, on which I have already enlarged, that it turns a glistening white in the fire that makes other things grimy, it has also a mysterious property of conceiving fire from fire. A lump, cold to the touch, has fire hidden within it, which, though it is not at once apparent to our senses, yet lies slumbering and, as an experiment will prove, is there even if it be unseen. For this reason we call it " quick lime ", as if the hidden fire were an invisible soul quickening the visible substance. How marvellous it is to think that this fire is being kindled at the very moment when it is being quenched ! To disengage its hidden heat the lime is moistened or drenched with water and then, though it was cold before, it becomes hot by the application of that which cools things which are hot already. The fire that was hidden appears, leaving the lump to breathe its last breath, and then the lime lies so cold in death that even the pouring on of water will not make it burn again, and what we before called " quick " we now call " slaked ". What more can be added to a miracle like this ? And yet there is a greater marvel still. If you treat the lime, not with water, but with oil, which is as fuel to fire, however much you drench or soak it the lime refuses to burn.

If it was about some stone from India that we read or heard these wondrous facts and were not able to test them by a practical experiment, we should obviously either think the tale a lie or be filled with extreme surprise. But things that present themselves daily to our eyes, though they be equally marvellous, are disregarded because they are common. Indeed, some products of India itself, which might be expected to rouse admiration, cease to do so as soon as they appear frequently amongst us The diamond for example, is a stone which many of us possess, especially if we are goldsmiths or jewellers, and it is so hard that neither iron nor fire affect it, nor, indeed, anything at all except goat's blood. But do its owners familiar with its qualities admire it as much as those to whom its power is shown for the first time ? Persons who have not seen it do not believe perhaps what they hear about it, or if

they do they merely wonder at it as being something outside
their experience ; and if they get a chance of testing it
they still only marvel at its strangeness until familiar
experience gradually takes off the keen edge of their
surprise.

Again, we know that the loadstone has a wonderful
power of attracting iron. When I first saw it I was thunder-
struck, for before my eyes an iron ring hung, attracted
and suspended from the stone. Then, as though the stone
gave its own power to the iron it attracted, this ring was
put near another and lifted it up ; and as the first ring
clung to the magnet, so did the second ring to the first.
A third ring was joined on in the same way, and then a
fourth, so that there hung from the stone a chain of rings
with their hoops connecting, but not interlinked, attached
together only by their outward surface. Who could not
be amazed at the power of the stone, not confined to itself
but passing through so many hanging rings and binding
them together by invisible links ?

I heard, however, an even more marvellous tale about the
magnet, from my brother bishop Severus of Mileris.
He told me that Bathanarius, formerly count of Africa,
when the bishop was dining with him one day, brought out
a magnet, and after putting a piece of iron on a silver plate
held the magnet underneath. Then as he moved his hand
with the magnet under the plate, the iron upon the plate
moved about accordingly. The intervening silver was not
affected, but however quickly the count moved the magnet
to and fro, so quickly did the iron on the plate obey its
attraction.

I have told you what I myself saw and what I was told
by one whom I trust as I trust my own eyes. I will now
tell you what I have read about the loadstone. When a
diamond is put near it, it does not attract iron ; or if it
has already attracted a piece, when the diamond gets
near, it lets it go. These stones come from India ; and
if we are ceasing to marvel at them because they are now

familiar objects, how much less must they marvel who get them so easily and send them to us. They perhaps pay no more attention to them than we do to lime, which, because it is common, we regard with indifference. And yet lime has the strange property of burning when water is poured on it, and refusing to burn for oil, although water puts a fire out and oil makes a fire blaze.

Nevertheless, when we proclaim the wondrous works of God past and yet to come, which we cannot put to the test of actual experiment, sceptics demand that we shall give a clear explanation of them. We cannot do so, for they are beyond human comprehension ; but if people think that therefore we are telling lies, they themselves ought to try and account for all the marvels that we can or do see. If they realize that this is beyond a man's powers, then they should acknowledge that it does not follow that a thing has not been or will not be merely because it cannot be explained, since there are things now in existence of which the same is true. I will not, then, detail the many marvels in books, not matters of past history, but existing to-day in certain localities. If anyone has the wish and the means to pay a personal visit he will discover for himself if they are true: but I am going now to give a few examples.

Salt at Agrigentum in Sicily, men say, becomes fluid, as if it were in water, when it is put into a fire : but if you throw it into water it crackles, as though it were on a stove. In the land of the Garamantes there is a spring of water, so cold by day that no one can drink it, so hot by night that no one can touch it. In Epirus there is another fountain which, like all others, quenches lighted torches, but, unlike all others, lights quenched torches. There is a stone in Arcadia called asbestos, because once lit it cannot be extinguished. The wood of a certain kind of Egyptian fig-tree sinks in water instead of floating like ordinary wood ; and, stranger still, after it has been lying at the bottom for some time, it rises to the surface again,

although when wet it should be heavier by the weight of
the water it has absorbed. In the land of Sodom apples
grow which arrive at an outward show of ripeness, but
when you bite them or squeeze them, the peel cracks and
they crumble into dust and ashes. The Persian stone
pyrites burns the hand if you hold it tightly, and so takes
its name from the Greek word for fire. In Persia also is
found another stone called selenite, because it has an inner
brightness which waxes and wanes with the phases of the
moon. In Cappadocia mares are impregnated by the wind
and their foals only live for three years. Tylon, an island
in India has this advantage over all other lands : none of
the trees that grow there ever lose their leaves.

These and countless other marvels recorded in history,
dealing not with past events, but with places still existing,
I might enlarge upon ; but it would be tedious for me to
do so, and beside my purpose. Let those sceptics, who
refuse to believe God's scriptures, explain them if they can.

(XI) Adam and Eve in Paradise

(XIV, 10–28)

We may fairly ask ourselves the question whether our
first parent or first parents (for there was a marriage of
two) experienced in their animal body before their sin
such emotions as we shall not experience in the spiritual
body when sin has been purged away and ended. If they
did, how could they have been happy in Paradise, that
wondrous land of bliss ? Who that feels fear or pain can
be called absolutely happy ? And what could they have to
frighten or hurt them amid such abundance of blessings,
where neither death nor any sickness was to be feared, and
where nothing was absent that a good will could desire,

THE CITY OF GOD

nothing was present that could vex a man in body or mind and disturb his happiness?

Their love to God was unclouded, their love for each other was that of partners living in sincere and faithful union; and from this love there flowed a wonderful delight, for the object of their love was always theirs to enjoy. Their avoidance of sin was tranquil; and so long as it was maintained no other ill could attack them from any quarter and bring sorrow. Or did they perchance desire already to touch and eat of the forbidden tree, but feared to die: and so even then in Paradise were they vexed by fear and by desire?

Far be it from us to suppose that such things could be in a place where sin had no existence. It is already sin to desire what the law of God forbids, and to abstain not through love of righteousness but through fear of punishment. Far be it from us to think that, before there was any sin there should have been committed with regard to the tree the very sin against which our Lord warns us with regard to a woman: " *Whosoever looketh on a woman to lust after her hath committed adultery with her already in his heart.*"

As happy, then, as were our first parents, vexed by no mental perturbations, and hurt by no bodily discomforts so happy would the whole human corporation have been, had they not introduced the evil which they have transmitted to their posterity, and had none of their descendants in iniquity committed sins worthy of damnation. Their first happiness would have endured, until in virtue of the benediction " *Increase and multiply* ", the number of the predestined saints was complete; and then another and a greater happiness would have been given, such as the blessed angels enjoy, a happiness in which there would have been the certain assurance that no one would sin and no one would die. Thus the saints would have lived, knowing nothing of labour, pain or death, as now after having endured all these things they shall live with bodies incorruptible in the resurrection of the dead.

As God foresaw all things and therefore could not be ignorant that man was destined to sin, we ought to consider the holy city in accordance with God's foreknowledge and ordainment, and not in accordance with something that we could not possibly know because it was not in God's ordination. Man by his sin could not disturb the divine plan, nor compel God to change what He had decreed. God's foreknowledge had anticipated both things; that is, both how evil the man whom He had created good was destined to become, and what good He Himself should even thus derive from him. For though God is said to change His decisions—so that the Scripture speaking figuratively even says that God repented—this is said with reference to man's expectation, or to the order of natural causes, not with reference to that which the Almighty had foreknown that He would do.

So God, as it is written, made man upright, and therefore of a good will. If he had not had a good will he could not have been upright. The good will, then, is the work of God; for God created him with it. The first evil will, which preceded all man's evil acts, was not so much a work in itself as a falling away from God's works to its own. Therefore, the resulting acts were evil, not having God but the will itself for their end; and so the evil will or the man himself, so far as his will was evil, brought forth evil works, just as the tree of evil brought forth evil fruit.

Moreover, though the evil will is not in accordance with nature, but rather in opposition to nature, since it is a vicious defect, it is still part of the nature of which it is a defect, and without that nature it could not exist. But it belongs to the nature which the Creator created out of nothing, not to that which He begot from Himself, as He begot the Word, by whom all things were made. For though God formed man from the dust of the earth, yet the earth itself and every earthly material was absolutely created from nothing; and man's soul also God created from nothing and joined it to the body when He made man.

But evils are so thoroughly overcome by good that though they are permitted to exist, in order to show how the righteous foresight of the Creator can make a good use even of them, yet good can exist without evil. We see this in the true and supreme God Himself and in every celestial creature, visible and invisible, above this murky atmosphere. But evil cannot exist without good, because the natures in which evil exists, in so far as they are natures, are certainly good. Evil is removed, not by withdrawing any nature or part of nature that has been introduced by the evil, but by healing and correcting that which has been vitiated and depraved. The will's judgement, therefore, is then truly free, when it is no longer the slave of vice and sin. Such was it when God gave it to us ; and this having been lost by its own fault can only be restored by Him, who was first able to give it. Therefore Truth says : " *If the Son shall make you free, ye shall be free indeed* " ; which is equivalent to saying : " If the Son shall save you ye shall be saved indeed." For He frees us from that wherefrom He saves us.

And so man lived according to God's rule in a physical and spiritual paradise. Paradise was not merely physical for the advantage of the body, and not also spiritual for the advantage of the soul ; nor was it only spiritual for man to enjoy it by his inner senses, and not also physical for him to enjoy it by his outer senses. Obviously it was both for both ends. But after the proud and envious angel (of whose fall as well as that of his fellows, who from being God's angels became his angels, I have said as much as I could in the eleventh and twelfth books of this work), fell from the spiritual Paradise, he essayed to creep with persuasive guile into the mind of man, whose unfallen state he envied now that he himself was fallen. He therefore chose the serpent as his mouthpiece in the physical Paradise where all the animals on earth were living with those two human beings, the male and the female, subject to them and harmless. And he did so because the serpent

Y

is a slippery creature who moves with tortuous windings and was therefore suitable for his purpose.

By the presence of his angelic nature, and by the superior force of his spiritual iniquity he subdued the serpent to himself and used it as his instrument of mischief. He then entered into guileful conversation with the woman, beginning with the lower link in the human alliance, so that he might gradually gain the whole, and not supposing that the man would readily believe him nor that he could be beguiled into error unless he was overborne by another's mistake. For even as Aaron would not give way to his erring people when they tried to persuade him to make an idol and yet yielded to forcible constraint ; and even as we cannot believe that Solomon was so blind as to think that it was right to worship idols but was only induced by women's blandishments to commit that sacrilege ; so, also, we must think that Adam was not beguiled into believing that the serpent spoke the truth and therefore transgressed God's law, but that he the one human being yielded to the other human being, the man to the woman, the husband to the wife, owing to the strength of the tie which bound them in partnership together.

Not vainly did the apostle speak when he said : " *Adam was not deceived, but the woman was deceived.*" He means that the woman accepted the serpent's tale as true, but the man could not bear to be parted from his one companion though it involved communion in sin.

Adam, however, was none the less culpable, since he sinned knowingly with his eyes open. And so the apostle does not say " Adam did not sin ", but " *Adam was not deceived* ". He shows that he sinned when he says, " *By one man sin entered the world,*" and immediately afterwards more distinctly, " *In the likeness of Adam's transgression.*" He meant that people are deceived who do not think what they are doing to be sin ; but Adam knew that he was sinning. Otherwise how will the words be true : " *Adam was not deceived* ? " He was perhaps so far deceived that, having no experience of God's severity, he thought his sin venial. Consequently, he was not deceived as the woman was deceived, but he was deceived as to the judgement that would be passed on his plea : " *The woman whom thou gavest to be with me, she gave me, and I did eat.*" Why say more ? They were not both deceived by credulity, but they were both entangled in the snares of the devil and made prisoners by sin.

It may seem strange why other sins do not alter human nature as it was altered by the transgression of that first human pair ; for as the result of it our nature now is subject to the dire corruption we feel and see, and to death, and is distracted and tossed by many furious and contending passions, and is certainly now far different from what it was before the Fall, even though in Paradise it still lodged in an animal body. But if any one is disturbed by this thought, he should remember that the sin was not a small and trivial one merely because it was concerned with food and that not bad or noxious food except that it was forbidden ; for in that place of happiness God could not have created or planted anything evil. By the precept He gave God commanded obedience, which is indeed the mother and guardian of all the virtues. For the rational creature was so created that submission is advantageous to it, while the fulfilment of its own will in preference to its Creator's is destruction. The command to abstain from one kind of food only in the midst of abundance was one so easy to keep and so little difficult to remember, especially as lust did not yet oppose will—for that was the after penalty of transgression—that the iniquity of breaking it was all the greater in proportion to the ease with which it might have been kept.

Our first parents had begun secretly to be corrupted before they fell into open disobedience ; for the evil act would never have been done had not an evil will preceded it. And what is the origin of evil will but pride ? " *Pride is the beginning of all sin.*" And what is pride but a craving for undue exaltation ? And undue exaltation is this, when the soul abandons Him to whom it ought to cleave as its principle and becomes a sort of principle for itself. This happens when it becomes over self-satisfied. And it becomes self-satisfied when it falls away from that unchangeable good which ought to satisfy it more than itself. This falling away is voluntary ; for if the will remained steadfast in its love for the higher and unchangeable good, which gave it light to see and ardour to love, it would not turn away to find satisfaction in itself, and so pass into the realms of cold and darkness. If their will had been firm, the woman would have not believed that the serpent spoke the truth, nor would the man have preferred his wife's wish to God's command, nor have supposed it to be a venial transgression of God's precept to cling to his life partner even in a partnership of sin.

The wicked deed, that is, the transgression of eating the forbidden fruit, was committed by persons who were already wicked. That evil fruit could only be brought forth by an evil tree. But that the tree was evil was not the result of nature ; for it could not, anyhow, become so except by the vice of the will, and vice is contrary to nature. Nature could not have been depraved by vice had it not been created from nothing. Because it was made by God, it is a nature : because it was made from nothing, it falls away from Him. Man did not so fall away as to become nothing ; but when he turned towards himself he became less than he was when he cleaved to Him who supremely is. To exist in oneself, that is, to be one's own satisfaction after abandoning God, is not quite nothingness, but it approximates to it.

Therefore in the Scriptures the proud are called by another name, " self-pleasers." It is a good thing to have one's heart uplifted : not to one's self, for that is pride, but to God, for that is obedience and a proof of humility. There is something in humility which strangely exalts the heart, something in pride which debases it. It seems

to be a paradox that loftiness should debase and lowliness
exalt ; but pious humility enables us to submit to what is
above us ; and nothing is more exalted above us than
God : therefore, humility by making us subject to God
exalts us.

Pride, being a defect of nature, by the very act of refusing
subjection and revolting from Him who is supreme, falls
low ; and then comes to pass what is written : " *Thou
castest them down when they lifted up themselves.*" For
he does not say " when they had been lifted up ", as if
first they were lifted up and then cast down ; but when they
lifted up themselves even then they were cast down—
that is, the very lifting up was already a fall. Therefore
it is that humility is specially recommended to the city of
God as it sojourns in this world, and is specially proclaimed
in the city of God in heaven, and in the person of Christ
its King ; while the contrary vice of pride according to
the teaching of the sacred writings specially rules his
adversary the devil. And assuredly this is the great
difference which distinguishes the two cities of which we
speak, the one being a society of godly men, the other of
ungodly, each associated with the angels that belong to
them, the one guided by the love of self, the other by the
love of God.

The devil would not have trapped man into the open and
manifest sin of doing what God had forbidden if man had
not already begun to be self-satisfied. It was this that made
the words pleasing, " *Ye shall be as gods* " ; a thing that
would have been better done by obediently cleaving to
their supreme and true principle than by proudly living
to themselves. For created gods are not gods by their own
truth, but by having a share in the true God. By craving
to be more man becomes less ; and by wishing to be self-
sufficing he falls away from Him who is truly sufficient.

This wicked desire which prompts man to be self-
satisfied, as if he were himself the light, and turns him
away from that light which he has only to accept and

become light himself, this wicked desire, I say, secretly came first and was followed by the open sin. For what is written is true. " *Pride goeth before destruction, and before honour is humility* "; that is, secret ruin precedes open ruin, the first not being counted ruin at all. For who counts exaltation as ruin, although the moment that the Highest is forsaken decline begins ? But who does not recognize it as ruin, when there is a plain and certain transgression of a commandment ?

Consequently God's prohibition had reference to such an act as when committed could not be defended by any pretence of its being lawful. I venture to say that it is useful for the proud to fall into some plain and open sin, which may make them displeased with themselves, seeing that they have already fallen as the result of self-satis-faction. Peter was in a sounder state when he was dis-satisfied with himself and wept, than when he was filled with self-satisfaction and presumptuousness. This is what the sacred Psalmist means when he says : " *Fill their faces with shame, that they may seek Thy name, O Lord* " ; that is, let those who pleased themselves in seeking their own glory be now pleased with Thee and seek Thine.

It is, however, a peculiarly evil and damnable form of pride that seeks refuge in excuses for a manifest sin. That is what our first parents did, when the woman pleaded, " *The serpent beguiled me and I did eat*," and the man said : " *The woman whom Thou gavest to be with me, she gave me of the tree, and I did eat*." There is here no word of entreaty for pardon, no imploring request for healing. Though they do not, like Cain, deny the deed, yet their pride seeks to attribute the guilt to something else, the woman's pride choosing the serpent, the man's the woman. Where there is a plain transgression of a divine command, to make such a plea is to accuse rather than to excuse oneself. For the fact that the woman sinned at the serpent's persuasion, and the man at the woman's offer, did not make the transgression less evident, as if there were anything whom we ought to believe or obey before God.

Therefore, as the command of God was treated with scorn, God who had created man and made him in His own image, who had set him above the other animals and placed him in Paradise, who had enriched him with abundance of safety and all good things, who had laid upon him neither great nor many nor difficult commands but to make a wholesome obedience easy had given one very brief and light precept whereby he reminded the creature whose service was perfect freedom that He was Lord, it was only just that condemnation should follow upon sin. And the condemnation was such that man who by keeping the command would have remained spiritual even in the flesh became now fleshly even in the spirit. Self-satisfied as he had been in his pride, he was now abandoned to himself by God's justice, not to live in the absolute independence he affected or to have the freedom he desired, but dissatisfied with himself to endure a hard and miserable slavery under the power of him to whom by sinning he had consented, doomed in his despite to die in body as he had willingly become dead in spirit, condemned even to eternal death, did not the grace of God deliver him, because he had forsaken eternal life.

Whoever thinks that such punishment was excessive or unjust is obviously unable to measure the greatness of sin's iniquity when sin might so easily have been avoided. As Abraham's obedience is deservedly proclaimed to be great, because the thing commanded, to kill his son, was very difficult, so in Paradise the disobedience was the greater because the precept given offered no difficulty at all. And as the obedience of the second Man was the more laudable, because " *He became obedient even unto death* ", so the disobedience of the first man was the more execrable because he became disobedient even unto death. Where the punishment of disobedience is great and the thing ordered by the Creator easy, who can adequately estimate how great a crime it is in a matter so simple not to obey the authority of so great a power which threatens such a terrible penalty?

In fine, to put matters briefly, when that sin was punished, what penalty save disobedience was laid upon disobedience? What else is man's misery but his disobedience to himself, so that as he would not do what he could he now wills to do what he cannot. He could not indeed do all things in Paradise before the Fall, but as he then only wished to do what he could do, he could do all the things he wished.

To-day, as we recognize in his offspring and as divine scripture testifies, " *Man is like to vanity.*" Who can count how many things there are which he wishes to do and cannot do, so long as he is disobedient to himself, that is, so long as his mind and his flesh do not obey his will? In spite of himself his mind is frequently disturbed, and his flesh suffers, and grows old, and dies, and bears all the other pains we endure, pains that we should not unwillingly bear if our nature absolutely and in all its parts obeyed our will. You may say that the infirmities of the flesh hamper it in its service. But what does it matter how its service is hampered so long as the fact remains that by the just punishment of God our Ruler, whom we refused to serve in subjection, our flesh, which once was subjected to us, now torments us by its insubordination, although our insubordination to God could not have caused any trouble to Him but only to ourselves?

He does not need any service from us as we need service from our body, and therefore what we did was no punishment to Him but what we receive is a punishment to us. The pains, moreover, which are called the pains of the flesh, are, indeed, in the flesh and from the flesh, but they are also pains of the soul. What pain or desire can the flesh feel by itself without the soul? When the flesh is said to desire or to suffer, the truth is, as we have explained, that the man himself does so, or some part of the soul which is affected by what the flesh feels, whether it be a harsh sensation causing pain or a soft sensation causing pleasure. Pain in the flesh is only a hurting of the soul arising from the flesh and a kind of shrinking in it from what the flesh feels, even as that pain of the soul which is called sadness is a shrinking from things that have happened to us against our wish. Sadness is frequently preceded by fear, which itself is in the soul and not in the flesh ; while bodily pain is not preceded by any kind of fear in the flesh, such as could be felt in the flesh before the pain. Pleasure, however, is preceded by a certain appetite which is felt in the flesh like a craving, as hunger, thirst, and that generative desire which is commonly called " lust ", although this is a general term for all desires.

Anger itself was defined by the ancients as simply a lust for revenge ; although sometimes a man is angry with lifeless objects which cannot feel his vengeance, as when one breaks a pen that is writing badly or crushes a reed. Yet even this, although somewhat unreasonable, is in its way a lust for revenge, a kind of shadow, so to speak, of the law of retribution, that they who do evil shall suffer evil. There is then a lust for revenge, which is called anger ; there is a lust for money, which is called avarice ; there is a lust for having your own way no matter how, which is called obstinacy ; there is a lust for self-advertisement, which goes by the name of boasting. There are, indeed, many and various lusts, some of which have special names and others have not. For who could easily find a word for the lust of ruling, which yet, as civil wars testify, has a powerful influence on the soul of tyrants ?

Therefore, although lust has many objects, yet when the word lust is used without the addition of any object, it usually suggests to the mind a lustful excitement of the body's obscene members. This lust takes possession of the whole body, not only without but also within, and moves the whole man with a passion in which mental emotion joins and mingles with carnal appetite, so that the ensuing pleasure is the greatest of all bodily delights. So enthralling is it, indeed, that at the moment of consummation all keenness of thought is suspended and lulled to sleep.

What friend of wisdom and holy joys is there who being married and knowing, as the apostle warns us, " *how to possess his vessel in sanctification and honour, not in the disease of desire, as the Gentiles who know not God*," would not prefer, if he could, to beget children without the intervention of lust ? Then in the business of begetting offspring the members created for that purpose would not be stimulated by the burning heat of lust but would act at the bidding of the will, in the same way as the other members serve for their respective ends. Even those who are enamoured of this pleasure, whether in the conjugal bed or in the filthiness of vice, are not moved to it at their own will. Sometimes lust importunes them when they want it not, sometimes it leaves them stranded in the act, and while their mind is burning with desire their body is cold and numb. So, strange though it seems, this passion not only fails to obey the will to beget offspring but also refuses to serve the caprices of lasciviousness ; and though it often opposes the mind's restraint with all its force, it sometimes is divided against itself, and while it moves the soul it cannot follow its own lead by moving the body also.

We are right in feeling especially ashamed of this lust ; and rightly, too, are these members themselves called " shameful ", seeing that lust moves or checks them, not at all according to our will but by a kind of autocracy of its own. It was not so before man's fall. For it is written in Scripture, " *They were naked and not ashamed*." It was not that their nakedness was unknown to them, but nakedness was not yet shameful because lust did not yet move those members without the will's consent, not yet did the flesh by its disobedience give witness to convict the disobedience of man.

Our first parents were not created blind, as vulgar ignorance imagines : Adam saw the animals to whom he gave names, and of Eve we read : " *The woman saw that the tree was good for food and that it was pleasant to the eyes.*" Their eyes then were open, but they were not open to this ; that is, they did not notice the service rendered them by the vesture of grace, for they had no consciousness of their members warring against their will. But when grace was stripped away, that their disobedience might be visited by a reciprocal penalty there began in the movements of their body a new shamelessness, which made nakedness indecent, and rendered them at once both observant and confused.

Hence, after they had violated God's command by open transgression, it is written of them, " *And the eyes of them both were opened, and they knew that they were naked and they sewed fig leaves together, and made themselves aprons.*" " *The eyes of both were opened,*" says the scripture, not to see, for they saw already, but to discern between the good which they had lost and the evil into which they had fallen. Therefore also the tree itself, which was to give them that discernment if contrary to God's command they touched it and ate, took its name from this fact and was called the tree of the knowledge of good and evil. For the pleasure of health is rendered more evident by some experience of the discomfort of sickness.

" *They knew,*" therefore, " *that they were naked* "— naked of that grace which saved them from being troubled at their bodily nakedness when sin's law offered no resistance to their will. And so they obtained a knowledge of which they would happily have been ignorant, if in trustful obedience to God they had not committed that offence which brought to them experience of the harm done by unfaithfulness and disobedience. And therefore, troubled at the disobedience of their flesh, the penalty which testified to their own disobedience, " *they sewed fig-leaves together and made themselves aprons* " ;

that is they made themselves cinctures for their privy parts. Shame modestly covered that which lust disobediently moved in opposition to the will, which was thus punished for its own disobedience. Consequently all nations, being descended from that one stock, have so strong an instinct to hide the shameful parts that some barbarians do not even uncover them when bathing, but go into the water with their drawers on. In the dark solitudes of India, also, though some philosophers go naked and are therefore called " gymnosophists ", they hide these members with a covering from which the rest of their body is free.

Lust requires darkness for its consummation ; and that not only in unlawful intercourse, where secrecy is necessary to escape betrayal, but even in dealing with prostitutes, a form of vice which the earthly city has legalized. Though lust there goes unpunished and unreproved, meeting no check in that city's laws, it still avoids the public eye. So much of modesty is demanded by nature and even brothels provide seclusion ; vice found it easy to break through moral prohibitions, but shamelessness found it impossible to do away with the veils that hide this turpitude from sight.

Even the foulest of men acknowledge the foulness of lust ; and though they love it they dare not display it. Does not conjugal intercourse, legitimate and honourable though it be, require a bedchamber free from all observation, even if its purpose is the procreation of children in accordance with the terms of the marriage contract ? Before the bridegroom begins even to fondle his bride, does he not shut out the household and even his own groomsmen and such relatives as close ties of kinship have till then permitted to be present ?

The greatest master of Roman eloquence says that all right actions desire to be set in the light ; that is, they desire to be known. This right action, however, if it seeks to be known, yet blushes to be seen. Who does not know what passes between husband and wife that children may be born ? It is for that purpose that marriages take place with such ceremony. And yet when the act of producing children is being done, not even such children as may already have been born to the pair are allowed to witness it. This right act, when it comes to being known, seeks mental, but shuns visual, notice. And why so, if not because the act, although seemly in itself as being an instinct of nature, yet brings with it a sense of shame as being the result of a punishment ?

Hence those philosophers even who have drawn near to the truth confess that anger and lust are vicious mental states because even when their objects are such as wisdom does not prohibit they move towards them in a turbulent and inordinate fashion and consequently need always to be regulated by the mind and reason. This third part of the soul, they say, is posted in a kind of citadel so that while it rules and these two passions obey man's righteousness can be kept safe without a breach. These parts, then, they acknowledge to be vicious even in a wise and temperate man, so that the mind by its pacifying and restraining influence must check and recall them from those objects to which they move unlawfully and allow them passage to those which the law of wisdom sanctions. Anger, for example, may be allowed to enforce a just authority and lust is permissible in performing the task of procreation. But these parts, I repeat, were not vicious in Paradise before the Fall, for they never moved then in opposition to a holy will towards any object from which it was necessary that they should be restrained by the guiding bridle of reason.

Even if now they move in this way and are regulated by a bridling and restraining power which men of temperate, just, and godly lives can exercise sometimes with ease and sometimes with difficulty, this is certainly not the health of nature but only the weakness of guilt. As for the fact that modesty does not hide the action of anger and the other passions, as shewn in word or deed, with the same care as it conceals the action of lust, shewn in the organs of generation, the only reason for this is that in all other cases the members are moved not by the passions themselves, but by the dominating force of the will consenting to them. An angry man who rails at or even strikes another could not do so were not his tongue and hand moved by the authority of the will, as they are moved also when there is no anger. But the organs of generation have been handed over in such servitude to the dominion of lust that they cannot move if lust fails them, or if it does not raise its head either of its own accord or when excited to do so. It is this which shames us : it is this which blushingly avoids the gaze of onlookers. And rather will a man endure a crowd of spectators when he is venting his anger unjustly on some one, than the eye of one man when he copulates lawfully with his wife.

The Cynics, those canine philosophers, failed to realize this fact when in contravention of all men's modest instincts they proclaimed their unclean and shameless opinion, fit only for dogs. They said that as the conjugal act is legitimate one should not be ashamed to perform it in public, even in a street or square. Instinctive shame, however, has proved too much for this fantastic doctrine. They say, indeed, that Diogenes once did it for show, thinking that the glory of his sect would be increased if his signal shamelessness were thus fixed in the memory of men ; but his followers in later days have not taken his example. Shame has had more influence with them, to make them blush before men, than error to make them affect a resemblance to dogs. Hence I am inclined to think that Diogenes himself, and such others as are said to have done this, rather feigned the movements of copulation than consummated the act in the presence of a crowd, and that the spectators did not know what was really going on beneath the shelter of his cloak.

Philosophers then did not blush to show themselves

desirous of a woman's embraces in places where lust itself
would blush to raise its head. And even to-day there are
still Cynic philosophers to be seen. They are the gentry
who are not content with their cloak for badge, but must
also carry a staff. And yet no one of them dares to do
what we speak of. If they did, they would be over-
whelmed, I will not say by showers of stones, but certainly
by the spittle of an indignant crowd.

Human nature is without doubt ashamed of this lust,
and it is right for it to be ashamed. In the disobedience
of lust, which has made the organs of generation subject
to its motions alone and has wrested them from the will's
control, we see clearly the punishment assigned to man's
first disobedience. It was fitting that this should appear
chiefly in that part of the body where is generated the
nature which by that first great sin was altered for the worse.
From the bonds of that sin no one can escape, unless
God's grace expiate in him individually the crime that
God's justice then punished, perpetrated, as it was, for
the destruction of all in common, when all were in
one man.

Far be it from us, then, to believe that our first parents
in Paradise felt that lust which caused them afterwards
to blush and cover their limbs, or that by its means they
would have fulfilled God's blessing, " *Increase and multiply
and replenish the earth* ". It was after sin that lust was
born : it was after sin that nature, having lost the power
it had once over the whole body but not having lost all
shame, perceived, noticed, blushed, covered. The blessing
upon that marriage, which bade them in union to increase
and multiply and replenish the earth, though it was continued to the sinners, was yet given before they sinned,
so that the procreation of children might be recognized
as part of the glory of wedlock, not part of the punishment
of sin.

To-day, being ignorant, of course, of the happy state
of Paradise, men suppose that children could not have

been begotten there in any other way than that with which they are familiar by experience ; I mean by the way of lust ; at which, as we see, even honourable marriage blushes. Some people do not simply reject but sceptically deride God's Scriptures, in which we read that our first parents after they had sinned were ashamed of their nakedness and covered over their privy parts. Others, while they accept and honour Scripture, would have it that the words " *Increase and multiply* " do not refer to carnal fecundity. They say that a similar expression is used of the soul : " *Thou wilt multiply me with strength in my soul* " ; and in the next passage of Genesis, " *Replenish the earth and subdue it*," they understand by " earth " the body which the soul fills with its presence and which it rules over completely when it is multiplied in strength. As for children of the flesh, they believe they could not then any more than now have been begotten without lust, which, after sin was born, noticed, blushed for, and covered ; and they think that children would not have been born in Paradise, but only outside it, as in fact happened. For it was after they had been expelled from Paradise that the pair came together to beget children, and begot them.

We for our part have no manner of doubt that to increase and multiply and replenish the earth in accordance with God's blessing is a gift of marriage as God instituted it in the beginning before man's Fall, when he created them male and female, a difference of sex plainly evident in the flesh. With this work of God His blessing itself is connected. For when the Scripture says, " *Male and female created He them*," it adds at once, " *And God blessed them, and God said unto them, ' Increase and multiply and replenish the earth and subdue it,' *" etc. Though the whole passage may not improperly be interpreted in a spiritual sense, yet the words " male and female " cannot be understood as a figure of speech, meaning that there is in a man one part that rules and another that is ruled. It is obvious that

we were created male and female for the purpose of
begetting offspring, and so increasing, multiplying, and
replenishing the earth ; and to argue against this fact is
the height of absurdity.

Our Lord when he answered the question put to him
was not speaking of the spirit which commands and the
body which obeys, nor of the rational soul which rules and
the irrational desire which is ruled, nor of the con-
templative virtue which is supreme and the active virtue
which is subordinate, nor of the understanding of the mind
and the sensations of the body : he plainly meant the
matrimonial union by which the two sexes are mutually
bound one to the other. They asked Him whether it was
lawful for any cause whatsoever to put away one's wife—
for, on account of the hardness of their hearts, Moses
permitted the Israelites to give a bill of divorcement—
and he said : " *Have ye not read that He which made them
at the beginning made them male and female and said ' For
this cause shall a man leave father and mother, and shall
cleave to his wife, and they twain shall be one flesh '. Wherefore they are no more twain, but one flesh. What therefore
God hath joined together, let not man put asunder.*" It is
certain, then, that from the beginning men were created
of two sexes, male and female, as we see and know them
to be now, and that they are called one, either on account
of the matrimonial union, or on account of the origin of
the woman, who was created from the side of the man.
And it is on this example and precedent, which God
Himself established, that the apostle admonishes husbands
to love their wives.

He who says that but for sin there would have been
neither copulation nor generation, says virtually that man's
sin was necessary to complete the full number of the saints.
If they by not sinning must have remained alone, because,
as some imagine, they could not have begotten children
had they not sinned, then certainly sin was necessary that
there might be not only two but many righteous folk.

z

And since that idea is absurd, we must rather believe that the number of saints due to complete this blessed city would have been as great, though no one had sinned, as it is now that the grace of God gathers its citizens from the multitude of sinners, so long as the children of this world generate and are generated.

Therefore, that marriage, worthy of the happiness of Paradise, if there had been no sin would have produced the fruit of love without the shame of lust. We cannot now show by any example how this could then have been possible ; but it ought not to seem incredible to us that that one member might have served the will then without lust, seeing that so many members serve the will to-day. When we want to do anything with our hands and feet we move them without meeting any resistance ; they are ready servants, as we see both in our own case and in that of others, especially among artisans employed in mechanical operations, where the slowness and weakness of nature is aided by industrious activity. May we not, then, well believe that as our other members now readily obey our will, so, then, the organs of generation might have discharged their function, even if lust, the penalty of the sin of disobedience, had been lacking ?

Did not Cicero in his " *Republic* ", when discussing the difference of governments, use a simile drawn from human nature, and say that the members of our body are so readily obedient that we lay our commands upon them as we do upon our children ; but that the vicious parts of the soul must be treated like slaves and coerced with a harsher authority. In the order of nature the soul certainly takes precedence of the body ; and yet the soul commands the body more easily than it commands itself. Still, the particular lust of which we are now speaking is the more shameful, inasmuch as the soul is neither master of itself therein, so as not to feel lust at all, nor is it master of the body, so as to keep those members of which we are ashamed under the control, not of lust, but of our own will. If that could be done, those members would not be held shameful.

As things are now the soul is ashamed that the body, subject to it by its inferior nature, should still resist its authority. In the case of the other emotions when it meets resistance it feels less shame, because the resistance is from itself, and although it is conquered it is itself the conqueror. The victory is a wrong one, and contrary to order, since it is won by those parts of the soul which ought to be subject to reason ; but still they are parts of itself, and therefore the victory, as I said, is its own. When, however, the soul conquers itself to a due subordination and its irrational motions are made subject to the intelligence and reason, which again are subject to God, then the victory is virtuous and praiseworthy. Yet the shame is less when the soul is disobeyed by its own vicious parts than when its will and orders are disobeyed by the body ; for the body is distinct from and inferior to the soul and without it its nature would have no existence.

So long as the other members are kept under the authority of the will, seeing that without them those organs which are excited by lust to resist the will cannot effect their purpose, chastity is preserved, and the delights of sin forbidden, though not foregone. Certainly had not culpable disobedience been visited with disobedience as penalty, the marriage in Paradise would never have known this struggle and rebellion, this strife between will and lust, the inadequacy of the lust as against the sufficiency of the will ; but those members like all the rest would have been obedient to the will. The field of generation would have been sown by the organ created for that purpose, as the earth is now sown by the hand. As things are, when we try to discuss this subject at all thoroughly, modesty bars the way and compels us to ask pardon with an apology to chaste ears. But it might have been that we should have no cause to do so. We might have discoursed and written freely, without fear of seeming obscene, upon all those points which occur to the mind when one is considering the organs of generation. There would not even have been any words that could be called obscene, but all that might be said of those members would have been as free of offence as what is said of the other parts of the body.

Whoever, then, comes to the perusal of these pages with an unchaste mind, let him shrink, not from the facts of nature, but from his own guilty thoughts. Let him blame what is the result of his own impurity, not the words that necessity compels me to use ; words for which every pure and pious reader or hearer will readily pardon me, while I expose the folly of that scepticism which argues only from its own experience and has no faith in anything beyond. He who is not horrified by the apostle's censure of the horrible vice of those women who " *changed the natural use into that which is against nature* ", will read all this without being offended, especially as I am not, like Paul, citing and censuring a damnable uncleanness, but am explaining the facts of human generation to the best of my ability while with Paul I am avoiding all obscenity of language.

The man, then, would have sown the seed and the woman have received it, as need required, the generative organs being moved by the will, not excited by lust. Not only do those members move at our bidding, which are furnished with joints of solid bone, our hands, for example, and feet and fingers ; we can also, when we wish, move those which are composed of soft and relaxed nerves : we can shake them or stretch them out, we can bend and twist or contract and stiffen them, as we do with the muscles of the mouth and face. The lungs, which are the most delicate of all the interior organs, except the brain, and are therefore carefully protected in the cavity of the chest, for all purposes of inhaling and exhaling breath or of uttering and modulating sound are obedient to the will as we breathe, exhale, speak, shout, or sing, just as the bellows obey the blacksmith or the organist.

I say nothing of the fact that some animals have the natural power to move any part of the covering with which their whole body is protected if they feel anything on it which they wish to remove—a power so great that by a tremor of the skin they can not only shake off flies that have settled on them, but even spears that have fixed in their flesh. Man, it is true, has not this power ; but is that any reason for thinking that the Creator could not have given it to all the creatures that he wished ? Man himself might have been able to claim obedience even from his inferior members, had he not forfeited it by his disobedience : for it would not have been difficult for God so to shape him that what is now moved in his body only by lust should have been moved only by will.

We know that some men are differently constituted from others and have some rare and remarkable faculty of doing with their body by an effort of will what other men cannot do at all and indeed scarcely believe when they hear of it being done. Some people can move their ears, either one at a time or both together. Some without moving their head can bring their hair down upon the forehead and move the whole scalp backward and forwards as they wish. Some by lightly pressing their stomach bring up an incredible variety of things they have swallowed, producing whatever they please quite whole as if out of a bag. There are persons who can so exactly mimic the voices of birds and beasts and other men that unless they are visible it is impossible to distinguish them ; and some can emit such rhythmical sounds from their fundament that without being offensive they produce the effect of singing. I myself have known a man who could break into a sweat whenever he wished ; and it is a recognized fact that certain people can weep at pleasure and even burst into a flood of tears.

Even more incredible is something which a number of the brethren saw quite recently. There was a presbyter called Restitutus belonging to the parish of the church of

Calama. Whenever he pleased—and he was often asked
to do so by people who wished to witness this strange
sight with their own eyes—if any one imitated the wailing
of mourners, he became so insensible and lay in a state so
like death that not only did he not feel pricks and pinches
but even when fire was applied and burned him, he had
no sense of pain except afterwards from the injured place.
That his body remained motionless not by any effort of
his own but because he was insensible was proved by the
fact that he breathed no more than a dead man. Yet he
said that if anyone spoke at all loudly he heard the voice,
but it seemed to come from a distance.

As, then, even now, though men lead a life of trouble
in the corruption of their flesh, in some cases the body
serves them by many remarkable movements and moods
outside the usual course of nature, what reason is there
why we should not believe that, before the sin of disobedience and the punishment of corruption that followed,
a man's members might not have served his will for the
propagation of children without lust ? Man has been given
over to himself, because in self-conceit he deserted God ;
and disobeying God he could not even be self-obedient.
Hence man's obvious misery : he cannot live as he would
wish. If he lived as he wished, he would think himself
blessed ; but he could not be so if he lived wickedly.

If we look closely, we see that no one lives as he wishes
but the blessed, and no one is blessed but the righteous.
Even the righteous does not live as he wishes, until he has
reached a place where he cannot die, be deceived, or hurt,
and until he is certain that this will be his eternal condition.
This is what nature demands ; and nature is not fully
and perfectly blessed until it attains what it seeks. But
what man now can live as he wishes, when it is not in his
power even to live ? He wishes for life and is compelled
to die. How, then, does he live as he wishes when he does not
live as long as he wishes ? Even if he wishes to die, how can
he live as he wishes, seeing that he does not wish even to live?

If a man wishes to die, not because he dislikes life, but that after death he may live better, he is not yet living as he wishes, but only has the prospect of so living when through death he reaches what he wished. Admit that he lives as he wishes because he has done violence to himself and bidden himself not to wish for what he cannot have but to wish only for what is possible—as Terence says : " Since you cannot have what you will, will what you can "—is he therefore blessed because he lives in patient misery ? A blessed life is not possessed if it is not loved. If it is both loved and possessed, it must necessarily be loved more ardently than all beside, for whatever else is loved must be loved for the sake of the blessed life. And if it is loved as it deserves to be—and the man is not blessed who does not love the blessed life as it deserves— then he who so loves it cannot but wish it to be eternal. Therefore it will only be blessed when it is eternal.

And so man lived in Paradise as he wished so long as he wished what God had commanded. He lived enjoying God and was good by God's goodness ; he lived without wanting anything and had it in his power so to live for ever. He had food that he should not hunger, drink that he should not thirst, the tree of life that old age should not break his strength. No corruption, existing in his body or issuing from his body, caused any annoyance to any of his senses. He feared no sickness from within, no violence from without. He had sound health of body, complete tranquillity of mind.

As in Paradise there was no immoderate heat or cold, so its inhabitants never had their good will disturbed by fear or desire. Nothing gloomy was there at all, nothing foolishly glad. True joy flowed ceaselessly from God who was loved " with a pure heart and a good conscience and an unfeigned loyalty ". The honest love of husband and wife made their partnership secure. Body and spirit worked harmoniously together, and God's command was kept without difficulty. No languor made their leisure   wearisome;   no   sleepiness   interrupted   their desire to work.

In this felicity, when things were so easy and man so happy, let us not admit the suspicion that children could not have been begotten without the morbid prompting of lust. Nay, at that time the organs of sex obeyed the bidding of the will like the other members of the body, and without any artificial stimulus of passion the husband fell into his wife's arms, his spirit tranquil and his body perfectly pure. A thing is not to be regarded as impossible because it cannot be put to a practical test, but since those parts of the body then were not inflamed by turbid emotion, but were brought into use when required by the will's spontaneous command, it may well be that the man's seed entered the wife's womb without rupturing the hymen, even as now a virgin loses a certain quantity of blood every month without suffering any injury. Obviously the sperm might pass through the same channel that now gives exit to the menstrual flow. A woman's body opened then at the hour of birth not with the groans of painful labour, but with the readiness of a ripe fruit, and when the child was conceived it was not lustful desire but a willed experience that brought male and female together.

We are speaking of things that are now held to be shameful, and although we are trying, as far as we can, to conceive them as they were before they became shameful, necessity compels us to confine our discussion within the bounds of modesty rather than to enlarge upon it with such humble powers of speech as we possess. For since that of which I speak was not experienced even by those who might have experienced it—inasmuch as their sin and their merited exile from Paradise came upon them before they ever joined together calmly in the task of generation— when sexual intercourse is spoken of now, what does it suggest to men's senses?   Surely not such a placid obedience to the will as we might conceive, but rather a turbid wave of lust such as we have all experienced. That is the reason why modesty prevents further speech, although my mind suggests further matter in plenty for consideration.

Almighty God, the supreme and supremely good Creator of all substances in nature, who helps and rewards every will for good and abandons and condemns every will for evil and orders both alike, certainly did not lack a plan whereby even from the condemned race of men He might people His city with the fixed number of citizens which His wisdom had fore-ordained. The whole mass, indeed, of mankind was damned, like the branches of a tree whose roots are rotten, but He discriminated not by merits but by grace and shows now to the redeemed how much He has bestowed, not only in their case but in the case of those who have not been delivered.

Everyone acknowledges that the goodness which has rescued him from evil is not something which he has earned but something that was given him free. He goes scathless, but he has been picked out from the company of those whose punishment he might justly have shared. Why, then, should God not have created those whom He foresaw would sin, since he was able to reveal in and by them both what their guilt deserved and what His grace bestowed, and since under His creating and disposing hand the perverse disorder of the wicked could not upset the right order of things?

Sinners, whether they be angels or men, avail not to hinder "*the great works of the Lord wrought to all his wishes*". He who by His providence and omnipotence distributes to each his portion knows how to make good use of the evil as well as the righteous. Thus God made a good use of the wicked angel, who in punishment for his first evil wish was condemned to an obduracy that prevents him wishing any good, when He allowed him to tempt the first man, who had been created upright, that is to say, with a will for good. He, indeed, had been so made that if he trusted in God's help man's goodness would overcome the angels' wickedness, but if in proud conceit he abandoned God, his creator and helper, he would be overcome. If his will remained upright resting on God's support he would have the good that he deserved ; if it turned perverse and abandoned God he would have evil.

Even this trusting in God's help could not be achieved without God's help, although it was in man's own power by yielding to self conceit to relinquish the benefits of divine grace. For as it is not in our power for our fleshly body to keep alive without the help of food, while it is in our power to refuse it nourishment and cease to live, as those do who commit suicide, so it was not in man's power, even in Paradise, to live well without God's help ; but it was in his power to live wickedly, although thereby his happiness would end and well-deserved punishment follow. As God was not ignorant that man would fall, why should He not have permitted the malignity of the jealous angel to tempt him ? He knew full well that man would be overcome, but none the less, He foresaw that by the man's seed, helped by divine grace, the devil himself in turn should be conquered to the greater glory of the saints. Therefore, neither did any future event escape God's notice, nor did His prescience compel anyone to sin : rather by a logical experiment He revealed to the intelligent creation, human and angelic, how great a difference there is between a man's private presumption and God's own protection. For who would dare to believe or say that it was not in God's power to prevent both man and angel from falling ? God preferred to leave it in their power, and thus to show what evil could be wrought by their pride and what good by His grace.

And so two cities have been created by two loves : the earthly city by love of self even to contempt of God, the heavenly city by love of God even to contempt of self. The one city glories in itself ; the other glories in the Lord. The one seeks glory from men ; the other finds its greatest glory in God the witness of conscience. The one lifts up

its head in its own glory ; the other says to its God,
" *Thou art my glory, thou dost lift up my head.*" In the one
among its princes, and the nations it subdues, the love of
dominion holds sway ; in the other princes and subjects
serve one another in love, the former by wise counsel, the
latter by obedience. The one loves its own strength as
shown in the persons of its rulers ; the other says to its
God, " *I will love Thee, O Lord, my strength.*"

Therefore, the wise men of the one city have
always lived according to man's rules and have
sought the good of their bodies, or of their minds,
or of body and mind together. Even those of them
who have known God, "*glorified Him not as God,
neither were thankful but became vain in their imaginations,
and their foolish heart was darkened ; professing themselves
to be wise*"—that is glorying in their own wisdom and
overcome by pride—"*they became fools, and changed the
glory of the incorruptible God into an image made like to
corruptible man, and to birds and four-footed beasts, and
creeping things*"—for they were either leaders or followers
of the people in adoring these images—"*and they
worshipped and served the creature rather than the Creator,
who is blessed for ever.*" But in the other city there is no
human wisdom save piety, whereby the true God is duly
worshipped, and it looks for its reward in the society of
holy men and holy angels, "*that God may be all in all.*"

INDEX

Achilles, 84

Ad Donatum, see *The World and its Vanities*

Adversus Nationes, see *Against the Heathen*

Against Helridius, 214

Against Jovinianus, 214

Against Marcion, 22

Against Rufinus, 214

Against the Heathen, 140

Alexander, 87

Ambrose, 10, 11, 13, 17, 173–8 ; hymns, 177, 180–9 ; on virgins, 190 ; on modesty, 196 ; on gait, 198 ; on dress, 199 ; on beauty, 201 ; on visiting, 202 ; on liberality, 203

Anacharsis, 89

Anaxarchus, 49

Antioch, the maiden of, 190

Apologeticus, see *The Christian's Defence*

apostasy, 133

Apuleius, 286

Arnobius, 16, 17, 139–41 ; on Roman gods, 142

Augustine, 1, 17, 18, 177, 178, 269–73 ; on pagan ideals, 274 ; on wonders, 276, 313 ; on eunuchs, 277 ; on the Manichæans, 279 ; on miracles, 281 ; on metamorphosis, 285 ; on Roman history, 289 ; on chastity, 297 ; on troubles, 301 ; on blessings, 305 ; on eternal punishment, 309 ; on sin, 318 ; on pride, 324 ; on lusts, 329

Aurelian, 7

Blesilla, 211, 212

Capito, Sisinnius, 164

Catinensians, 86

Cato, 19, 84

Cato Major, 160

chastity, 61, 169, 226, 297

Chateaubriand (quoted), 14

Christian Church, rise of, 4 ; persecution of, 6 ; organization of, 9 ; recognition by the state, 10 ; heresies in, 14, 15, 174, 270, 279 ; spread of, 38 ; ritual, 40, 43 ; unity of, 112

Christians, charges against, 26, 44, 46

Christian's Defence, The, 5, 16, 22, 23

Chronicle, The, 214

Cicero, 50, 160, 338

circus, the, 103, 161

City of God, 16, 271, 272

Cleomachus, 86

Cloak versus the Toga, The, 23, 24

Confessions, 177, 271

Constantine, 1, 10, 11

Cyprian, 13, 16, 17, 95–8 ; on virgins, 97 ; on the circus, 103 ; on the theatre, 104 ; on law courts, 106 ; on the vanities of the world, 108 ; on the unity of the Church, 112 ; on apostasy, 133

Damasus, 12, 211

De Catechizandis Rudibus, 271

De Doctrina Christiana, 271

De Ira Dei, see *God's Anger*

De Lapsis, see *On those who lapsed from the Faith*

De Virginibus, see *On virgins*

Deaths of our Persecutors, The, 157

Decius, 6, 7, 95

demons, 36

Diocletian, 1

Diogenes, 42, 87

Divine Institutions, 158

Domitian, 6

dress : women's 23, 52, 88 ; men's, 82 ; the cloak, 84, 90 ; the toga, 89 ; demanded by modesty, 199

Duchesne (quoted), 270

Printed in Great Britain by Stephen Austin & Sons, Ltd., Hertford.